Welcoming the Word in Year C
With Burning Hearts

Verna A. Holyhead, S.G.S.

LITURGICAL PRESS
Collegeville, Minnesota

www.litpress.org

Extracts from poems "God's Grandeur" (2 lines), "As kingfishers catch fire" (3 lines), "The Blessed Virgin compared to the Air we Breathe" (6 lines) from *Poems of Gerard Manley Hopkins* by Gerard Manley Hopkins, eds. W. H. Gardner and N. H. Mackenzie (1970). By permission of Oxford University Press on behalf of the British Province of The Society of Jesus.

"Annunciation to the Shepherds from Above" by Rainer Maria Rilke, trans. J. B. Leishman, from *Selected Works: Volume II,* © 1960 by New Directions Publishing Corp. Reprinted by permission of New Directions Publishing Corp.

"A whistle from the clay of my throat" by an anonymous poet in Baxter Detention Centre. Used with permission.

Extract from "Great things are done" from *William Blake: Selected Poems,* ed. Michael Mason (1994). By permission of Oxford University Press.

"Let the links of my shackles snap" by Rabindranath Tagore in *The Bible Through Asian Eyes,* eds. Masao Takenaka and Ron O'Grady (Pace Publishing, Auckland, New Zealand in association with Asian Christian Art Association, Kyoto, Japan, 1991). Reprinted with permission.

Extract from "Via Negativa" by R. S. Thomas, from *Collected Poems 1945–1990* (London: Orion Publishing Group, Ltd., 2002). Used with permission.

The Scripture quotations are from the *New Revised Standard Version Bible,* Catholic edition, © 1989 by the Division of Christian Education of the National Council of Churches of Christ in the U.S.A. Used with permission. All rights reserved.

Cover design by Ann Blattner.

Library of Congress Cataloging-in-Publication Data

Welcoming the word in Year C : with burning hearts.
    p. cm.
  ISBN-13: 978-0-8146-1835-6 (set)
  ISBN-13: 978-0-8146-1834-9 (alk. paper)
  ISBN-10: 0-8146-1834-0 (alk. paper)
  1. Church year meditations.   I. Holyhead, Verna.   II. Title.

BX2170.C55W58 2006
242'.3—dc22   2006005796

Contents

Introduction

Every eucharistic assembly is an "Emmaus" event of extraordinary hospitality where Christ opens the Scriptures for us and breaks bread with us. As with the disciples at Emmaus, he has vanished from our sight too, but he is an absent presence in these gifts. The purpose of this commentary is to help the reader respond to the Word of God that is proclaimed at the Sunday Eucharist, or at Sunday worship without a priest, with a personal and communal welcome that overflows into mission.

Listening is the primary response to the word. This word resounds from the cosmic obedience of Genesis, through its incarnation in Jesus Christ, the Firstborn from the dead, who challenges "anyone who has an ear [to] listen to what the Spirit is saying to the churches" (Rev 2:7), and into our present assemblies.

At Emmaus, the risen Christ is also and first a listener—listening to the disillusioned and failing disciples who have turned their backs on Jerusalem, the city of salvation; listening to what these disciples perceive as bad news, and then revealing it as his own good news. There is a continuing challenge for the Church to explain the Scriptures in this Christ-like way that integrates the hopes and realities of people's lives, offers them the possibility of compassion and forgiveness for their fears and failings, and gives them hope for the future. Luke's Gospel ends with Jesus' instruction to his disciples to wait for the promise of the Father, and his Acts of the Apostles (Part 2 of Luke's Good News) begins with this promise, the Holy Spirit, shaking, burning, blowing them out into the world to proclaim the Word. The Spirit is the memory and future of the Church, and so is both conservative and creative. Whenever we read the Scriptures reflectively, hear them proclaimed in the liturgical assembly, or preached and interpreted in the homily, it is the Spirit who helps us to stretch our lives between the two poles of "remember" and fidelity to the tradition of the Church and "today," which is a discovery of how the Word of God speaks to us in the present.

For most Christians, their only regular encounter with the Scriptures is in the Liturgy of the Word. Sometimes we may be unreceptive to the Word, all too ready to turn our backs on what seems an unwelcome, boring, or irrelevant intrusion into the real business of living and working. We may even smolder away . . . but yet we still gather. And then there are the good times when we experience being in communion with the Scriptures and with each other; when we enter easily and even eagerly into conversation with the Word of God; when we are so challenged that our hearts do truly burn within us and we want to hurry out and share the biblical story and our faith in it. I hope that these reflections for Year C, the first in the series that will also cover Years A and B, may contribute something to such communion and challenge for those who live and witness, teach, and preach the Word of God.

As the gospel reading has preeminence in and is the climax of the Liturgy of the Word, the reflection on the gospel of the day will be given greatest attention, although comments about the first and second readings and the responsorial psalm are also included. There is emphasis on the images, phrases, and themes of the gospel that recur, especially in the first reading that is usually most closely related to the gospel reading.

As a woman whose life has been influenced by the Rule of Benedict, I am aware of the many people who find in that ancient text of a spiritual master a wisdom that has endured for over fifteen hundred years, and still helps them today in their seeking of God in ways of life that are very different from the original monastic context. At the beginning of his Rule, Benedict says that the search for God is always to have "the Gospel as our guide" (Prologue to the Rule of Benedict 21). And in his last chapter he repeats his conviction that the Old and New Testaments are "the truest of guides for human life" (RB 73.3). Therefore, as a Supplement to the weekly Lectionary reflections, I have added for those who may be interested in them, a brief weekly reflection for the Rule that can be mixed with the biblical Word as an additional leaven of hope. In a very real way, this was a personal challenge: to test for myself, at least from Sunday to Sunday, the truth of Benedict's biblical foundations of his Rule. He has, of course, passed with flying colors. My success, I leave to the reader to judge.

It is told of John Wesley that he was once asked how he attracted such large and enthusiastic crowds to hear him preach. Wesley replied: "I set myself on fire, and they come to see me burn." May what follows in this book strike a tiny flame to help us burn with and witness to the Word of God as we journey through the Sundays of the Church's year of grace.

Verna A. Holyhead, S.G.S.
Melbourne
September 2005

1

The Season of Advent

As our civil year is drawing to a close, the Christian community is celebrating its liturgical "New Year," and this makes it a kind of "beginning-end" time, a season of contradictions and challenge.

Advent is the greening of our earth with hope that springs from the tired dryness of the old church year; a greening with the hope that there is an end not *of* the world but *for* the world when human history will come full term, and God will be everything to everyone (1 Cor 15:28).

Advent is preparing to give birth to the One who has come and yet is coming, mindful that it is our life's work to conceive Christ in the Spirit, to swell pregnant as a church with the holy seed of God's grace, and to bear Jesus to our world.

Advent is a stirring in the womb of our complacency: a time for turning and returning, for straightening crooked paths in our relationships with God and with our sisters and brothers, for filling in the holes and removing the stumbling blocks that trip us up on our journey of discipleship.

Advent is welcoming and befriending the vulnerable, the stranger, the desert places in myself and others. It is preparing a way into and through those deserts, believing that it is there that God stirs and saves.

Advent is the season of a Midwife God preparing to deliver into our hands the care of the wrinkled infant kingdom whose name is Son and Savior.

First Sunday of Advent

• Jer 33:14-16 • Ps 25:4-5, 8-9, 10, 14 • 1 Thess 3:12–4:2 • Luke 21, 25-28, 34-36

On this first Sunday of the church year, many of us will gaze on the single burning flame that is lit on the Advent wreath. It seems so small and insignificant against the background of world events, and even of our own lives. We are often so physically and mentally exhausted at the end of the year that we may be inclined to be skeptical about this tiny, flickering flame and the illumination it can offer us. But as we enter this season, the Church encourages us to have hope in the promises of God that can so easily flicker in and out of our consciousness. At first hearing, Luke's Gospel may seem to be proclaiming a message of fear and doom; its truth, however, is different. Just as at the first Genesis creation God brought a new cosmic ordering, a new liberation from the chaos of nothingness, so will Christ, in his Second Coming as the glorious Son of Man, liberate the cosmos and all humanity from fear and menace. Luke uses large, symbolic language for large events. It is the only way to speak of events that have not yet been experienced.

Many people in our world commit themselves to what has not yet happened and to long-range hopes. Medical researchers speak about positive outcomes in decades ahead; ecologists are concerned not just for our planet at this moment, but for its future in the centuries to come; astrophysicists conjecture about developments in terms of millennia. We accept these long-range forecasts and hopes, yet we may feel uncomfortable with, and even dismissive of the emphasis on the future at the beginning of Advent. We don't mind thinking, with comfortable nostalgia, about the past coming of "baby Jesus"—but that is not where the Church wants us to start Advent.

When we take our first plunge into this season we seem to be caught in a liturgical riptide that drags us away from the comparatively safe and familiar shore of the present into the uncharted end of human history and reflection on the second, and as yet unrealized, coming of Christ.

Advent challenges us to let our hopes reach beyond cozy domesticity to the huge and human hope of a new creation. Just as a woman watches for the signs that the birth of her child is imminent, so Jesus urges his disciples to be alert to the birth pangs of the reign of God in all its fullness. In our present time, in the womb of human and cosmic history, God is nurturing and preparing for the birth of the new heaven and new earth. Although the images of this may startle and even frighten us, such responses are caught up into the mystery of Christ by the two most important words in this Sunday's gospel: "liberation" and "confidence." In the midst of any personal suffering, international tension, opportunist politics, or natural disasters that we might experience during these Advent weeks, the Word of God urges us to be people of hope. Nor are Christians to be the captives of frantic seasonal consumerism. We are called, rather, to be a people awake and alert to the promises of God already revealed, grateful for what has been liberating for us as Jesus' disciples in the year just past, and confident in the gifts of God that are yet to come. Luke proclaims to us the same good news as was spoken by Jesus to the bent-over woman (cf. Luke 13:10-17). Touched by Jesus, the woman who for eighteen years had only looked at feet and dust was able to "stand up straight" and be free to see the Sabbath stars shining on his face. Today, we too are urged to lift up our heads and have faith that we will see our redemption drawing near in the Son of Man.

If the gospel reading had continued for one more verse, we would have heard that Jesus himself does what he spoke about. After a day of teaching in the Temple he goes to spend a night in prayer on the Mount of Olives, praying perhaps for readiness to meet his own future, his own end-time of death, confident in the liberation that his Father would offer him on the other side of death. For each of us, our death is a personal *parousia*, a coming of Christ at the end of our individual human history and a final invitation to enter into new and eternal life.

In the Spain of 1937, Republican forces loyal to the newly elected government were under attack from a fascist coup led by Generalissimo Francisco Franco. He had promised prosperity and stability to the people but delivered only death and destruction. Desirous of a bold visual protest against Franco, representatives of the democratic government came to the Paris home of the Spanish artist Pablo Picasso to ask him to paint a mural for the Spanish Pavilion of the 1937 World's Fair in Paris. Three months later, while Picasso was still deciding what he would create, news came of the bombing of the small village of Guernica in northern Spain during a "practice" Fascist raid. The village burned for three days, and sixteen hundred of its civilians died or were wounded. When the stark black and white photos of its destruction filled the front pages of Paris newspapers, the appalled Picasso immediately began the huge mural, *Guernica*, which would become modern art's most powerful antiwar statement. In the middle of a dark canvas full of twisted, broken body parts and agonized animals, an arm holds a lighted lantern; and at the bottom center there pushes through the rubble a new shoot of a fragile plant. Both light and plant are prophetic signs of hope in Picasso's apocalyptic landscape. The words of Jesus are light and life to us in today's biblical landscape.

In the first reading, the prophet Jeremiah is imprisoned by King Zedekiah, but he is urged by the consoling spirit of God to paint his hope in prophetic words and images. His personal sufferings do not blur Jeremiah's vision of God's promises. Just as with Picasso's icon of both social protest and hope, biblical prophetic hope is never just vaguely otherworldly and private; it is also hope that is communal and practical, sustaining both the prophet and his people in their present, while dreaming forward to future possibilities. Jeremiah proclaims that one day a Just One will come; a new Branch will spring from the stock of David, pushing through the rubble of failed kingship and guaranteeing in his person the continuance of the messianic family tree of David. When this day comes, justice and integrity will flourish on earth, and Jerusalem, city of conflicts and destruction, will be newly founded and renamed as "the Lord-our-righteousness." She will stand before the world as icon of and witness to the glory and transforming mercy of God. This new life that comes out of pain is not the dream of only prophets and poets and artists. It is also dreamed in contemporary prison and torture chambers, in communities that experience persecution, beside the beds of the terminally ill, and by every parent who holds the fragile life of their newborn. For us, the Scriptures are like a magnifying glass that not only enlarges experience but also focuses the heat that ignites for us a holy hope, realized in Christ.

It is love, Paul writes to his church at Thessalonica, which will confirm our hearts in holiness and make us ready for the great dream of the Second Coming of Christ. This love is not only for those who are near and dear to us, as Paul was to his church, but also for fairly neutral associates. Our love is to be a hugely generous love that embraces the whole human race. Radical and mature, such love can transcend all personal, religious, and cultural boundaries, and so is a reflection of God's own universal and unconditional love that will be revealed in its fullness at the end of time. But, ever a realist, Paul recognizes that in our efforts to love in this way we walk a tightrope that is stretched between the "now" of God's salvation and the "not-yet" that we are still awaiting. Neither shortsighted pragmatism nor impractical futurism will enable us to keep our balance. It is fatal for us tightrope walkers to look down, so with the antiphon of the responsorial Psalm 25, we profess what will steady us: "To you, O Lord, I lift up my soul."

Second Sunday of Advent

• Bar 5:1-9 • Ps 126:1-6 • Phil 1:4-6, 8-11 • Luke 3:1-6

Against a backdrop of geography, politics, and history, Luke ushers the adult John the Baptist onto the Jordan stage. Last Sunday's Gospel announced the advent or "arrival" of Jesus at the end of human history; today, as watchman and awakener, John announces the advent of salvation and consolation to the people and proclaims that their hope for the dawn of messianic time is near. In searching for ways in which to communicate John's significance, Luke and the other gospel writers found it most appropriate to use (with minor alterations) the words of Second Isaiah with which that prophet begins his "Book of the Consolation of Israel" (Isa 40-55). John's is the voice that, after four centuries of prophetic silence, heralds the coming of God's salvation not only to Israel, but also to all humankind. In an insignificant and troublesome pocket of the Roman Empire, John starts to shout his message throughout the district around the Jordan River.

Son of the priest Zechariah though he may be, John dissociates himself from Jerusalem and the Temple and chooses the place where Israel crossed over from its wilderness wandering into the Promised Land. John will call the people to make another crossing: from the exile of unfaithfulness to God into the forgiveness of their sins. He proclaims a baptism of repentance, a conversion of heart (*metanoia*) that looks to future commitment and not merely to regret for the past.

We are used to heavy earth-moving equipment and technology that can speed travelers on their way—cutting out sharp bends, smoothing treacherous bumps, straightening dangerous curves to give us a clearer and safer view of what is ahead or oncoming. Advent is the season of Christian "road works," with John the Baptist as our overseer. With John's voice, the church asks us, both personally and communally, to level and straighten out whatever is an obstacle or danger on our journey to God. What are the "potholes" in our discipleship, those sins of omission? From what do we need to be converted if we are to make the way smoother for others who find it difficult to travel to God because of our intolerant or erratic behavior? Do we indulge in outbursts of destructive "road rage" toward our sisters and brothers as we all try to follow the way of the gospel? Have we a kingdom vision that can enable us to see around the twists and turns of personal tragedy or ecclesial failure and recognize there an advent of Christ—his presence with us in the suffering, dying, and rising from these painful realities?

In the first reading, Jerusalem is imaged by the prophet Baruch as a grieving mother whose children have been carried off and scattered by her enemies, leaving her without a future and a hope. But her history will be transformed by God who is "mistress of the robes" in the drama of salvation. God will strip the city (often a symbol of the whole people of Israel) of her mourning garments and dress her with something of God's own beauty. Baruch offers no reason for this transformation except the mercy of God. Newly clothed in this mercy, Jerusalem will also be given a new name that suggests her response to God's mercy: "Peace through integrity, and honor through devotedness." Then from her high vantage point, Jerusalem will witness the fulfillment of her hopes as she sees her children returning from exile, escorted by God who causes the rough places to be leveled, the mountains flattened and the valleys filled in. Like a royal procession, shaded not only by trees but also by the glory of God, Israel comes home. Advent is a time when Christians are called to consider ways in which they can commit themselves to "peace through integrity" on behalf of those who are in physical or psychological exile—in different ways, in different places.

Our response to the reading from Baruch is the beautiful Psalm 126, a hymn of praise to God for hopes fulfilled and dreams realized. From the seed of tears has sprung a harvest of joy; from mouths silenced in sorrow come shouts of jubilation. That the Lord has done great things for his people is witnessed to the nations, and the psalmist continues to pray for God's grace to flow in unexpected ways and places, using the imagery of streams that would transform the Negev Desert. Together the assembly prays for the transformation of our own tears, our own inner deserts, and our own thanks for the great things already and so often done for us by God.

From the desert of his prison, Paul writes to the church at Philippi in words that the liturgy now addresses to us. It is a hopeful letter, full of Paul's confidence in the fidelity of this church to continue in the way of the gospel so that Jesus Christ may bring his work in them to completion by the time he comes again. Out of his tender compassion, Paul prays a threefold prayer: that the Philippians may continue to grow in mutual love; that its members may be discerning of the demands of their Christian life; and that they may be vigilant for Christ's Second Coming, "having produced the harvest of righteousness that comes through Jesus Christ for the glory and praise of God" (Phil 1:11). First love, then understanding, then ethics—these are Paul's priorities, for where would the last be without the other two?

Third Sunday of Advent

• Zeph 3:14-18a • Isa 12:2-6 • Phil 4:4-7 • Luke 3:10-18

The Word of God is not just a word spoken centuries ago—certainly admirable, possibly nostalgic, but definitely distant and far away in the irrelevant past. It is a word that, proclaimed and heard in the Sunday assembly or prayed in our daily sacred reading (*lectio divina*), should be the cause of our joy. This Third Sunday of Advent has traditionally been called *Gaudete* (Latin for "Rejoice") Sunday, because joy is what is expressed so obviously in the first two readings, and with a louder but more subtle challenge in the third. There is also an element of joy in our drawing closer to Christmas and the joy to the world that came with the birth of the Word made flesh.

The prophet Zephaniah is daring in his image of God as the dancing partner of the beloved daughter, Zion-Jerusalem, leading her in a vigorous *hora* to celebrate her liberation from her enemies. Under the reforms of King Josiah (c. 630 B.C.E.) and the diminution of the Assyrian threat, the grip of despair on the people was loosened. Then both the nation and her God shout, sing, and dance with the exuberant yet intimate joy characterizing a wedding feast. Such joy, says Baruch, should overflow into Israel's liturgical feasts in which the people remember and renew their love of God who is tenderly, faithfully dwelling with his people. It is such memory and joy that should be even more present in our Christian liturgy.

Paul, too, wants his church at Philippi to be happy as he is happy, even though he is in prison. Such happiness is not the superficial cheerfulness that can permeate so much of the commercialism, consumerism, and partying of the pre-Christmas weeks. It is joy "in the Lord," which comes from a deepening relationship with Christ and the gentle acceptance of our sisters and brothers. In such relationships the Lord is truly near to us and so, in our own small histories, we are preparing—or not preparing—for the final welcome that we will receive from Christ when he comes at the end of our individual lives, and at the end of human and cosmic history. To maintain this joy and hope, Paul stresses the importance of prayer: prayer as thanksgiving to God, prayer as supplication in times of great need, and prayerfulness as a constant attitude of mind and heart. This gives witness to our total and confident dependence on God and protects us from useless anxiety.

In the Gospel another shout is heard: urgent, loud, seeming at first to be discordant with the joy of the other readings. John the Baptist is with us again, a lean and eager man, his life pared down to essentials by his wilderness experience, his tongue sharpened by silence. Listening to his prophetic and passionate words, the crowds wonder if he might be the long-awaited messiah. They come to John with their practical questions: "What must we do?" they ask, and John has practical answers for them. He does not suggest that they dissociate themselves from their everyday lives, but rather that they be converted to just living and sharing in their ordinary relationships. John does not call them into the desert, but urges them to be sensitive to the wilderness of poverty around them and among them, responding by clothing the needy with their extra tunic and sharing food with the hungry.

There is nothing of elitism in the Baptist's ministry. In the crowds are two of the most despised groups in Palestinian society: tax collectors and soldiers, both of whom worked for the Roman occupying force. The tax collectors are not told to resign, but to stop exploiting the people; the soldiers (probably police who served as security guards for the tax collectors) are not commanded to leave the force, but to avoid violence, intimidation, and grumbling about their pay; they at least get a wage. One way the imperial system of Rome or any global power then or now can be changed is by the change of heart of those within it or concerned about it, or by informed, responsible voting for or against it. This is gospel "people power."

John comes to us this third week of Advent as the awakener of our sense of social justice, the one who points to the clutter of selfish concerns and materialism that can suffocate our practical love for our brothers and sisters in the stale air of indifference or greed. We are called to be concerned not only with the material clothing of the naked, but also with covering with love the naked vulnerability of someone in need. To feed the hungry is not only to be concerned with the soup kitchen, but also to nourish one another with our compassionate concern. How can we, individually, or in our families, parishes, or other communities, respond today to John the Baptist? How can we plan ways in which we can give Christmas back to the ones to whom it really belongs: to the homeless, the refugees, the elderly, the sick, the hopeless young people, those with disabilities, all of whom are so often discarded like our cast-off Christmas wrappings?

What John casts off are any pretensions to public adulation. To accept this is a subtle temptation, especially for the successful minister. If we are not awake and alert to our own limitations and God's generous gift giving, we can be almost imperceptibly deformed from God's servants into God's proprietors and controllers, parceled up in our own self-importance. But faced with the crowd's growing excitement that he might be the longed-for messiah, John contrasts himself humbly, definitely, and negatively with the One who is to come. His baptism, says John, is heir to the Jewish purification rites of repentance and cleansing. John will encourage the people to wash their hearts in the Jordan River, but the Coming One will baptize with the Spirit and with the transforming fire that will refine and purify for the end time when the wicked will be separated from the just like the insubstantial chaff that is threshed from wheat. The people will have to thresh out their right choices for God and throw away the useless husks that clutter up their lives. He himself, says John, is not even worthy enough to undo the sandal strap of the Coming One and handle the dirt and smell of his feet. And he rejoices in this good news, content to be best man to the bridegroom (cf. Luke 5:34), the one whose mission is to lead the bride Israel to Christ.

It is not easy to hear prophetic voices over the outer noise of the shopping centers or the inner noise of our thinking about what still needs to be done by Christmas Eve. Yet these are the days when we are encouraged by Isaiah, whose song is today's responsorial, to take at least some short time to be water-drawers as well as shoppers. In the few moments of prayer or sacred reading, we can reach into our inner depths where the well of salvation flows, and drink joyfully and confidently from its sustenance. Or we can draw water so that we may quench the thirst of a brother or sister for companionship, for compassion, for something to hope for—and discover that, in our so doing, God renews the springs of his grace within us.

Fourth Sunday of Advent

• Mic 5:1-4a • Ps 80:2-3, 15-16, 18-19 • Heb 10:5-10 • Luke 1:39-45

The large mysteries of the first three weeks of Advent converge this Sunday into the truth that the Christ who will rule the cosmos was carried in the small world of Mary's womb. John the Baptist, whose strong voice we heard on the Jordan bank last week, today has no voice, and can only announce the good news of Jesus' equally silent advent by an exultant leap of joy in Elizabeth's womb. There are no crowds pressing forward, asking questions. There are only two pregnant women as the first and most intimate audience for the meeting of the Messiah with his precursor, and the one question Elizabeth asks of Mary is: "Why has this happened to me, that the mother of my Lord comes to me?"

As the ark of the covenant was being taken up to Jerusalem, David had danced before it in joyful reverence for the sacred artifacts of Israel which it contained (2 Sam 6:14-15). John now dances before Mary, the new "ark" of a new covenant, sealed in the flesh and blood of the child she carries in her womb—the most holy possession of Israel. When the six-month-old baby leaps in Elizabeth's womb, she too becomes a prophet. Filled with the Holy Spirit, she reads the signs of the times, the "something more" of an ordinary human event—the stirring of the child in her womb—and proclaims the blessedness that God has bestowed on Mary and the One she carries.

In the meeting of Mary and Elizabeth, the generations embrace one another. The older woman of autumn grace and the young woman of the springtime of salvation need each other, as the generations still do. Mary's prompt visitation to her cousin was surely not just an act of love and readiness to help Elizabeth in her pregnancy. If Elizabeth needed her young energy, Mary must have needed Elizabeth's mature companionship. Both are women of extraordinary faith: the one believing in the message of an angel who had then departed, leaving Mary to her God and her future; the other trusting in her mute husband who somehow, perhaps in the unspoken love of their marital embrace, communicates Gabriel's Temple message and their longed-for child is conceived. Through the overwhelming favor of God, these two women are weavers of the life that shuttles back and forth within them, stitching the Old Testament to the New, with seamless grace.

The Advent mystery tells us so clearly that God has a special love for apparently unimportant people and places: for backwater Nazareth and its young woman; for the unnamed village of an old country priest and his aging wife; for the Bethlehem town of Ephrata which, by the time of the prophet Micah whom we heard in the first reading, had been eclipsed by Jerusalem in importance, despite the fact that the former was David's birthplace. The word of the Lord that came to Micah in the eighth century B.C.E. announces that a new future awaits this town for, like a woman in labor, its pain (of neglect) will be changed when it brings forth a future king who will fulfill the dreams as yet unrealized by the Davidic lineage. The one to come will be shepherd of his flock, caring for them in the strength of the Lord, and bringing peace and security. In such unimportant places and in unexpected ways, the Son of David will be born as this fulfillment of the dreams of his people. In us, too, such dreams will be fulfilled if we offer Jesus the hospitality Gerard Manley Hopkins describes:

> . . . O marvellous!
> New Nazareths in us,
> Where she shall yet conceive
> Him, morning, noon, and eve;
> New Bethlems, and he born
> There, evening, noon, and morn.[1]

Do we recognize the glory of God in unimportant people and places? Or do we drop a veil over the poverty and pain that can exist not only in far-off places, but also nearby, and even in our own hearts? Some people dread the approach of Christmas. The loneliness, for example, of those suffering the pain of broken relationships or distance from loved ones is intensified by the joyful companionship and family gatherings of those around them. In many places the statistics of suicide and domestic violence are higher during this "season of goodwill" when not much goodwill is experienced by some people. This is a challenge to our parishes and families, and one that many Christians are meeting with great generosity and hospitality.

Under our Christmas trees are mysterious packages of all colors and sizes and shapes, waiting to be unwrapped. God has also given us the most wonderful of Christmas gifts: his own Son, wrapped in our human flesh. But the whole Christ, head and members, is not yet fully formed. Until the end of the ages, he continues to wrap himself in the love and fidelity of his disciples.

Christ has come in the past in the days of his flesh, is coming to us in the present in his grace, and will come again in his final and glorious advent.

Notes

1. From Gerard Manley Hopkins,"The Blessed Virgin compared to the Air we Breathe" in *Poems of Gerard Manley Hopkins,* ed. W. H. Gardner and N. H. Mackenzie (Oxford: Oxford University Press, 1970). By permission of Oxford University Press on behalf of the British Province of The Society of Jesus.

2

The Season of Christmas

A notable poet was once asked in an interview to explain the meaning of one of his poems "in ordinary terms." He replied that if he had wanted to communicate meaning in that way, he would not have written a poem.[1]

The biblical authors must have felt the same way when they wrote about the mysteries that make up the Season of Christmas, because what we hear in the Liturgy of the Word during these few weeks is not the language of "ordinary terms."

The words of Luke's Gospel, like the season itself, come quickly upon us: bundling us off to Bethlehem; hastening us with the shepherds to obey the urgent angelic voices and go to see the child lying in a manger; keeping us on the move up to Jerusalem and back; hurrying through the childhood years of Jesus until it is time to stand on Jordan's banks with the crowds, the prayer, the water, and the voice that claims him as "my Son, the Beloved."

The readings from the Old Testament night continue to shine in the darkness to reveal the child and servant whose voice will one day be heard both throughout the vastness of the cosmos and in the intimacy of the human love of parents and children.

The great birth that we celebrate at Christmas is not only the unique birth of Jesus, but also the birth and ongoing growth to maturity of our faith in him. This is what we are also called to by the New Testament letters that are proclaimed at Christmastide. The authors try to remind us, in the midst of our preoccupation with gift giving and receiving, that Jesus is the greatest gift, the "wonderful exchange" between humanity and divinity that prolongs the Christmas mystery throughout human history.

Flesh and spirit, concealment and revelation, time and eternity, divine glory and human vulnerability: these contradictions are all wrapped in the holy gift of Christmas. The Word of God speaks of them, reconciles them, and makes of them a poem "in no ordinary terms."

Christmas Day

Midnight Mass

• Isa 9:1-6 • Ps 96:1-3, 11-12, 13 • Titus 2:11-14 • Luke 2:1-14

It comes down to this, down to all this littleness, to the tiny, fragile flesh of a newborn child in whom God dares to immerse himself in human history: fully human and fully divine. Luke's Gospel genius brings together heaven and earth, human longing and divine response, in a narrative that cuts through often incomprehensible discussions of the divine sonship of Jesus. The story of the birth of Christ is told as a nighttime event, and so we celebrate Christmas with candles and lights and under the stars. But none of these eliminate the darkness; they shine within it. So it is with this Child. Here is a mystery of divine concealment and divine revelation, darkness and light. Luke's words weave together the threads of his good news: the census, the birth of Jesus, and the proclamation of this to the shepherds.

A census as described, called by the emperor Augustus, is not recorded in history; when there was a census this was regional. But Luke's concern is not the recording of political history but the interpretation of salvation history. He sets the birth of Jesus in the world of Augustus and the *pax Romana* to express the faith that it was not the emperor who was the savior and peacemaker, as some of the inscriptions on his monuments proclaim. Rather, it was this powerless child, in an insignificant corner of Palestine, who would be what Isaiah had hoped for: Prince of everlasting peace, Davidic descendant, with the whole world as his domain—if it would accept him, if we would help spread this peace in our own small worlds of family, friends, workplaces. And how easy and quick it can be to discard the peace and joy of Christmas Day, tossing it away with the discarded wrappings and insubstantial tinsel.

Jesus was not born in the familiarity of his own home, not surrounded by celebrating family and friends. Mary's birth pangs and Joseph's shared pain come as they are on a journey and among strangers. The traditional interpretation of "no room for them at the inn" has been one of negative refusal to help an obviously pregnant, near-to-full-term woman and her husband, something that would be abhorrent to Middle Eastern hospitality. Could it be that Luke is already emphasizing that it is the poor who are willing to give what they have, even if this is only the humble hospitality of a room shared with the animals and a feeding-trough bed for the new-born rather than more conventional guest accommodation? Given that he is writing fifty or so years after the resurrection of Jesus, Luke has surely experienced this, been moved by it, and challenges his more affluent communities with it. How often, to our shame, have the poor witnessed this to us in our own times?

The child is twice described as "wrapped in swaddling bands," revealed as bound into a real, enfleshed humanity by the birth customs and culture of his particular time and place. As the Book of Wisdom proclaims, these are the same for king or commoner (Wis 7:4-5). Yet what is concealed is sung to the shepherds by the peaceful militia of angels: "to you is born this day in the city of David a Savior, who is the Messiah, the Lord." And this is a great joy for all the people. This is the good news that will turn the shepherds from a terrified, ostracized huddle on a Bethlehem hillside into seekers and proclaimers of what they find.

By the proclamation to the shepherds Luke again chooses to make the poor and marginalized the first people who hear the good news of Christ's birth. For the first time in his gospel he uses the word "today." When we hear this word as a eucharistic assembly, it becomes a present call to us to respond out of the poverty of our human and holy longings: to go and find the child of peace, to share the joy of our finding, to gaze with the eyes of faith on what the shepherds saw, to glorify and praise God—and go home changed. We find the Child laid "today" not only in the feeding place of the eucharistic table but also in our sisters and brothers, those to whom we also say "Amen" when we receive the body of Christ, and especially those whom Luke's Christmas Gospel is all about: the hospitable, the peaceful, the poor and disregarded.

There was blood and sweat and pain that night. As Isaiah had hoped, but never saw, it was not the blood and pain of war and death, but that of birth. The light that gleams on the birthing woman's sweat, the glistening womb-wet child and the gentle, calloused, and midwifing hands of a carpenter will become the great light for those who walk in darkness. In this beginning, the Wonder-Counselor, Mighty-God, Eternal-Father—the Word made flesh—can only whimper and fill his mouth with his mother's breast. His newborn eyes do not yet focus on the world beyond the womb. And we respond to Isaiah's words with joyful faith: "Today is born our Savior, Christ the Lord."

The short second reading from the Letter to Titus calls us to a practical response to the revelation of God's graciousness that has appeared in Christ Jesus. The divine grace, which was Isaiah's hope and which took flesh most radically in Jesus, is incarnate in the quality of our human relationships. The author of the Letter describes these as the avoidance of "worldly ambitions," disciplining ourselves with "self-restraint," and living "good and religious lives."

We live in hope of another Appearing, a Coming at the end of human history, when the birth pangs of the new creation will come upon the cosmos. Then Jesus will gather to himself, and reveal in a way beyond our imaginations, all those who have given him the hospitality of their hearts and the blood and sweat and pain of their faithful discipleship.

For many people without much love in their lives, Christmas can be a hard season. Suicide rates go up, family quarrels break out, the loneliness of the bereaved and the friendless is felt more sharply. War may seem to be more actively pursued than peace, and the "hosts" are not an angelic good news chorus, but invading military militias or terrorists. How true does the Christmas story ring in a personal or global night that is starved of stars and carols? Yet perhaps our traditional celebration of Jesus' birth at midnight is a reminder that the darker the night, the more joyous the dawn with which it is pregnant.

Sunday in the Octave of Christmas

Feast of the Holy Family of Jesus, Mary, and Joseph

• 1 Sam 1:20-22, 24-28 • Ps 84:2-3, 5-6, 9-10 • 1 John 3:1-2, 21-24 • Luke 2:41-52

This feast has wandered through the liturgical calendar for just over a century since Leo XIII established it in 1893 as an optional celebration for what was then the Third Sunday after Epiphany. It was a call to the church to remember the holiness of family life and morality in the face of social changes of the nineteenth century that were a threat to it. Eventually it was made a feast of the universal church by Benedict XV and, in accordance with the liturgical reform of the Roman calendar by Vatican II, has finally settled on the Sunday after Christmas (or December 30, if there is no Sunday between December 25 and January 1).

"Family" today has many cultural and moral connotations and challenges for Christians. We are familiar with those who may belong to separated, divorced, blended, or single parent families. Discussion of same-sex "family" takes place in legislative bodies, churches, and gay groups. The public, and parents above all, are horrified by child abuse and pornography that can reach its tentacles into home, school, church, tourism, and the Internet to disrupt and destroy family relations. For some people, therefore, the "Holy Family of Jesus, Mary, and Joseph" may seem to exist on another planet or, at least, be light years away from twenty-first century relevance. Yet the gospel truth that the Word of God for this feast affirms is that family life is "a kind of school of deeper humanity"[2] that is penetrated by the spirit of Christ. It is a challenge to live in mutual respect and love: for parents to honor the dignity of their children, and children respect the dignity of their parents, each one bound to the other in the love that God has lavished upon us, as John writes in today's second reading.

Our understanding of what we usually call "the finding in the temple," has often been sabotaged by artistic depictions of a precocious child Jesus, haloed and white-clad, lecturing (and even berating!) the religious teachers. Yet if we are attentive to the text, Jesus is described as first *listening* to the Temple teachers before asking questions at what was a customary festival and Sabbath question-and-answer session (as opposed to a judicial one). "Searching" and "finding" are important gospel themes in Luke. They reflect the human experience that so often our questing involves questioning, in the hope that we will find that something more: more love, more wisdom, more truth.

Any parent can appreciate Mary and Joseph's desperate search for and relief at finding Jesus, but there is another search, another finding that is of central importance. It hangs painfully on Jesus' response to his mother's question (v. 48), "Child, why have you treated us like this?" The first words of Jesus in Luke's gospel are his response: "Why were you looking for me? Did you not know that I must be busy with my Father's affairs?"—the affairs that will take Jesus through a life of obedience, through another Passover of pain, another three-day loss in the tomb and into his new and risen life. The most significant developmental task of adolescence is the search for and gradual finding of one's identity, and as R. Alan Culpepper comments: "What defines one's identity—family ties, religious experience, a sense of vocation, a personal creed, or one's dreams and ideals? Jesus found his identity by affirming his relationship with God."[3]

For Mary and Joseph, as for all parents, there is the pain of allowing this child his independence, his identity, loving him, not possessing him or punishing him, but not fully understanding him. Surely a sword passes also through Joseph's heart as, in response to Mary's words about "your father and I," and as if gently contradicting her, Jesus refers to "my Father." For us, as for Joseph, commitment to gospel priorities will always cause some pain. Parents know this in a special and poignant way. For now, this "passover" of the adolescent Jesus is a theological sign of what is to come.

After this, Jesus returns to Nazareth with Mary and Joseph and is obedient to them. In the verse preceding this Gospel (Luke 2:40), Luke had written of the growth of Jesus in human and divine wisdom after his presentation in the Temple. The last verse of this Temple incident with which Luke ends his narrative of Jesus' childhood is again a comment that it was in this human family that such growth continued. An aspect of doing his Father's will was his openness to being graced by the precious relationships of his family at Nazareth. Children and parents in every age and culture are meant to be grace for one another.

In the first reading, Hannah is also a woman for whom motherhood involves generous dispossession. She offers back to temple service her son, Samuel (Hebrew "lent by God"), the child born to her after her desperate prayer in the same temple (1 Sam 1:9-18). Sustained by the love of her husband Elkanah, despite her infertility, she had long prayed for a child, and God answered her prayer. Many generations later, Mary and Joseph, sustained by their mutual love, must also accept to be dispossessed, to lose the son who one day will be not only in the temple, but the very Temple itself. Happy are we who dwell in this Temple, built into it as living stones by our baptism.

Just as every family is called to be a "domestic church,"[4] so the church is called to be a "family of God." In his First Letter, John reminds his communities that they are God's children. Mary and Joseph could not fully understand who Jesus was; we cannot even understand ourselves as God's children, says John, for what we are to be so wonderfully in the future has not yet been revealed to us. So we live in faith and hope that one day we shall be like God, seeing him as he really is. Our faith and hope must be expressed in obedience to God and the love of one another, as Jesus has told us and the Spirit enables us.

Octave of Christmas

Solemnity of Mary, Mother of God

• Num 6:22-27 • Ps 67:2-3, 5-6, 8 • Gal 4:4-7 • Luke 2:16-21

The liturgical emphasis of this day is on the octave of Christmas rather than on the fact that it is the civil New Year for those who follow the Gregorian calendar. The Gospel is a repeat of the Christmas dawn Mass, with the addition of the verse that describes the circumcision and naming of Jesus. This is Luke's first emphasis on the Jewishness of Jesus, and on Mary's and Joseph's obedience to the Mosaic law. The first obedience Luke describes, however, is that of the shepherds. For the sake of their flocks, they were familiar with reading the skies and stars and listening to the singing of the winds; then one night they hear and see hosts of angels leading them over to Bethlehem.

Marginalized by the self-righteous who considered them irreligious because of their handling of their animals, and especially because their work did not permit them to leave their flocks unsupervised in order to participate in regular worship, these are the first people who are called to a new "worship," to a new "leaving all" of their flocks in order to go to the Christ Child. They risk a hasty journey down from the hills to the town. Perhaps it is the unexpectedness of the choice of themselves, poor and marginalized ones, as hearers of the angel's proclamation, that urges them and opens them to faith in what they see there: a man and woman with a newborn child, "a Savior, who is the Messiah, the Lord" (Luke 2:11). And when they return to their flocks, to their ordinary life, they return as people of praise, giving glory on their small piece of earth to what the angels had glorified in the vast heavens above them.

In his "Annunciation to the Shepherds from Above," Rainer Maria Rilke has the Christ himself speak to the shepherds:

> Look up you men, Men at the fire there, you
> familiar with the skies unbounded ways,
> star readers, hither! Look, I am a new
> uprising star. My being is one blaze,
> so filled with light the firmament is too
> small now to hold me and my powerful rays,
> for all its depth. Do let my splendor throw
> its beams right into you: oh the dark sight,
> the gloomy hearts, destinies black as night
> that you're brim-full of. Shepherd, I am so
> alone in you. Yet now there's room for me.
> . . . To you I can speak out,
> you have discretion; straight souls, free from doubt,
> you hear tongues everywhere.[5]

Mary hears what the shepherds repeat to her and, in contrast to their rush and excitement, around her there is silence. For a second time, she "ponders" what she has heard. The Greek word that Luke uses is from *symballo*, with the meaning of "throwing together," "discussing." Mary tries to "throw things together": her own human experience, the divine power which she knows is working in her, the vulnerable child of her womb, and what the shepherds have told her—the holy, messianic naming of the Son. Before her there lies a lifetime of such pondering. She is surely the model for our pondering of the Word, for the times of reflective silence that we all need to find, for the challenge that disciples of Jesus accept: to constantly try to treasure the good news about Jesus, and treasure this in spite of the often contradictory voices we hear.

Mary had already been greeted by the angel of the annunciation as "favored one," and by Elizabeth as "blessed." The first reading chosen for today is the most solemn blessing of the Old Testament, a Jewish blessing that, by its transplantation into the liturgy of this feast, serves to bless Mary as the one upon whom God's face has shone in a unique way; the woman whom God has favored with the joy and pain of the motherhood of Christ and the members of his body; the woman to whom God gives not just the peace of Christmas, but also that of the Resurrection morning.

For those of us for whom today is not only the Octave of Christmas but also the civil New Year's Day, this is a day of partying and pleasure, of seeing out the old and seeing in the new. What this newness also means for Christians is reflected in Luke's portrait of both the active, excited shepherds, obedient to the word of God, and in his cameo of Mary, still and silent with the Word made flesh. Both activity and excitement, stillness and silence are needed in our lives if we are to recognize the Christ and tell this good news to others throughout this year and the years to come.

Eight days after his birth, in accordance with the Jewish law, the flesh of Jesus is marked with the "covenant of circumcision." In his humanity he is truly of Abraham's seed, and is called by the ritual to renew this covenant in his flesh (Gen 17:9-14). For the first time, Jesus' blood flows in covenant making. Like no other Jew before or since, Jesus will reaffirm his covenantal living every day of his life, and at his death when there will be another flow of blood, another covenant which Jesus will make in his body and blood (Luke 22:20). As with all Jewish sons at their circumcision, Jesus is also named— named with the name that was announced by the angel to Mary before he was conceived and which sums up his person: Jesus, "he who saves."

In his Letter to the Galatians, Paul makes his only statement about the humanity of Jesus. He is "born of a woman," and he is born Jewish, "under the law." But he is also Son of God. For Paul, this is a matter of faith, not the beginning of a theological discussion. He continues with an almost ecstatic profession of the consequences of this faith: our adoption, through Christ, as free sons and daughters of God whom we recognize as "Abba," "Father," because the Spirit of Jesus is naming this in our personal depths. In our eucharistic assembly we will profess this faith when we pray in the words that Jesus taught us: Our Father . . . .

We cannot see what the year ahead holds for us, do not know what joys or sorrows we will inherit. But as children of God, and therefore heirs to the riches of his grace, we struggle to become, day after day, what we really are. The woman of whom Christ was born, whose solemnity we celebrate today, will mother us, too, into this maturity.

The Epiphany of the Lord

• Isa 60:1-6 • Ps 72:1-2, 7-8, 10-13 • Eph 3:2-3a, 5-6 • Matt 2:1-12

This is a feast for seekers and stargazers, for wanderers and wonderers who refuse to allow themselves to settle into comfortable indifference. It is a story of hypocrisy and political intrigue and the outwitting of them. This feast may bring us back home, contemporary "Babylonian" exiles that we are (cf. the first reading), to love and wisdom—out of the consumerism of after-Christmas sales and overdrawn credit cards or the vague feelings of guilt toward those to whom we wished Christmas blessings more out of social pressure than personal regard. Historically, the development of this feast has taken different turns, but it has always come back to being a feast of revelation, of appearing or "epiphany," as the word suggests. In the East, the baptism of Jesus and the first of his miracles at Cana are also remembered, as they are at the gospel canticle antiphon for Evening Prayer II in the Western church.

The Magi may be historically controversial, but there is no doubt about the way in which they thrill our imagination and make us wonder about their visit to the child. Wonder and excitement about journeying to Jesus are important for every Christian, king or commoner. It is not from the Bible but from a legend recorded by the eighth-century saint and first English historian, Bede the Venerable, that we have numbered and named them Melchior, Caspar, and Balthasar. And the twentieth-century operetta, *Amahl and the Night Visitors*, reinforced this nomenclature. Artists, especially after the discovery of the New World, have often made the Magi a multiracial trio, with their black, red, and yellow faces, and the presumption of a one-to-one correspondence with their three gifts. The scholars may rightly debate historical issues; as listeners to the biblical word proclaimed in the assembly, and prayed in our sacred reading, we simply accept the narrative of the feast as story, but as story laden with symbols and rich in theological associations. And a story is often the surest, straightest line to the truth.

Guided by their natural and scientific wisdom, equipped with wealth and readiness to take risks, the Magi—learned ones, possibly Persian astronomers—discover that following a star and searching for the truth can lead one into a political minefield. (Some things never change!) It was a widespread belief that heavenly portents marked the birth of great leaders, and so they come to Jerusalem to look for a baby whom they describe as the "infant king of the Jews." Panicking at the suggestion of any threat to his power, Herod gathers around him his "yes" men, those whom Matthew names as the same opponents of Jesus in the passion narrative (Matt 26:57), and inquires of them where the Messiah was to be born. For his own theological purposes, Matthew modifies the prophet Micah's text with the Davidic text from 2 Samuel 5:2 to add a royal note to the search for the newborn King. The wisdom of the Word of God in the Hebrew Scriptures is thus offered and accepted by the Magi. They have the humility to know that they are not self-sufficient, that they need help on their search; and they have the discernment that sees through Herod's hypocritical and vicious suggestion that, when the Magi have found the child, they return to tell Herod the whereabouts of the child so that he, too, can go and pay him homage.

In the Gentile Magi, the divisions of culture, religions, and nation are reconciled because: "Lord, every nation on earth will adore you," as we respond with the antiphon to Psalm 72. If we believe that every nation, every religion has some gift to offer God, can we dare refuse to accept the gifts that strangers bring us? A multicultural society and church is a witness to the inclusiveness that Christ asks of us.

The most important gift we can offer Christ, the gift that is richer than any gold, frankincense, or myrrh is, of course, the wealth of our love and the fragrant readiness of suffering which this will inevitably entail. This is beautifully shown in O. Henry's short story, "The Gift of the Magi." Jim and Della, husband and wife, decide to give each other special Christmas presents. They are poor, but each has a prized possession. Della's is her lovely long hair; Jim's is his fob watch. Della cuts her hair and sells it in order to buy Jim a platinum chain for his watch. Jim sells his watch so that he can buy a set of pure tortoiseshell combs for Della's hair. Then comes the moment of "epiphany," the revelation of the love behind both of their sacrifices that is the most precious gift. O. Henry ends his story with the affirmation of the loving wisdom of Jim and Della as gift givers.[6]

In the gifts that the wise ones offer to the Christ child there is again the hint of the paschal mystery: the myrrh of embalming, the frankincense that fragranced the Temple sacrifices and burned before the Holy of Holies, the gold of precious value. The Magi go home by another route when they realize that they are being manipulated by hypocrisy and jealous power-seeking. It is, Matthew suggests, often the strangers and outsiders—and today read the asylum seekers or the unpretentious poor or those who work for justice—who reveal to us, as individuals and as nations, how and what we should be seeking and how to come home to this truth. This is movingly expressed in the anonymous poem written by an asylum seeker in an Australian detention center:

> I do not know what will happen after I die.
> I do not want to know.
> But I would like the Potter to make

a whistle from the clay of my throat.
May this whistle fall into the hands
of a cheeky and naughty child
and the child blow hard on the whistle continuously
with the suppressed and silent air of his lungs
and disrupt the sleep
of those who seem dead
to my cries.[7]

In Isaiah's prophetic vision, the heart of Jerusalem expands and throbs with joy as not only her own sons and daughters stream into her from their exile in Babylon, but other nations bring the gifts of economic prosperity to her. The allusion to the gifts as gold, frankincense, and myrrh and to the givers as kings is an obvious reason for the Lectionary's choice of the first reading. But Jerusalem's rising from the ruins is above all because of the wealth of love God has for his people.

The author of the Letter to the Ephesians also proclaims the revelation of God's love in Jesus Christ. Regardless of where people come from, all people may inherit the same divine promises, be recognized as parts of the same body of Christ Jesus, through the free workings of the Spirit. Do we really accept, do we want, such a revelation? Are we ready to live the consequences of this Christmas gift of God's revealing grace throughout the coming year?

The Baptism of the Lord

• Isa 40:1-5, 9-11 • Ps 104:1b-4, 24-25, 27-30 • Acts 10:34-38 • Luke 3:15-16, 21-22

Hopefully, we have often witnessed it: the priest rolling up his sleeves in readiness for the ministry of the waters, the invitation of the children in the assembly to gather around the font, the reverent taking of the naked, tiny, and vulnerable scrap of humanity and the holding up of him/her to the people into whose faith this child will be baptized. Then there is the triple immersion: in the name of the Father, the Son, and the Holy Spirit— sometimes with slightly outraged protest, more often with the quietness of pleasant familiarity with the waters of the womb. Then another elevation, and this child of God is shown with a new christened identity to the assembly. There is always applause, always a smile on even the most bored faces, and a moment in which human and holy solidarity is felt, not only by the proud parents but also by the gathered local church. It is a moment that is truly "sacramental," a sign of some greater and hidden mystery of God's extraordinary love; and it is a humbling realization. The child has done nothing to deserve this, except for the wonderful obedience of being born. One can almost hear the biblical question echoing down the centuries, with all its hopes and fears: "What then will this child become?" (Luke 1:66). In Luke's Gospel, that question had been asked about John the Baptist at his circumcision. It is the adult John that we meet again in today's gospel, and it is in the context of water and baptism.

The solidarity of a parish baptism, the communal event that it is, reflects Luke's narrative. Jesus is surrounded by people who had been baptized by John. The Baptist is humble, for when the people express a wondering expectancy that he might be the promised messiah, John is strong to resist the temptation to self-aggrandizement, quick to dispel any illusions about his status. He is only a servant, he says, who is not even worthy to perform the menial task of doing up the sandal straps of the coming One. He points out to the crowd the differences between himself and the One who is to come: his is a baptism of water and repentance; the Messiah's will be a baptism of transformation through fire and the Holy Spirit. Probably the Baptist is referring to the end time, but Luke announces this with the insight of a post-Pentecost evangelist and the experience of the transformation of that fire and wind-struck day (Acts 2:1-4).

To the good news of solidarity and humility, Luke adds the significance of prayer. Several times in his gospel Luke sets important events in Jesus' life and mission in the context of prayer (e.g., Luke 6:12-13; 9:28; 22:42-46). Jesus dies with the words of Psalm 31:5 on his lips. The baptism of the Lord could be called a prayer event, for Luke does not describe the moment of baptism but rather its aftermath. It is Jesus' prayer that tears open the heavens for the descent of the Holy Spirit and the revelation of his true identity by the Father's voice that acclaims him as the Beloved Son on whom God's favor rests.

It is the same for us. Prayer is a necessary part of our identity as baptized sons and daughters of God. It opens heaven to us and reveals who we are for, in a very real sense, we are who we pray. At prayer we struggle to hear what God is calling us to be, to know who we are in our deepest truth, at the still point where the Spirit has descended into our depths and anointed us for mission.

The responsorial Psalm 104 is a praise of God's creation, and the baptism of Jesus is a revelation of the new creation as the Spirit of God broods over the Jordan waters that are parted by the humanity of Jesus. It is seen to be very good, and we cry out: "Oh, bless the Lord, my soul!" The liturgy also presents this psalm as an acclamation of the God who is described in the first reading from the prophet Isaiah, the God who "recreates" the people of Israel, transforming them from exiles in Babylon to "home-comers" to Jerusalem. It is especially the weak ones, those who need loving care like that which a shepherd gives to newborn lambs and their mother ewes, who will be carried home by God's gentle strength. It is this same gentle power that, in Christ, embraces every child who is recreated in baptism.

In the reading from the Acts of the Apostles, Peter also refers to John the Baptist and Jesus' anointing with the Holy Spirit and with power. He is speaking in the house of Cornelius, a Roman centurion and "God-seeker," to whom he has been summoned after the experiences described earlier in Acts 10 and which would culminate in one of the most significant "recreations" of Peter and the early apostolic church. This context needs to be explained (and preferably read). Peter, too, had heard a voice from heaven that had disturbed his noontime prayer on the rooftop. Hungry and sleepy, he has a vision of a tablecloth that descends from heaven containing living creatures that were considered ritually unclean by the Mosaic Law. All his life these had been forbidden as food to Peter, so when he is commanded by the voice (which he recognizes as the Lord's) to get up and eat, he protests vehemently. Then comes the triple injunction that will transform the early church: "What God has made clean, you must not call profane" (Acts 10:15). As the tablecloth of unclean creatures is whisked away, it is replaced by three "unclean" men, Gentiles, who come from Cornelius to beg Peter to come down with them to the centurion's house. Cornelius, too, has heard God's voice telling him to send for Peter. With the realization that God has no partiality, that the divisions of clean and unclean apply neither to food nor to people, Peter takes the huge step over the Gentile threshold and witnesses there to Jesus. In the verses that follow today's reading, and before Peter has finished speaking, the transforming Holy Spirit falls upon the Gentile household and, with Peter's humble assent, they are baptized in the name of Jesus.

Deaf and blind from the age of nineteen months, seven-year-old Helen Keller had learned the finger spelling of many words during the four months since meeting her partially blind teacher, Annie Sullivan, but she did not connect them with any reality. One day in 1892 when they were passing a water pump, Annie placed Helen's hand under the running water and pressed into it the word: W-A-T-E-R. From that moment, Helen became a "new creation" who began to connect the alphabet of the deaf with real objects, and a person who would eventually amaze and inspire so many through her work for people with disabilities, especially the visually impaired.

As we conclude the Christmas cycle with the solemnity of the Baptism of the Lord, "water" is the word that we should press into our Christian consciousness. We *are* (not were) baptized, called into new connections between the reality of our world and the water of our baptism. Do we respond with blessing for God's gifts to us as his baptized people, his beloved in the Beloved? Do we really believe that God shows no partiality and so respects all people, no matter what their religion, ethnicity, or culture? Are we a church of a shepherding God, with a care for the weak and helpless? Day after day, we are called to become what we are: people of the water and the Holy Spirit.

Notes

1. Brian Linard, ed., *A Way to the Heart of Christmas* (New York: New City Press, 1991) 7.

2. Vatican II, *The Church in the Modern World*, art. 52.

3. R. Alan Culpepper, "The Gospel of Luke: Introduction, Commentary and Reflections," in *The New Interpreter's Bible*, vol. IX (Nashville: Abingdon Press, 1995) 78.

4. Vatican II, *Dogmatic Constitution on the Church*, art. 11.

5. Rainer Maria Rilke, "Annunciation to the Shepherds from Above," in *Selected Work: Volume II*, trans. J. B. Leishman, copyright 1960 by New Directions Publishing Corp.

6. O. Henry, *Treasury of World Masterpieces: O. Henry* (London: Octopus Books Limited, 1983) 649–653.

7. An anonymous poet, Baxter Immigration Facility, Port Augusta, South Australia. Used with permission.

3

The Season of Lent

We are fond of logos. Schools, businesses, sporting clubs and teams, community groups, travel agencies, all use them to say—often superficially: "You belong to us, and we belong to each other." As we prepare to enter into the Season of Lent, the Church presents us with a "logo." Not a very elegantly designed logo, this cruciform smudge of ash on our foreheads, but then neither was the crucifixion of Jesus elegant. Nor is the cross of ash gentle and fragrant like the first cross that was traced on us with the oils of catechumens and chrism at baptism. Our first liturgical fingerprinting recorded our identity as "Christian," as one committed to living and dying and rising with Christ. The cross another brother or sister traces on us today is rougher, grittier, dirtier than the cross of baptismal oils—because that it how our lives have become. As we receive the ashes, the words of both options are stark and urgent: "Repent and believe in the gospel," or "Remember that you are dust, and unto dust you will return." Remember what Lent is all about.

The ritual of Ash Wednesday speaks of realities that our glossy personal and social masks usually try to hide, and perhaps so many people come to receive the ashes because it is a relief to admit in ritual what we find so difficult to put into words: that there are the "tears of things" within and around us: the grief and tragedy, the despair and deaths that are part of the dust and ashes of human life. Ideally, people bring their last year's palms to the church on the Sunday before Ash Wednesday and incorporate the burning of these into the liturgy to provide the ashes with which they will be anointed in three days' time. Here are the palms that we held in our hands a year ago when, on Palm Sunday, we sang our "Hosannas." And yet we know that so often we have been unfaithful to the King we hailed and whose coming we called blessed. Many times our commitment to Christ has become as insubstantial as ash. But as those who live in bushfire-prone areas know, ash is also the regenerating remnant of what was once alive and can again bring forth prolific new life.

Many things that were once alive in us have probably died and turned to ash: loved ones have died, illness has struck, friendships may have been broken, illusions about ourselves or others have been destroyed. It is out of such ashes that we hope Christ will raise us up to new life with him at Easter. In the season of Lent, therefore, the Church calls us to traditional Christian practices: to prayer that is not wordy or ostentatious; to fasting that is not cosmetic but an expression of our action for and solidarity with those who hunger for justice; and to almsgiving that is not a hypocritical trumpeting of or subtle hinting at our good works and generosity. The Japanese have a beautiful proverb that says: "Something of the fragrance of the flowers lingers on the hands of the giver." Whatever we do in Lent should seep unobtrusively into our world and relationships, and yet it will also transform us with the lingering "fragrance that comes from knowing him" (2 Cor 2:14) and our attempts to live his mystery more deeply during this season.

Just as in every human birth there is the breaking of the waters and the flowing of blood, so it is when we have been carried in the womb of the Church through the days of Lent to the three-day feast of the Easter Triduum. In those days, for which all the Lenten days are a pregnancy, we will again participate in the mystery of our passage through the water and blood as we are reborn in the spirit of the risen Christ.

First Sunday of Lent

• Deut 26:4-10 • Ps 91:1-2, 10-15 • Rom 10:8-13 • Luke 4:1-13

The First Sunday of Lent always leads us into the wilderness, into that biblical place of contradictions for the sons and daughters of God: the place of covenant making and covenant breaking, of freedom shouts and discontented grumblings, of exhilaration and exhaustion. At the beginning of Lent, the Church challenges us to reflect on how, as God's people, we still live our lives in such a wilderness. Yet it also asks us to do this in the company of Jesus who endured the wilderness temptations, who was challenged to make choices about his identity and how and if he would live as "beloved Son." Jesus is the image of and supreme challenge to our humanity about which we are reminded on Ash Wednesday.

In the first verse of the gospel, the *Spirit* is described as leading Jesus into the wilderness to be tempted by the devil, and the last verse announces that, after Jesus had withstood the temptations, the devil left him—but only to return when the *opportunity* (the Greek *kairos*) is right. That poignant and tragic opportunity will come again on the eve of Jesus' passion when Judas decides to betray his master (Luke 22:6). We might ask ourselves if we ever put ourselves into today's gospel in the role of the tempter. Do we dare to believe that we can be stumbling blocks, obstacles to the Christian commitment of our sisters and brothers? For us, as for Jesus, temptation is not over after one successful struggle; it is a process of ongoing choices that either strengthen or weaken our Christian commitment.

Throughout his public ministry, Jesus confronted the temptations that are telescoped here into one event: the temptation to be a convenient "bread-making" messiah; to seek power rather than powerlessness; to be delivered from a suffering servant's death. The tempter is personal, direct, confrontational. Whether literally or symbolically, Luke depicts Jesus at a most vulnerable "desert" moment, the first of many during his life. He is at the end of forty days of fasting. He has not yet preached one sermon, cast out one demon, healed one sick person. He is alone, hungry, poised at the edge of decision making before his Father and his own truth. With perfect timing, the tempter arrives with three attractive propositions.

Each temptation begins with "*If* you are the Son of God. . . ." But just before Luke has led us into the wilderness event, he has given us the genealogy of Jesus that is climaxed with the statement that Jesus is "son of Adam, son of God" (Luke 3:38). Now he will be tested in his obedience to that identity. For Jesus to turn stones into bread would mean great personal and social advantages: neither he nor the poor of the land need be hungry anymore, the tempter implies! But Jesus answers that it is not bread alone, but the Word of God that is life-giving food. People of every generation must transplant the wilderness temptations into their own life and times, and the first contemporary temptation is to neglect the Word of God and allow ourselves to be seduced by so many other words: mobile phones, faxes, mass media, the flood of computerized information, our often mindless and heartless inner and outer conversations. The Word of God feeds our deepest hungers. Our obedience to this Word is expressed in our attentive listening to its proclamation, especially in the Sunday liturgy, in our prayerful reading of Holy Scripture (*lectio divina*), and our efforts to make this Word "living and active" (Heb 4:12) from day to day.

The people of first-century Palestine who were living under the oppression of the Roman Empire were hoping for political redemption. If Jesus seizes power and glory, suggests the devil in his second temptation, what he could do for them! But Jesus knows what this would mean: power and authority handed to him by the tempter would bring with it oppression and violence (Luke 4:1-14). Instead, Jesus will go the longer, less immediate and more sacrificial way of service to others rather than domination over them. He will wait to receive the kingdom from the hand of his Father rather than from the devil, the ruler of a "counter-kingdom." Jesus will establish a healing reign over sick bodies, tormented psyches, and a troubled cosmos. We are only too familiar with scenarios of unjust wars and political compromise in the lust for power. We certainly need to take a stand against these, but perhaps we are less conscious of the compromises in ourselves: of that bargaining for a little more status and authority at the expense of others and the effect that this has on world history—whose time we share. We can often be tempted to serve personal success rather than fidelity to God, our own reputation rather than the needs of our brothers and sisters, political expediency rather than justice. "God only shall you serve" will involve Christians in the self-sacrificing obedience of Jesus.

The third temptation is for Jesus to launch his messianic career with a spectacular stunt—throwing himself from the high point of the Jerusalem Temple. The tempter assures Jesus that, as a privileged Son, God will certainly deliver him from any human and airborne limitations by sending angels to catch him and carry him to safety. And what religious authority his survival would give him! But Jesus will be true to his sonship not by flamboyant acts but by suffering an impoverished death on a cross, a commonplace punishment for criminals. Only then will come Jesus' leap of faith, not from the Temple pinnacle, but from the raised cross on Calvary; not into angels' hands but into the hands of his Father (Luke 23:46) who will lift him up in the Resurrection. Often we would like God to treat us as "different," "special" people who deserve miraculous intervention and deliverance from the limitations of our humanity. This will be offered to us, but only in the way in which it was offered to Jesus: by the way of suffering, dying, and rising with him.

The tempter subtly manipulates Scripture, picking and choosing words, quoting them out of context for his own ends. Each of Jesus' responses to the devil is also a quotation from the Hebrew Scriptures, but correctly used and Spirit-filled, his strong weapon against evil. From his childhood, Jesus had been formed by the creed and creativity of the Old Testament, and in this encounter Luke gives us no other dialogue except: "It is written. . . ."

The first reading is one of such formative creedal statements of the Old Testament. It was part of the ritual for the Festival of Ingathering, a late summer festival in which a basket of first fruits was offered to God as a symbolic acknowledgment that the land that had brought forth this harvest was a gift of God to the ancestors of Israel. And it was a gift to a vulnerable, hungry people who had suffered at the hands of the Egyptians and were called out of slavery into the wilderness experience under the protection of the "mighty hand and outstretched arm" of their God. This is the God to whom Jesus was obedient in his wilderness experience, and our God to whom we pray in the responsorial Psalm 91: "Be with me, Lord, when I am in trouble." As in all liturgy, there is a sense of solidarity, a present identification with the past for the sake of and hope in our future.

As Paul explains to his church at Rome in the second reading, Scripture is the word of faith, the word that comes from the heart of God, to be welcomed into our hearts, spoken to our world, and lived daily. We still need to be alert to the misuse of Scripture, especially its fundamentalist interpretation.

In *The Interpretation of the Bible in the Church* (1993) the Pontifical Biblical Commission reminds us that:

> The fundamentalist approach is dangerous, for it is attractive to people who look to the Bible for ready answers to the problems of life. It can deceive these people, offering them interpretations that are pious but illusory, instead of telling them that the Bible does not necessarily contain an immediate answer to each and every problem. Without saying as much in so many words, fundamentalism actually invites people to a kind of intellectual suicide (art. 110).

It is another "treasonable" temptation to be avoided.

Second Sunday of Lent

• Gen 15: 5-12, 17-18 • Ps 27:1, 7-9, 13-14 • Phil 3:17–4:1 • Luke 9:28b-36

> Great things are done
> when men and mountains meet.
> This is not done
> by jostling in the street.[1]

So wrote William Blake.

Jesus has been "jostling" with his disciples in the first prediction of the Passion that immediately precedes the gospel that we hear today. It is to that prediction that reference is made in the first half of the beginning verse (omitted in the Lectionary): "Now about eight days after these sayings. . . ." The disciples could not understand a vision of a suffering messiah that was so alien to their own preconceived ideas. Talk of rejection, killing, and rising again was all too much! Worse still was what seemed to be Jesus' invitation to follow him into these dark and terrifying experiences. To be faithful to him, they would need some sustaining ray of light, some vision of truth that was, as yet, invisible in Jesus' humanity. And so Jesus takes them up a mountain, away from the "jostling" of crowds and their own inner turmoil. Mountains are places of new perspectives on the familiar plains, of further seeing and harder breathing which, in the Scriptures, are symbolic of so much more than the physical or geographical. But the mountain can also be a place of danger and death.

Luke describes what we have come to call Jesus' "transfiguration" as happening "while he was praying," so emphasizing the power of prayer to mediate the presence of God and the consequent transformation of the one who prays. For a passing moment, the light of the glory of God, the personal reality of Jesus, is unveiled in his face and clothing—two symbolic indicators that still say something to us about a person. Then Jesus is joined by two of his ancestors, Moses and Elijah, two "mountain men" and men of forty-day experiences of both joy and sorrow. They talk with him about his departure, his "exodus," which he was to accomplish in Jerusalem. The first of these, Moses, had to cope with his people who frequently grumbled about their exodus into freedom out of Egyptian slavery. After passing forty days on Mount Sinai where he had been called by God to receive the divine teaching, Moses was transformed by his encounter and his face had become so radiant that when he came down from the mountain to his people he needed to veil himself lest his brightness blind them (Exod 34:29-35). Elijah had encountered God in the sheer (or "thin") silence outside the cave on Mount Horeb/Sinai after his forty-day flight from Jezebel, his too vicious slaughter of the false prophets she favored, and his arrogant ignoring of the other fifty true and hidden prophets of God (1 Kgs 18-19). Like ourselves, Jesus needed the support of others with whom he could talk of his own journey through life and death into glory. With his half-asleep disciples there was no such conversation or understanding. By this encounter with Jesus' Old Testament ancestors, Luke also witnesses to both continuity between the two Testaments and discontinuity in the preeminence of Jesus that will be revealed by his Father.

The glory of the Transfiguration eventually penetrates the fog of sleep that has been the result of the disciples' mountain climb. As it will be in Gethsemane, such sleep is the faithless opposite to watching and praying—a reality with which we may be all too familiar. As Moses and Elijah leave, Peter has what he considers his own moment of dazzling brilliance. He does not want to take any holy risks. A safer, more familiar solution, he suggests, would be to "house" the glory of Jesus, Moses, and Elijah in three tents (or "tabernacles") set up on this mountain. As observant Jews, Jesus and the disciples had all celebrated the Feast of Tabernacles/Booths from their childhood. That feast commemorates not only the wilderness wandering of Israel when the people lived in fragile, portable tents, but also the later dwelling of the cloud of God's glory, the *shekinah*, in the Jerusalem Temple. We have often been very pious about Peter's words, "Master, it is good for us to be here," but inattentive to Luke's following comment that Peter did not know what he was saying. Jesus' disciples are never to be frozen in the familiar. For Peter, James, and John, there is another mountain to be climbed, another transfiguration in blood and pain to be experienced before the glory of the Resurrection is revealed.

Then God, not Peter, takes the initiative—tenting over Jesus and the disciples with divine glory, overshadowing them with a cloud and calling them into its mystery. Over Moses on Mount Sinai, over Daniel's Son of Man, over Mary of Nazareth, the cloud was witness to and symbol of God's transfiguring presence. Now it embraces the tabernacle of Jesus' body along with those who are his companions. Terrified, they enter and hear the Father's assurance, given only to Jesus at his baptism but now announced to disciples of all times: "This is my Son, my Chosen; listen to him!" Then there is silence and Jesus alone is with them. They will go down from the mountain, onto the plain; and the struggle to understand Jesus goes on. On the plains of our everyday life, we struggle to respond to the Father's command: to listen to the Son, to become children of the light in his light, brothers and sisters who are ready to risk the unfamiliar and new because we are enveloped in the security of God's presence and promise. After the mountain of Jesus' transfiguration comes the hill of his crucifixion. Our pilgrim legs have to be strong for both climbs, and though we may not always recognize it, the "mountain top" experiences are often occasions where God allows us to catch our breath for the next and harder ascents.

In the first reading, God promises Abram (his name is not yet changed to Abraham) that despite his present childlessness, he will have descendants as many as the stars in the heavens and a land to call his own. Abram puts his faith in the One who is described symbolically at the beginning of this chapter as his "shield," the protective carrier of defense who went before the one at risk in battle. God then "cuts" a covenant with Abraham while he is in deep darkness, overwhelmed by a sleep that, in this instance, is a symbolical biblical assurance that all the initiative is with God. With the symbolism of smoke and a traveling torch of fire, God moves through a passage of divided animals to enact an ancient ritual that proclaimed that if promises are not kept, the same destruction may fall on the failing covenant partner (Jer 34:18-20). Here it is a divine and unilateral promise, and God, of course, will be faithful. One day a descendant of Abram, the bright Morning Star, will shine eternally in resurrection glory, a flash of which is glimpsed in the transfiguration of

Jesus. And as for the Land? Our prayer might continue to be offered in the words of the responsorial Psalm 27: "Hear, O Lord, when I cry aloud" for peace, for the two nations who both have Abraham as their father yet are so often "breathing out violence" against one another. In every darkness, personal, communal, or national, the Lord is the faithful promise maker who will be what the psalmist proclaims: our "light and our salvation."

Paul may sound arrogant when he tells his church at Philippi to imitate him, but these words need to be heard in the context of what he has written just a few verses before our Lectionary reading begins. For Paul it is also "Jesus alone," and he regards everything else in his life as rubbish so that he may gain Christ. This, and not any personal glory, is the commitment he wants to witness to the Philippians. For many people today, the cross is reduced to a fashionable, external piece of jewelry. For Paul, the cross is the way in which Christians will be transfigured in their inner depths into the mystery of Christ's death and resurrection. Abraham was promised a homeland; to us, says Paul, is promised the homeland of heaven if we live faithfully and trustfully in Christ. We can well imagine Paul praying today's psalm for himself, his dear Philippians, and for our Sunday assembly: "Wait for the Lord; be strong, and let your heart take courage."

Third Sunday of Lent

• Exod 3:1-8a, 13-15 • Ps 103:1-4, 6-8, 11 • 1 Cor 10:1-6, 10-12 • Luke 13:1-9

In today's gospel the crowd reminds Jesus about the tragedy of what happened to a group of Galileans who had been standing at the altar worshipping God when they themselves became sacrificial offerings at the hands of Pilate's henchman. Although not historically recorded outside the gospel, this would have been an incident as politically explosive as those that are still too tragically familiar in volatile and unreconciled parts of our world and in acts of indiscriminate terrorism. Jesus recognizes the unspoken but implied question: "Big sinners, big suffering?" and answers with an explicit "No." He himself raises the issue of eighteen people who were killed when the tower of Siloam accidentally collapsed on them for no known reason. Neither of these incidents, says Jesus, is about God's punishment of the victims' sinfulness, although human nature is sometimes and mistakenly quick to make such a judgment. They show, rather, the fragility of our lives and the suddenness with which death can overwhelm us. We can be tempted to query, privately or publicly, the truth of our response to Psalm 103, "The Lord is kind and merciful," but the laws of nature are not to be equated with the laws of morality.

Jesus uses these events to make one point: what happened was sudden, with no time to avoid the catastrophes. But there is a much greater catastrophe on which the people need to focus: their unpreparedness for the merciful yet just judgment of God. So Jesus tells a parable about an unproductive fruit tree. A healthy fruit tree is interdependent, not self-sufficient; it takes nourishment from the soil in which it is planted and is further nourished by the work of the gardener who fertilizes it. In turn, the tree gives back fruit.

In the judgment of the vineyard owner, time has run out for the tree that had not borne fruit for three years, and it deserves to be cut down. It is all "take" from the soil that must also nourish the other trees, and no "give." But the gardener begs his master to be patient and allow him another year of extra effort, of digging round and fertilizing the tree to see if it will bear some fruit. If it still does not, then it can be cut down. By choosing this reading for Lent, the Church suggests that the loving patience of our God is giving us another chance to do some seasonal gardening on ourselves: to loosen the soil around our personal and communal earthbound roots with the tools of prayer, fasting, and almsgiving; to fertilize our lives with the rich Lenten liturgy of word and sacrament; and to strengthen, not weaken, one another, by mutual care and kindness.

The tree is a fig, a sturdy tree. Unlike some of our indoor plants, fig trees do not droop and die overnight. It takes a long drought, continuous and insidious gnawing at the roots, or protracted neglect to make a fig tree barren. And what about us? What has gradually dried up and withered our Christian lives? Are there small infidelities that are gnawing away at the roots of our baptismal commitment? Are we failing to cultivate or prune our discipleship so that the sap of the Christ-life may continue to rise within us? Like the Galileans and the victims of the Siloam collapse, we can never be sure how many "next years" lie ahead of us. "Today," this Lent, is the important time of conversion.

In the first reading we meet Moses in the midst of his ordinary job of looking after his father-in-law's ordinary sheep in the ordinary wilderness around Horeb. Then into this ordinariness there comes an extraordinary intervention by God who takes possession of another tree, a worthless bramble, and transforms it by fire and voice into an unconsumed sign of divine presence. Moses' first movement toward the conversion of his life is when he notices the flames and takes the trouble to "turn aside" to see why the bush is not burned up. From the burning but unconsumed bush a voice is heard, calling Moses into its presence. Moses is told to take off his protective shoes and feel the new and holy ground on which he is being asked to walk. God names himself as the Genesis God of Moses' ancestors, the God of Abraham,

Isaac, and Joseph. This is the God who keeps promises: to the old and infertile who bear children, to the child of the promise who is saved from the knife for life and love, to the lamed trickster who becomes patriarch of the tribes.

But this God is not only a God concerned with the past. This is a God who is attentive to the present suffering of the Hebrews, who desires freedom and justice for them. Then the God who has spoken in the first person, the "I," suddenly switches to "you." The Lectionary omits the important verses 9-12 where, to his surprise and consternation, Moses discovers that in the liberation planned for his people God also plans to have Moses very much involved! God is not interested in Moses' personal ability, but in his availability. God will brand him with holy fire, not for slavery but for freedom, and will show him the compassion and strong love of which the responsorial Psalm 103 sings. In all the deeds of justice which God makes known from the burning bush, he will be with Moses.

Moses asks God what name he will tell the Hebrews when they ask him by whom he has been sent to lead them out of oppression. God replies with "I AM WHO I AM," which can also be translated "I WILL BE WHO I WILL BE," for Moses, and for all God's people until the end of time. This does not tell Moses much. It rather challenges him to commit himself to a great mystery, so God again reminds Moses of his ancestors to whom God was presence and power. What God was for them, he is and will be for Moses. God can break into our ordinary lives, too, and can call us to protest about the unjust status quo and ask us to be his instruments of liberation for our sisters and brothers. It will not be as dramatic as the Exodus encounter, but in our joys and sorrows, in the voices of our friends and even our enemies, and in contemporary historical events, we may one day hear God saying, "So come, I will send you."

In his Second Letter to the Corinthians, Paul remembers his ancestors of the wilderness generations in what is something of a cautionary genre. He reminds his church about the past that has present relevance for their lives in Corinth. Their ancestors experienced God's salvation through water when they passed through the Sea of Reeds, and their thirst was twice quenched by water from the rock in their desert wanderings (Exod 17:1-7; Num 20:2-13). Interpreting the past by the present, Paul calls Christ the rock from which the saving waters flowed. He also refers to the manna, the bread from heaven, by which God fed them in the wilderness. In this Letter, Paul is concerned with the waters of baptism and the bread of the Eucharist, and he warns the Corinthians that these sacraments are no more a guarantee of salvation than was the desert food and drink if they, too, are a sinful and grumbling people like many of those who were led by Moses.

Each Lent should draw us deeper into the mystery of the paschal fire which is the light of Christ, the "I AM" who is resurrection and life; into the waters that flow from his pierced side and to which we again commit ourselves when we renew our baptismal promises at the Easter Vigil; and into the bread baked hard in his passion and broken for us, a broken people, to make us one body in the risen body of Christ.

Fourth Sunday of Lent

• Josh 5:9a, 10-12 • Ps 34:2-7 • 2 Cor 5:17-21 • Luke 15:1-3, 11-32

In Year C, the gospel for this Sunday is repeated on the 24th Sunday in Ordinary Time. In this reflection, the focus will be more on its Lenten context and its relation to the other Lectionary readings.

The journalist Marina Cantacuzino founded in England the Forgiveness Project, a group that works with grassroots organizations for reconciliation, conflict resolution, and restorative justice through victim support. In 2004 they held what they called "The F Word" exhibition in the Oxo Gallery of London's South Bank. It was neither pornographic nor a study of popular slang usage. The "f" stood for "forgiveness," and consisted of a collection of photographs matched with twenty-six personal stories of forgiveness and reconciliation from South Africa, Rumania, Ukraine, Israel, Palestine, Northern Ireland, and England. The Forgiveness Project continues to build and expand such words and images, and is a traveling exhibition. Marina comments that for some people, "forgiveness" is still a "dirty word." One of the exhibition's patrons is Archbishop Desmond Tutu, much experienced in the South African Truth and Reconciliation Commission. In today's gospel, Jesus gives us his own words and a memorable image of forgiveness and reconciliation in the parable of the Prodigal Son.

The compassionate love of God in Christ is always ready to forgive sinners and welcome them home. This is the challenging truth that Jesus proclaims—to the consolation of the tax collectors and sinners, and the dismay of the Pharisees and scribes who were his audience. Today we are Jesus' Lenten audience. We are called to listen to the story of two brothers, neither of whom really knows what it means to be the son of a father who is prodigal in his love.

In *The Spiritual Life*, Evelyn Underhill commented that much of our lives revolve around the actions of "to Want, to Have, and to Do," to the neglect of "to Be."[2] The parable begins with the "want" of the younger son, a demand to have his share of his inheritance. In Middle Eastern context, this amounted to wishing that his father was dead, since that was the rightful time for inheritance. As a foolish lover, the father gives not only the younger son what he demands, but also gives a share to "them"—so including the older brother. In fact, the latter, as the elder, would receive double the share (Deut 21:17-21). This son, therefore, skulks selfishly, hypocritically in the background until he is revealed for what he really is at the end of the parable. Even though he remains physically at home, he is also in the "far country" of misunderstanding and intolerance of either his father or his brother. As well, and contrary to social expectations of an elder brother in his culture, he does nothing to promote understanding or reconciliation between them.

The father is only concerned with being a loving father, and so he allows his younger son the freedom to reject his love. The wants of this boy lead him where he certainly did not intend to go when he left home: to enslavement to a Gentile boss in a Gentile pigsty, to starvation, and to physical and spiritual impoverishment. By looking after pigs he makes himself ritually unclean, so squandering a second inheritance, his Jewish faith. At this crisis point, the boy sits down and "comes to himself"—works it all out in the first person: "I" will do this and that; "I" will go home and do the work of a hired hand so that "I" can pay back my debts; "I" will explain everything to my father and express my regret at what "I" have done. But coming to himself will not reconcile the son; coming to his father will.

During Lent, the Church calls us to remember the gifts of God that we have squandered and that have led us into the small or greater mess of our spiritual "pigsty." With great wisdom, she also knows that we need this time of heightened awareness of our compassionate Father who embraces us in the outstretched arms of the Crucified.

And so the son begins his homeward journey. Jesus' audience would not have been prepared for his reception, for the second demonstration of the father's love. No doubt the eyebrows of the townspeople were raised at the father's unpatriarchal, undignified rush to meet the wastrel for whom he had long been waiting. For his son it was unexpected, and before he had a chance to launch into his prepared speech, the father's eager, compassionate welcome squeezes out of him everything that he planned to do. He finds that what actually happens is that he is greeted for what he still is—son of his father—and not for what he had done. And so he accepts to be found and forgiven, a most significant aspect of reconciliation. We are challenged to hear and respond to the call to trudge out of the degradation of sin back to an Easter homecoming. We are asked to allow the grubby rags of our unfaithfulness to be stripped off so that our Father may clothe us anew in our baptismal commitment, give us the signet ring which seals God's trust in us, and enable us to walk tall in the sandals of the free.

Gospel reconciliation is an occasion for communal rejoicing, something that we hope would be obvious in the way we celebrate the sacrament of reconciliation, especially during Lent. But the elder son will not join in any celebration for the son and brother who "was dead and has come to life; he was lost and has been found." Again the father shows his love when at the risk of offending his guests, he leaves them to beg his elder son to join the festivities. This boy, too, has to allow himself to be found by love, has to learn what he now reveals he has not understood: that he is a son and not what he bitterly describes himself as—one who "has been working like a *slave*" for his father. He refuses to say "my brother," speaking only of "this son of yours." He exaggerates the sins of his brother, accepting no responsibility for his own broken relationships. With him we are left on the threshold of a Lenten choice: to be reconciled or unreconciled with our Father and our brothers and sisters and so go into the Easter celebration of Jesus, our brother, who "was dead and has come to life, . . . was lost and has been found" in the new and risen life which he offers us.

Paul is adamant about this new life. "In Christ," he writes to the Corinthians, there is "a new creation," a continuing transformation, and it is all at the initiative of God. In these two phrases Paul summarizes the gospel of salvation. Like the prodigal son, we cannot work out reconciliation for ourselves; we can only accept it as the wonderful action of God in Christ on our behalf. Although without sin, Christ became a sin offering for our sinfulness, and so through this Righteous One we share in the righteousness of God. This reconciliation extends beyond humanity, to all creation. Paul has been called to be an ambassador for this reconciliation, and in this Lenten season the Church attunes our ears and hearts to his message so that we may continue to cross over more and more deeply into reconciliation with God, with one another, and with the whole cosmos.

In the reading from the Book of Joshua another "crossing over" is described. Israel has crossed over from the wilderness into Gilgal on the east border of Jericho. Now they can freely and openly celebrate their Passover; now they no longer need to eat the wilderness food of manna, but can harvest their own crops and feed off the produce of their own land. The goodness of the Lord of which the responsorial Psalm 34 sings will be tasted now in a different way, for God has "rolled away" for his people the shame of Egypt, like stones are rolled away. This is a wordplay on the connection between the Hebrew *gll*, meaning "to roll" and the cairn of twelve stones that Israel rolled out of the Jordan and set up to commemorate their crossing of the river and entry into the promised land (Josh 4:20-22). Just as the Jewish Passover ritually celebrated this crossing into freedom, so in our

Christian Passover we remember and celebrate our crossing from death to life when the stone of the tomb is rolled back and Christ rises to the glorious freedom that he shares with us—if we are willing to accept its demands. Ours is the privilege to respond today to our "crossing over" from the wilderness of sin in the words of the psalmist. And this we can do with a gratitude that was not possible before Christ: a radiant gratitude for our rescue by him from all our distress.

Fifth Sunday of Lent

• Isa 43:16-21 • Ps 126:1-6 • Phil 3:8-14 • John 8:1-11

The story of the woman used to trap Jesus is variously described as having "floated" or been "shoved" into the Gospel of John, and sometimes is more properly considered as belonging in another Gospel, perhaps Luke's. Both descriptions suggest that its acceptance was an inspired but not easy integration, just as women's stories are often not readily acceptable today. This gospel is not to be heard as a cautionary tale about sexual ethics, but as the good news of Jesus' mercy and his power to transform people from the inside out.

In the seventh chapter of John, Jesus had been involved in controversies with his opponents as he taught in the Temple, and from there he had gone to spend the night on the Mount of Olives. Lonely and verbally assaulted by his enemies, he needed to go into the healing presence of his Father in prayer. Then in the morning there is another confrontation. A woman has been dragged from the very act of intercourse with a man not her husband, and now cowers in the Temple court in the midst of her accusers, the scribes and Pharisees. They approach Jesus with the dilemma they have carefully orchestrated. Jesus is actually the first one they want to put on trial.

With mock reverence for the "Teacher," they put the case to Jesus. If Jesus argues that the woman should not be stoned, he violates the Mosaic teaching and the community tradition. If he says she should be stoned, he will violate his own compassionate teaching and be regarded by many as a charlatan who preaches one thing and does another. Moreover, he can be accused as a revolutionary who usurps the Roman right to order capital punishment (John 18:31). "Now what do you say?" they ask Jesus. The stones that the Mosaic teaching dictated should be hurled at *both* the woman *and* her male sexual partner (Lev 20:10; Deut 22:22) are already heaped up in the hearts of her accusers. They are ready to be thrown not at the offending male (who escapes any charge) but at another man, Jesus. That Jesus would dare to continue to teach the crowds in the Temple, which the religious leaders regarded as their own territory, was an ongoing cause of animosity between them. The trap is set for him, and what more disposable, despicable trigger could they use than this woman in whom they have no interest whatsoever except as a lure for Jesus.

His answer is silence, and bending over he writes on the ground. There have been many suggestions about what he wrote, but surely it was nothing but doodling—the scribble we do on the telephone pad or notebook when we are bored with what is going on and the words that are being churned out. There are so many words in the legal books, so many prescriptions about good order, but it is what is written in the human heart that Jesus reads (John 2:25). Bent over, silent, eyes fixed on the ground, Jesus assumes the same stance as the woman. But then he straightens up and tosses at the accusers of both of them the insistence that: "Let anyone among you who is without sin be the first to throw a stone at her" (John 8:7). Jesus has taught others not to judge or condemn without mercy so that one will not be judged or condemned oneself (Luke 6:37; John 7:24), but now he not only says these words; at a moment of dangerous challenge, he lives them, and dares to be angry in the holy place before the merciless ones who were considered holy men. Then he again bends over and continues his doodling, waiting for those around him to read what is written in their own hearts. Did Jesus' words strike the memory of their own Scriptures which say: "Surely there is no one on earth so righteous as to do good without ever sinning" (Eccl 7:20)? The scribes and Pharisees realize suddenly that they themselves are now on trial. In a culture where honor and shame are a powerful ethic, they are fearful of exposure by the fearless man who confronts them. One by one they drift away. Is their exit according to seniority, a last clutch at remnants of their respectability? Or is it that the older they are the more they may have to read in their hearts about a wife, a daughter, a granddaughter, an unknown woman in a brothel?

Now, for the first time, the woman is addressed as a human being. Jesus speaks to her as more than just a heap of evil that has been dumped in the Temple and must be cleaned out as soon as possible. He refuses to judge by appearances or by legalisms; he has nothing to fear about his own sexuality; he can look straight at her and speak intimately to her. There is only one stone thrown in this incident: the stone of mercy which Jesus casts at the devastated and violated woman as he assures her that no one has condemned her, especially not himself. His concern is more for the woman's future than for her past: "Go your way, and from now on do not sin again" (John 8:11). This is no moralizing lecture, simply the powerful command of love lived for her at a moment of great risk for both of them.

Sometimes, especially as we read and pray the Scriptures reflectively, we can allow our imagination to lead us deeper into the heart of Jesus, into his human memory and experience. Reflecting on this gospel, might we wonder if, on that Temple morning, he remembered what his own mother had told him: the fear—holy yet human—she must have experienced, the gossip she probably endured about her pregnancy. And did Jesus also remember the gentle and just man named Joseph, who would not cast a stone?

Far away from the Temple, in our own experience, are we tempted to use the sins of others to mask our own self-righteousness, our personal failures and limitations? What attitude do we show to those who consider they have the right to be arbitrary dispensers of death by war, capital punishment, euthanasia, abortion, or subtle defamation? Are we brave enough to oppose their ethic, in personal encounter or by the ballot box? Do we pray that they will read their own hearts and change them? And are some of us still most condemnatory about those who sin against the two commandments that seem to be written larger than the other eight in our Christian psyches because they are concerned with things sexual? What we need to heap up in our own hearts and in our church is compassion that heals, not stones that hurt.

In the reading from Second Isaiah the prophet addresses his people who have been ravaged by exile and deprived of hope. Isaiah announces that God has not finished with them. When the prophet tells the Babylonian exiles not to dwell on the memory of God's deliverance of his people through the Sea of Reeds, he does not mean that he wants them to forget and discount God's past faithfulness, but rather to encourage them in their faith and hope. What God has done in the past he will do even more wonderfully in the future, their future. God will continue to do new things for his people. In their trek home across the wilderness there will be no need to worry about how they will find their way, because God will make a road for them; no need to fear the wild animals, for these will be tamed to honor God; no need to dread the desert thirst, because God will release streams of water for them to drink. They will become a people of praise for the mighty deeds of their God. This is the God who is revealed in Jesus, and who does the most radical "new things," especially for the outcast, as we hear in this Sunday's Gospel.

Jesus shames the scribes and Pharisees into a silent acknowledgment of their sinfulness. Paul's encounter with the risen Christ had done that for him to such an extent that everything prior to this he now regards as "rubbish." Although he too was made a radically new person by Christ, it is still a daily struggle for Paul to remain true to this identity and accept that he must share in the sufferings and death of Christ if he is to share in his resurrection. Only Christ, not any law, can give him the strength for this.

To encourage his Philippians in their own struggles, Paul compares himself to an athlete, a runner who, if he wants to win the race, must never look back but keep his eyes fixed on the finishing line ahead. And God is cheering for Paul, urging him on to receive the prize of life in and with Christ Jesus. With Paul and the Philippians, we are in the same race for the same prize. But we are competing not against our running partners but against ourselves and whatever tries to hold us back from Christ.

Does all that the readings proclaim this week seem like a dream to us? Is the good news of God's word "back there," in the past, and not very relevant for our present or our future? Or have we the Lenten faith to believe that, if we too share in the sufferings of Christ, we will be like the image of the reapers of the responsorial Psalm 126 and come to Easter singing and carrying the sheaves we have harvested in these weeks of prayer, fasting, and good works?

Palm Sunday of the Lord's Passion

Procession Gospel

• Luke 19:28-40

Today we begin the Great Week of the church's year, the one we call "Holy," and our perspective on this is from the back of a donkey. On what we call Palm Sunday, Matthew, Mark, and Luke all present us with the same image of Jesus in the Gospel that is read before the procession. The donkey-riding Jesus recalls how Solomon rode to his anointing as king, feeling under himself the gentle plodding of a donkey, a humble work animal, and not the powerful muscles of a warrior's charger (1 Kgs 1:38). Such a ride reminded the king that his main work was the defense of the poor and disadvantaged, not the search for power, and the making of peace, not war. That most of the kings failed in these tasks contributed greatly to the downfall of the monarchy. The way that we are to enter into the New Jerusalem and the reign of God is the way in which Jesus, the Messiah King, rode into his city: in humility and peace, ready for self-emptying service to others, even unto death.

In this year's processional reading from the Gospel of Luke (19:28-40), there are no branches thrown down on the road. It is their cloaks that the crowd places beneath the feet of the colt as the briefly-triumphant Jesus rides into Jerusalem. Who were these crowds who praised and acclaimed him? They were not the people of some status who, in the person of the Pharisees, strike the only discordant note in the narrative, demanding that

Jesus silence his disciples. He replies that if he did do this, the very stones would take over the chorus of praise. It seems right to imagine the crowd as the poor, the healed outsiders, the forgiven sinners, those who didn't have much except the dignity or health that Jesus had restored to them. But because of this they were ready to give away even their precious clothes—many of them probably no more than dusty, sweat-stained rags—to make a royal carpet for *their* king. It is these people, not a chorus of angels as at the birth of Jesus (Luke 2:13-14), who now sing out praise and peace: the peace of heaven that is among them on earth in this man on a donkey.

As we walk in the Palm Sunday procession, what we are participating in is not a folkloric restaging of the gospel. Rather, it is a remembering of what we are: a community of fragile, poor people, who have experienced the saving love of Christ. Metaphorically, what we must spread in the dust and under the Master's feet are not our clothes, but our very selves. Just a few verses on in Luke's narrative, we confront other alternatives; Jesus will weep over his city, and more prestigious voices will say nothing about blessedness or peace, but will shout for crucifixion.

The Mass

• Isa 50:4-7 • Ps 22:8-9, 17-20, 23-24 • Phil 2:6-11 • Luke 22:14–23:56

After the exultation of the processional gospel, we are reminded of the suffering so soon to come by the Lectionary's choice of the third Suffering Servant song as the first reading of the Mass. During the coming weekdays of Holy Week, the first and second Songs are read, and the culminating fourth Song is proclaimed on Good Friday. The identity of the servant is a mystery, variously suggested to be Zion, the exiled people, a prophet, someone present or yet to come who will suffer greatly. By its use on this Sunday, an ancient text from the sixth century B.C.E. is used to direct our hearts to the memory of the Servant whom Isaiah never knew, and about whom he could not write. But we today listen as a privileged assembly, knowing that what Isaiah was searching and hoping for became brutally explicit in the passion of Jesus.

The servant is daily attentive to the Word of God. With unplugged ears he listens before he dares to speak, and those to whom he speaks are the weary and poor. His words make him a target for insult and physical attack. Fists fly at the mouth that comforts; those whom the servant's truth enrages spit out lies and injustice. Through it all, the servant is calmly confident and nonviolent because the Lord is his strength. In his suffering, God is present and proclaimed. This is true, also, of all those who, for the sake of justice, and especially for those weary of vicious political regimes or human degradation, have suffered and will suffer physical and psychological torture. Some, like Jesus, we can name; many are nameless, like the Isaian servant. Countless numbers of these servants have found the courage to suffer because of the words that they have heard from their God and recognize as revealed in the suffering Servant Jesus. The words of the responsorial Psalm 22 can be spoken by all the suffering ones—but with the rhythm that moves from despair to hope, from pain to praise of God's steadfast love. In the last verses of this lament, this praise is proclaimed to the whole assembly of God's people.

The passion and death of Jesus was not unique as a historical execution. But what makes it more than just a regrettable act of brutal injustice and tragic failure for one man is that God had opened the ears of his Son and Servant to the cosmic proportions of his obedience and love. So, unashamed and confident in God's love, Jesus goes to his death and makes what we have come to call "Good" Friday, truly "good" because it is a triumph of life-giving love. This is what Paul praises in the exultant hymn in the Letter to the Philippians that is today's second reading.

To the Philippians Paul writes that Christ emptied his divinity *into* our humanity; he did not leave this state of divine equality behind or discard it. "God became completely human, omitting nothing that belongs to our nature. He was without sin, because sin does not belong to our nature."[3]

Jesus Christ reveals God by what God does in him. Jesus' humanity is the most definitive, most understandable Word that can be spoken to other human beings through a life that was lived without any power-seeking, identified above all with the poor and with those with no status or with those who sought justice for such people. This made it a vulnerable life that would take Jesus, acceptingly and lovingly, to his death on a cross. And for this loving obedience to God and commitment to humanity, God raises his Son over all creation. He is now "Lord," to be reverenced by heaven and earth, by the living and the dead, by all of us who are in Christ and are called to share in his obedience and love.

On the First Sunday of Lent, we read that Satan left Jesus at the end of the wilderness temptation, but only to return at "an opportune time" (Luke 4:13). Just before the Last Supper, "Satan entered into Judas called Iscariot" (Luke 22:3), and we recognize that the sword of Simeon's prophecy hangs over those whom we meet in the Last Supper narrative. Even with his chosen disciples, some will fall, some will rise, some will both fall and rise. We can identify with all of them in large or small ways. Jesus sits at table and announces at the beginning of the meal that this is to be his last. Throughout his life, he had celebrated the Passover meal and its memories for his people, but this one is different: a supper celebrated *"with you,"* his chosen companions, and not to be celebrated again on this side of the kingdom. Bread and cup become an event of body and blood, of the whole person and presence of Jesus, which establishes a new relationship of participating in and sharing his life. Tonight the disciples recline around the table with him; tomorrow they will decline to be guests at the board of the cross. When arguments break out among them over who is the greatest, it is as though their ears are blocked and they have heard nothing of what Jesus has said. Peter is overconfident, crowing about his fidelity, but soon to hear the devastating cock announce his betrayal.

And then it is off to the Mount of Olives: to agony among the generations of olive trees where Jesus lies among them like a protruding root, struggling in prayer to surrender to his Father's will. For the three apostles with him, it is escapism into sleep. Then comes the pain of betrayal by a friend, the sword-slashing panic by the awakened apostles, and the command of nonviolence from Jesus. Arrested and parceled up in false accusations, Jesus is sent from one judgment seat to another: from the high priest to Pilate, from Pilate to Herod, from Herod back to Pilate, wrapped in insult.

All Jesus' friends are scattered; even Peter follows only "at a distance." He too is put on trial by a servant girl outside Pilate's courtroom, and a cock brings in the verdict of shameful guilt. But when Jesus is brought out, he passes by Peter, turns to him and looks at him . . . and Peter is saved. He realizes that his master will never turn away from him. Then he remembers his master's words and weeps bitterly at their truth and his untruthfulness. The same realization, the same remembering, the same tears, will save every disciple.

Scourged and mocked, Jesus is led out to his death—the innocent, nonviolent victim of the sin of the world. A man from the country, Simon of Cyrene, is made to help him carry his cross, but Jesus is the Servant who will still reach out to others. When some of the women of Jerusalem follow him like a mourning chorus, Jesus ministers to their grief, but begs them to make it a larger lamentation for all those who are unfaithful to their God. On Golgotha, Jesus ministers also to the poor criminal who recognizes him as a just one. Lover of sinners to the end, Jesus allows this thief to "steal" paradise from him. Then Luke puts on Jesus' lips the words of Psalm 31: "Into your hand I commit my spirit," a more gentle dying prayer than Mark's or Matthew's cry of "My God, my God, why have you forsaken me" (Ps 22:1). Quietly, Jesus escapes, like a bird freed from a trap, into his Father's hands.

For a moment, then, we go down silently on our knees, rising up to hear the faith of a non-Gentile proclaim before the human wreck of a dead man: "Certainly this man was innocent." This is the faith that will take us through Holy Week and through the killing fields in our own world. Hopefully, too, we will minister like Joseph of Arimathea: taking the wounded body of Christ, our suffering sisters and brothers, off their crosses, wrapping them in our compassion, and advocating for them before the powerful with gentle but brave persistence.

Notes

1. William Blake, *Selected Poetry of William Blake*, ed. Michael Mason (Oxford: Oxford University Press Inc., 1994) 267.

2. Evelyn Underhill, *The Spiritual Life* (London: Hodder and Stoughton, 1937, Morehouse reprint 1995) 20. Referred to by Robert T. Brooks in his homily for this Sunday in *Preaching Through the Year of Luke* (Harrisburg, PA: Morehouse Publishing, 2000) 34–36.

3. Michael Casey, *Fully Human, Fully Divine: An Interactive Christology* (Mulgrave, Victoria, Australia: John Garratt Publishing, 2004) 4.

4

The Season of Easter

The Easter Triduum

From the evening of Holy Thursday to the evening of Easter Sunday, we celebrate the three-day feast that is really one day and one feast, but which is so awe-inspiring that chronologically we need three days to enter into its mystery: the Passion, Death, and Resurrection of Jesus Christ. The celebration of the paschal mystery is like a precious jewel that crowns the church year, catching different lights and colors of its facets as we turn it through these days. On Holy Thursday we celebrate the paschal mystery from the perspective of floor, table, and the garden of the Mount of Olives; on Good Friday, from Golgotha and cross; and at the Easter Vigil and on Easter Sunday, in another garden transformed by dawn and an empty tomb.

We have been carried in the womb of the Lenten Church up to Jerusalem. On Thursday when we go to the evening Mass of the Lord's Supper, Lent has come full term, and it is time for us to be born into the Triduum. These are the days of euphoria and treachery; days of the smell of oils and our own humanity; days of taking another's feet in our hands and of tasting bread and wine on our tongues; days when we kiss wood and splash water; days when we gather around the newly lit fire and straggle after it through the darkness until we catch fire from it; days when we sit around the fire and tell stories; days when we become a community able to make "Alleluia!" our song in praise of the Easter Light of the world.

Holy Thursday

Evening Mass of the Lord's Supper

• Exod 12:1-8, 11-14 • Ps 116:12-13, 15-18 • 1 Cor 11:23-26 • John 13:1-15

Tonight we do not hear a Synoptic Gospel with a narrative of the institution of the Eucharist. The institution tradition is left to Paul to proclaim in the second reading. The Gospel we hear is John's description of the last meal that Jesus shares with his friends, his washing of their feet, and his command that his disciples, like him, be loving servants of one another.

The backdrop to this night is the description of the Jewish Passover and the memory of this feast of freedom for God's people. The ritual is outlined in detail in the first reading: the date of its celebration as a spring moon feast; the selection, slaughter, and eating of the unblemished lamb or kid: the marking of the Hebrew houses with its blood so that God would pass over them and not destroy them. The ritual had probably evolved from that of nomadic Bedouins who, on the first full spring moon and under the safe cover of darkness, prepared to take their flocks, with the vulnerable newborn lambs, to the spring pastures. It was a dangerous migration. To ward off evil, the nomadic community marked their tent pegs with the blood of one lamb that had been sacrificed for the sake of the whole flock, and was then roasted and eaten. Liturgical genius added (as it still does) elements of already established rituals and transformed them into the celebration of God's protection and deliverance, for Israel was about to become God's nomad in search of the new pastures of freedom. They were to go forth quickly, not delaying to leaven their bread, unencumbered with anything but the bare necessities of staff and sandals to help them on their journey.

The Passover was to become the defining experience for Judaism. It testified to the truth that human beings are meant to be free and that God is concerned when they are not. But it also meant that God required an active response from the oppressed people: not passive acceptance of the status quo, but a willingness to set out on a dangerous way, trusting in God's protection. The fact that the people called Israel had once been strangers and slaves in Egypt who were liberated by their God, was to have historical, religious, and ethical reverberations for the Jewish people down through the generations. They were to remember liturgically this Jewish Passover in every generation, a remembrance that pulls past, present, and future into a personal and communal "we" and a glorious but demanding "today."

Every Eucharist is a celebration of the Passover of the Lord, accomplished definitively in the blood of Christ, the Lamb of God, which marks us for salvation. As a nighttime community we come together on this Holy Thursday to share the meal of salvation and commit ourselves once again to the journey into which Christ calls us: into freedom and away from the slavery of sin (Gal 5:1,13). With the words of Psalm 116 on our lips we toast the goodness of God, no longer as the psalmist does from a cup of sacrificial libation at the Temple, but from the blessing cup of the sacramental blood of the risen Christ. We pledge ourselves publicly in the liturgical assembly to keep our promises to God.

It is Paul in his First Letter to the Corinthians who proclaims the words of institution of the Eucharist. With the Jewish remembrance of the Passover, the story becomes Paul's story; so the memorial of the broken bread and the poured cup becomes the Corinthians' own story, their own covenant with Christ. Christ says that the bread is his body "which is for you," a communion with all the members of his body. And as Paul writes to the Romans, "If God is for us, who is against us?" (Rom 8:31). From this moment, through Christ's death and resurrection until his return at the end of the ages, God in Christ is *for us*. When we, the members of his body, live the mystery we celebrate, and if, like Christ, we are bread broken and consumed for others and wine poured out for the thirst of the world, we witness to the world the holy mystery of this night.

In the Gospel, John tells us what life in communion with Jesus should be like. John is writing near the end of the first century C.E. Christians have been living the tradition Paul describes for three generations. But did John's community, like ourselves, too often forget what the Eucharist (or the "breaking of the bread" as it was first called) really meant? John reminds them by the washing of the feet. It is "the hour," the beginning of the time of privileged opportunity when Jesus will pass over from this world to his Father. He wants to celebrate it as a night of friendship, for friends are those with whom we can share joys and sorrows, hopes and fears, successes and failures. Friends are those with whom we can think out loud or make gestures that well up from our most precious and intimate depths. And this is how Jesus begins this last meal with his friends, and with a friend become his enemy. Tonight Jesus rises and lays aside his garments; tomorrow he will lay aside his own life. Tonight he ties a towel around himself; tomorrow he will be bound and stripped naked by others. Yet the resurrection note is also sounded here: for three days later Jesus will rise unbound from death, clothed in his risen body.

In his hands Jesus takes the holy vessels: a bowl of water and his disciples' feet. These are the poignant, humble, and so human symbols of the "everything" that Jesus knew the Father had put into his hands. Then he kneels down on the floor and begins to wash his disciples' feet. Leadership becomes loving service. Jesus comes to Peter, and Peter objects mightily to having his feet washed. He does not want his Lord and Master to abase himself. As a gesture of hospitality, a host would offer water to a guest to wash his own feet, or command a slave to do this. But is that all? Is there also, perhaps, the dawning realization that in Jesus' role reversal there might also be some implied message for Peter himself? If Jesus does this, would he, Peter, also be expected to be a humble servant? Jesus, as their host, offers to his disciples an intimate gesture of hospitality, a promise of welcome into his Father's house that he is soon to enter through his death and resurrection (John 14:2).

Peter fails to understand the foot washing in terms of the quality of relationships. After Jesus' strong words that unless he allows Jesus to wash his feet Peter will have no share in this hospitality, Peter swings, desperate and still uncomprehending, to a wildly quantitative response. Well then, not only his feet, but hands and head as well! But it is accepting the servanthood of Jesus, and the *quality* of one's life as a servant, that will bring salvation. Jesus has also washed Judas' feet; physically, he, too, is "clean," but his heart is polluted by betrayal and his rejection of his Master's love. And so Jesus tries to explain: "Not all of you are clean."

The foot washing is a self-revelation of Jesus, so he returns to the table to help his disciples understand that "you also should do as I have done to you." Some commentators have called these words the "Johannine words of institution," and they explain why this Gospel is chosen on the night when we remember the institution of the sacrament. The Eucharist is about sharing in the life of Christ who humbled himself, even to death on a cross. It is a revelation of the Master who descended into our humanity and will remain with us in the sacramental bread and wine. It shows us a Servant who handles our humanity with love, despite our friendship or enmity with him. And it asks us to follow his example: to get down, metaphorically, and serve one another, despite the dust and smell and misunderstandings; to be hospitable to our sisters and brothers and in communion with them. Then we, too, will have part with Jesus in the hospitality that his death and resurrection offer us.

Good Friday

Celebration of the Lord's Passion

• Isa 52:13–53:12 • Ps 31:2, 6, 12-13, 15-17, 25 • Heb 4:14-16; 5:7-9 • John 18:1–19:42

Today we gaze at Jesus, the Suffering Servant, exalted and raised up on a cross. On this day when we hear John's passion narrative, it may seem bleak and dark, but it is transformed by the memory of what this evangelist wrote in his prologue: "What has come into being in him was life, and the life was the light of all people. The light shines in the darkness, and the darkness did not overcome it" (John 1:3-5). This day is a day of the Triduum, the celebration not only of death, but also of life and light. We come to the liturgy as hungry people keeping the Easter fast, which reminds us that we have all surely experienced a time when we did not want to eat. Perhaps we were greatly in love or deeply in mourning, perhaps we couldn't put down the wonderful novel we were reading or stop writing the article or book that might make us famous. Whatever, we were filled with something that was more important than food at that moment. The Easter fast is intended to make us feel, in our bodies and our hearts, that what is most important is to be utterly hungry for and filled with God as revealed in the Passover of his Son.

The first Word of God that we hear today is the fourth Servant Song. The song opens with the announcement of what God promises the Servant: exaltation to great heights, even in his humiliation and degradation. It closes with the reason for this: the Servant is blessed because of his willingness to suffer for the sake of others. No crime is specified, no attackers identified, no word is spoken by the Servant; there is no attempt at violent retaliation. The followers of the Servant do speak. They not only describe his suffering, but also admit that their guilt and the disregard in which the community held the Servant have added to the pain of this dehumanized one. The images used underline this: he is like a root pushing up through the dust, useful for nothing but falling over and being kicked, or like a lamb that is led without protest to slaughter. From his disfigurement, the people hide their faces.

The Suffering Servant "will make many righteous" for, in spite of everything, the Lord will give him the capacity to draw others to himself. By the use of this Servant Song in the Good Friday liturgy, we become those generations, the people at the ends of the earth who have laid on the Servant Christ our iniquity but who, on this day especially, will not be allowed to hide our faces from the cross of the exalted one who is our future and our hope. Nor can we despise those who, in him and with him, suffer the contemporary diseases of body and mind or are crushed by the tyranny of the powerful. The example of the Servant invites us to put our lives at risk for the healing of the world. When we are called up to touch the wood of the cross, we also commit ourselves to these suffering ones—or we perform an empty ritual.

Through the lens of the Letter to the Hebrews, Jesus, as the High Priest who intercedes for us, is brought into sharp focus. On the annual Jewish Day of Atonement, their high priest passed through the veil of the Temple to sprinkle the blood of the sacrificial goat on the mercy seat and to make intercession for the people. Through the blood of Christ's sacrifice, our humanity, with all its shared weakness, has been taken into the merciful presence of God. "In the days of his flesh," Jesus brought his grief, his disappointment, his desolation and confusion before God in his agonized prayer. And he was heard because of his obedience to which he struggled in pain and tears. We can well imagine the responsorial Psalm 22 running through the heart and mind of Jesus. In its combination of lament and praise, suffering and celebration, death and resurrection become the one mystery of the Living One who dies and the Crucified One who lives. So we have the witness of Jesus himself that the prayer closest to our deepest hurts is honest, painful, and acceptable prayer.

At the beginning of John's passion narrative, there is no identifying and treacherous kiss. Jesus goes forward on his own initiative to meet those who have come to arrest him, announcing himself as "I AM (he)," to the helpless confusion of his enemies. Yet Jesus uses the protection of the Divine Name not for himself, but for his disciples. "No one," he had said earlier, "will snatch them out of my hand" (John 10:28b). The night and day will unravel but Christ will be knotted in pain and secured to the cross. One way in which we might reflect on this passion is to ask ourselves if and how we, today, can identify—or identify *with*—those whose story John tells.

There is Annas, the powerful ex-high priest who had managed to insinuate into that role five of his sons and his son-in-law, Caiaphas, then the high priest. People like this have been described as "the logicians of history," and not only past history. They arm themselves with apparently good arguments and zealous words that whip up seemingly rational political arguments for damage control. It is always preferable, they maintain, for one individual to die in order to prevent greater damage to the people as well as the unstated damage to their own corrupt ambitions. They speak hot words about the greater good out of frozen hearts.

There is Peter, huddling in the high priest's courtyard, seeking the comfort of light and warmth with the enemies of Jesus. He is on dark trial outside while the "light of the world" is on trial inside. Inside, Jesus receives a blow from an "outsider," one of the arresting officers; outside, an "insider" delivers to Jesus the blow of his denial that he is one of his disciples. Peter gives us the tragic witness of how quickly a disciple can betray the Master and then try to bluster out of such betrayal—until the cock crows to announce the darkest dawn Peter will ever know.

Close to the political power brokers are the bureaucratic functionaries, the Pilates. These are soft, pliable "jellyfish" who wobble from one opinion to another. They disguise their weaknesses with undignified bluster, fearful of making a mistake that would cause them to slip out of favor with higher authorities. In the end, it is simpler just to hand over the responsibility to someone else who can be bossed around. So Pilate hands Jesus over to the soldiers to be flogged. At least this will be some punishment for one of the troublesome Jewish people among whom he has to keep some imperial order. But given this order, the soldiers are only too ready to go further by mock coronation and pseudoroyal robing. With Jesus delivered back to him, Pilate announces to the crowd: "Behold the man!" And we too behold the height and depth of the human potential for good or evil as we gaze on the suffering Son of Man.

Self-possessed and undefeated, the Son of God strides toward the accomplishment of his Passover. John has no Simon of Cyrene; Jesus carries his own cross, the cross that belongs to him and which, for that very reason, will be raised up as a sign of victory. On the cross is the description of Jesus' "crime": "Jesus of Nazareth, King of the Jews." Written in Greek (the language of trade and commerce), in Latin (the language of Roman government), and in Hebrew (the language of Jesus' own Jewish people), John makes out of what Pilate wrote to salve his conscience a proclamation of Christ's universal kingship. On either side of Jesus hang "two others," named neither as criminals nor insurgents as in the other gospels. They are merely two attendant shadows who fade into anonymity in Jesus' royal presence.

The Crucified is dispossessed of everything: first of his clothing, then of his mother and the beloved disciple, the woman and man who are his two ideal disciples. But this hour of patient pain and separation will become the hour of new communion as these two are given into each other's care by the dying Jesus. Here is the model for the Johannine church and every Christian community: women and men as equal disciples, welcoming each other and caring for each other in Jesus' name and as his gifts, and all this under the shadow of the cross which is the glory tree. Then Jesus "knew that all was finished." Thirsting to the end, he is offered sour wine on a sprig of hyssop. John is here deliberately evoking the "Lamb of God" memory, for it was with the fern-like hyssop that Exodus describes the sprinkling of the doorposts on the night of the Hebrews' Passover (Exod 12:22).

In this Gospel, there is no dying cry, only the silent triumph of one who has accomplished that for which he came into the world. Jesus hands over his breath to his Father, the breath that will animate the new creation. No bones of this Paschal Lamb are broken, no cosmic darkness falls over the earth. From Christ's pierced side flow blood and water, John's signs of the Eucharist and Baptism through which all peoples and nations will enter into the new temple of the body of the Crucified and Risen One.

With deliberate irony, John proclaims that it is with the dead body of Jesus in their arms that hesitant Israel first finds life and faith. Joseph of Arimathea and Nicodemus bind Jesus in the swaddling bands of death, surround him with the amount of costly spices and oils that would be considered a fitting extravagance for a king's burial, and, in a solemn cortege, place

Jesus in a garden and a new tomb. Hidden in the heart of the earth, carried there by friendship, the grain of Christ's body awaits the ripening of Easter morning.

Then we go up to venerate the cross: young people glad to be doing, something, adults walking independently, children carried on their parents' shoulders, the frail aged and disabled heading with determination for what they are so familiar with. Together we become the people who pass by, looking and remembering that there is no sorrow like this sorrow. We kiss or touch or reverence the cross, and hope that its sap will drip salvation on us. This is Easter Triduum; this is our paschal faith.

Today the Church is even dispossessed of the eucharistic action, offering us the hosts that were consecrated at last evening's Mass. And so we leave the church to wait for the night of nights. . . .

The Easter Vigil

• Gen 1:1–2:2 • Gen 22:1-18 • Exod 14:15–15:1 • Isa 54:5-14 • Isa 55:1-11 • Bar 3:9-15 • Ezek 36:16-28 • Rom 6:3-11 • Luke 24:1-12

It has been the great empty and profoundly silent day of the church year, a day of waiting. And then in the dark, the Easter fire erupts to set our hearts alight. Lest we forget the cross, the presider traces it on the paschal candle and pierces it with five fragrant "nails" of incense. The date of the current year and the Alpha and Omega are also traced, and with our attentive presence we commit ourselves again, this year, to the risen Christ who is the Beginning and the End of our lives. Carved with our faith, the wax column of fire leads us, a happy, rather unruly community, into the womb of our church. Here, on this night of nights, Mother Church will bring us forth to new life. Having exultantly praised Christ, the Light of the world, symbolized by the paschal candle, we sit around this fire to tell stories from the two Testaments which affirm our identity as God's people brought from the darkness of sin into light and life. If we are privileged to listen to these stories and respond to them in song in the presence of those who are about to receive their new identity in the waters of baptism, there will be an added joy and significance to this Liturgy of the Word.

In the first reading from Genesis, the Word of God broods over the primeval chaos and brings forth life to the repeated rhythm of God speaking, naming, seeing, and blessing. Into the world prepared by the Spirit's creativity, God calls forth humanity, male and female, made in the image of God and given stewardship of creation. Then on the seventh day, there is the "sabbath," the day of contemplative, mutual presence of God to all that is created and creation to its God. It is all "very good," but one day it will be so much better in the new creation, in Christ.

Then the Word of God announces what does not seem very good, what in the Jewish tradition is called "the binding of Isaac" and is referred to constantly in the liturgy of the Jewish High Holy Days and the daily prayer of Jewish men. Abraham is the pioneer of faith who shows us the way to hope against hope (Rom 4:16-18) when burdened with immense grief. By telling Abraham to take his only son, Isaac, and make of him a burnt offering on Mount Moriah, God asks Abraham to destroy all the divine promises made to him, all his and Sarah's future that lie in this son. There is no reason except: "God says." But Abraham is obedient to God because he believes that at the core of his being is not the self, or what is born of oneself, but the radical commitment to his Creator. And so Abraham passes the test of faithfulness. Isaac is saved, and Abraham becomes what we name him in the first Eucharistic Prayer, "our father in the faith." In *The Binding*, the Jewish artist, Marc Chagall, painted a crucifixion which looms over Abraham and Isaac in the painting's shadowy background, and tonight we remember the obedience and deliverance that lay so many centuries ahead of the Genesis story in the deep shadow of another only Son and his Father.

The story of the passage of the Hebrews through the Sea of Reeds must always be read on this night, for it is part of the foundational story for the identity of Jesus the Jew and his people, the "rich root of the olive tree" onto which we have been grafted (Rom 11:17). God the Liberator leads his people through the waters of chaos. Moses' outstretched arm and staff, the protection of the angel, the pillar of cloud that is both guide for and buffer between the Hebrews and the Egyptians, all these are instruments of God's deliverance. Remembering these waters, tonight we sing our praise for the greater salvation that has been won for us by the waters of the flood of death that overwhelmed Jesus, his passage through these, his deliverance from its chaos in his resurrection, and our baptism into this mystery of God's salvation in and through Christ.

Isaiah gives us a moving description of the fidelity of God to his people. He uses the imagery (patriarchal in that era) of God as a faithful husband to his bride Israel. Despite Israel's unfaithfulness and the divine disappointments, despite temporary separation, anger, and upheavals, the relationship endures. And not only does it endure, it is transformed. The everlasting love of God builds a more beautiful relationship with his people with the tools of forgiveness, integrity, and peace. This is how Jesus will rebuild our lives after we have failed by our sinfulness to be faithful covenant partners of God.

Again we hear Isaiah speaking of God's love. It is like water for the thirsty, food for the hungry, wine and milk for the poor. Because of such love, the covenant made with David has been extended to embrace all the people who listen carefully to God and are open to the mysterious accomplishment of the divine will. The word of God that expresses this will goes forth throughout the generations, to bring forth new life, but nowhere and in no one was this word and will so fully expressed as in Jesus, the Word made flesh and the Covenant Maker, in his own body and blood.

The reading from the prophet Baruch, Jeremiah's secretary (Jer 36:4), is a hymn of praise to Wisdom. She is the gift of God to Israel and, with her assistance, the people are to rebuild their lives on the foundation of God's commandments. This Wisdom is practical, not speculative. She will be a companion who leads the people out of the exile of sin and restores them to the youthful love and peace of their earlier relationships with God. The cosmos itself is a witness to the creativity and wisdom of God that comes with obedience to his word. "Turn," "seize," "walk": all these are vigorous words that Baruch uses to encourage Israel to make the right choices in life and death situations. Such right choices were made preeminently by Jesus who reveals God's wisdom made flesh among us (cf. Matt 11:19; Mark 6:2; Luke 11:31).

By their infidelity, the people of God had defiled themselves and desecrated the holy name to which they should have given witness before the nations. God, however, will re-create them in ways that will cause praise of God's loving holiness to rise from all the countries to which the Jews have been scattered and from which God will rescue them. The re-creation of the people is described symbolically by Ezekiel, first as a ritual washing which cleanses them of any defilement, and then as a biblical "heart transplant." Only God can be the delicate surgeon who removes people's hearts of stone and replaces them with warm and living hearts that will beat with love for and obedience to their God. Then God will resuscitate the exiles with his own spirit/breath to make of them a renewed, regenerated people. For us, as a Christian assembly, this is the great night of our washing and regeneration.

Paul is explicit about this regeneration. It is in the waters of baptism that we go down into the death of Christ so that we may rise up with him to new life. We *are* baptized, continually called to live this new life of holiness. Through his crucifixion, Christ put to death the slavery of sin for the sake of our freedom; in his descent into the waters of death, he transformed them into the means of life. These are the great exodus themes of the Christian story within which we live and find our identity. Tonight we will again pronounce our determination to come out of sin when we renew our baptismal promises and stand in mutually reassuring solidarity with the newly baptized. After this reading, and for the first time in seven weeks, we respond with "Alleluia!" to praise the love of God that has no end. It is such love that made Jesus, the rejected cornerstone (Ps 118:22), into the keystone of the new Temple into which we are built as living stones by our baptism.

Like all the gospel narratives of the resurrection, the vigil reading from Luke proclaims that there is no place for triumphalism in the community of the Risen One. The Gospel centers on the "little ones": on women who were so culturally and religiously insignificant that their testimony had no validity. Silently, attentively, but disregarded, the women who had faithfully followed Jesus from Galilee (and had not found their men around) have noted the place of burial so that they can return after the Sabbath and complete the burial rites.

It is dawn, and the first cosmic light is breaking. Soon the inner landscape of the memory and faith of these women will also be enlightened. They are doing what they should do according the Jewish funeral ritual, but they are about to enter into the new and most profound ritual that is at the service of the new Temple of Jesus' risen body. At first there is just empty space, an empty tomb, in which the women are disoriented and do not know what to do. Then the two dazzling messengers of God proclaim to them the Easter message that will echo down the ages, to be heard with all its consequences by every Christian community that also enters into the mystery of the Resurrection: "Why do you look for the living among the dead? He is not here, but has risen. Remember . . . ."

The Church gathers us tonight so that we too will remember—after the fire and song and joy of this Vigil are over. When unexpected, unthinkable sorrow has intruded into our joy; when perhaps we have laid the body of a loved one in the grave; when the loss of self-esteem or friendship or health seems to cut us off from any good future or past happiness: then we need to remember both Jesus' Galilee predictions of his passion, his words about the new life that would rise from pain and death, and the Easter Gospel where prediction becomes proclamation.

Galilee, say the Lukan messengers, do remember Galilee—and all the little, unimportant people to whom Jesus gave new healed bodies, new peace of mind, new hope. These graveside women are Galilee women (Luke 23:49), and they do remember. It is this remembrance that returns them eagerly back to "the eleven and all the rest" with the good news of the Resurrection. Poignantly, Luke reminds us that his dearest followers are no longer the Twelve but eleven. With them, however, is a larger, more inclusive group that has been gathered into their company. On the execution place of the skull, Luke did not name any of the women who "stood at a distance." Now, no longer distant from but in the midst of the mystery of the crucified and risen Jesus, three of these women are named as Mary Magdalene, Joanna, and Mary the mother of James.

As it will be in the Emmaus narrative, "return" is a missionary word for Luke, but then as so often today, the women's witness on their return is regarded as "an idle tale," not worthy of serious consideration. Yet they have personally experienced the reality of resurrection, not by seeing the risen body of Jesus but through faith in the words of God's messengers and the memory of the Galilee experiences. To give Peter credit, Luke describes him as surrendering his male superiority (of which he would not have much left after his betrayal), and running to the tomb. He sees the linen burial cloths, but his response is described as amazement, not faith. Not until Luke 24:34 is the Lord's appearance to Peter announced, and with this personal experience, no doubt is left.

The gospels do not ground our faith in empty tombs or discarded burial cloths. Gospel faith in the Resurrection is built on the presence and witness of the risen Lord in human experience, in women and men who have received God's gift of faith and have had it nourished in the community of believers. This is what the newly baptized tell us tonight by their presence in the midst of our faith community; this is the responsibility we have to one another; this is the truth to which, as Church, we will loudly and constantly sing "Alleluia" for the next fifty days.

The Sundays of Easter

We have celebrated the paschal mystery for the three days of the Triduum—but even that is not enough. So the Church gives us fifty days, from Easter Sunday to Pentecost, to be celebrated "in joyful exultation as one feast day, or better as one 'great Sunday'"[1] The weeks are named "of" Easter, not "in" Easter because, unlike Advent or Lent, they do not prepare for a feast but prolong the celebration of Christ's resurrection and his presence among his people through the Spirit and in the time of the Church. Every Sunday is to the Christian week what the Easter season is to the liturgical year, for throughout the whole year we must never forget that we are a water-drenched and Spirit-filled people who have passed over into new life in the risen Christ.

As we are accompanied by the Liturgy of the Word on these Sundays of Easter, it is as if the Church leads us, a pilgrim people, to different lookouts from which we can gaze on the gospel landscape, which is transfigured by the light of Christ's resurrection. There is a wonderful intimacy about this

Easter traveling. In Year C, Jesus is in our midst: holding out to us the wounds of his risen body; breakfasting with and befriending those who had deserted him; calling us by name to follow him as our Shepherd Protector; lingering long with us at the table as the Host who gives us, his friends, the love commandment; promising us the gifts of the Spirit, the memory and future of the Church; breathing into the chaos of our lives his own peace that the world cannot give. Then, ascended to his Father, Jesus sends upon his disciples the wind and fire of Pentecost that shakes them into the world with burning urgency to proclaim to the ends of the earth that Christ is risen, he is truly risen.

During the Easter season, the first reading is not from the Old Testament but from the Acts of the Apostles, in order to highlight the emergence of the Church as the witness to the new things that God does in the risen Christ who is present in his Church through the Spirit. Every Christian community belongs to the lineage of the faithful witnesses we meet in Acts, and we are called every day, everywhere, to live what we hear and to sing our "Alleluias" for this privilege.

The Book of Revelation (or the Apocalypse of John), chosen for the reading on the Sundays of Easter in Year C, is not meant to be a source of esoteric word and number games or a futuristic code to be cracked so that the date of the end of the world can be confidently calculated. That there will be such an end, and that life in this world is a preparation for it and the new creation that will be born from it is the concern of John the seer (sometimes called the "elder," and not the apostle). John is passionately committed to "the kingdom of the world" becoming the "kingdom of our Lord and of his Messiah" (Rev 11:15). It is the Easter Jesus, the Alpha and Omega, the Beginning and End of our personal and global history, who makes the revelation to John that will help the Church, the Bride of the Lamb, to say a faithful "Yes" to the call of the Spirit.

Second Sunday of Easter

• Acts 5:12-16 • Ps 118:2-4,13-15, 22-24 • Rev 1:9-11a, 12-13, 17-19 • John 20:19-31

A dispirited, frightened group of disciples huddles together behind closed doors on the evening of Easter Day. "For fear of the Jews," says John, but we need to remember that he is writing for second and third generation Christians at the end of the first century. This is after the destruction of the Jewish Temple by the Romans that tore the hearts out of Judaism and precipitated a widening gap between the church and the synagogue. Consequently, Judaism became wary of anything which could be seen to weaken it still further. We often forget that Jesus' first disciples were themselves Jews.

The disciples have realized, only too painfully, that by deserting Jesus in the hour of his passion and death they have also betrayed themselves. They are wounded people who may believe that Jesus has risen from the dead, but what that means, and what it means *for them*, given their unfaithfulness, leaves them in panicking ignorance. Then the Tomb Breaker himself, with his wounded, living body is among them, breaking not only into their closed room but also into their despair.

The first gift of his resurrection that Jesus offers them is peace. The biblical opposite of "peace" is not war, but "chaos," and over this chaotic, bewildered little gathering their Lord says, "Peace be with you." This is not a passive, consoling peace, not peace as the world gives it (John 14:27), and as if to remind his disciples of this, Jesus immediately shows them his wounded hands and side. In the presence of their risen Jesus, the disciples respond to these words and wounds with joy. Then Jesus tells them that his gift of peace is also mission: the continuation of the mission on which his Father had sent him and for which they must be enlivened by his Spirit. Jesus breathes on them, and the word that John uses here for "breathe" is used nowhere else in the New Testament. It has all the nuances of the spirit/breath/wind of Genesis, which brooded over the primeval chaos to bring forth new life (Gen 1:2). In Genesis, too, the Creator God breathes into the nostrils of human dust, and this dust becomes a living person (Gen 2:7). When Jesus breathes over the disciples, the chaos of their lives becomes a new creation; their humanity is raised from the dust of disappointment and fear. This Easter Day is the first day of the new creation (or the "eighth day" in the Genesis time line). John also seems to suggest that this action is the ultimate sending forth of the prophetic breath that Ezekiel breathed over the valley of dead bones that stood up again as a living community, ready for action in obedience to the Word of the Lord (Ezek 37:9-10). Reconciled and raised by Jesus' Spirit/Breath, the disciples are to continue the mission on which he had been sent by the Father: the reconciliation of sinners.

On the following "eighth day," there is also a new beginning for Thomas, the disciple who was absent the week before. Nowhere in the gospels is Thomas ever described as "doubting." He has been outspoken, generous, ready to go to death with his master (John 11:16). At the Last Supper he is honest enough to say aloud what the other disciples were most likely thinking: that none of them *are* sure where Jesus is heading. But like his companions who did not accept the testimony of Mary Magdalene about Jesus' resurrection, Thomas also wants a personal experience. His postresurrection challenge is "not to be unbelieving but believing." In both his disbelief and his faith, Thomas represents us, the future generations who, like the generations in the Johannine communities, are called to blessedness because we believe without having seen Jesus in the flesh.

Jesus invites Thomas to stretch out his hand to the wounds in his risen body, for in this opened body is the way, the truth, and the life that Thomas was seeking (John 14:5-7). As Jesus and his disciple stand before each other in the midst of the community, it is Thomas' faith, not his hands, that dig deeply into the mystery of his risen Lord, and he cries out the most profound and personal proclamation of gospel faith: "My Lord and my God!" In return, Jesus blesses Thomas, but then speaks the greatest of all beatitudes that will resound beyond that Jerusalem room, into our assembly today, and to the end of the ages: "Blessed are those who have not seen and yet have come to believe" (John 20:29).

A visitor to the Vietnam Veterans Memorial in Washington, DC, described how he watched a man stand before the wall into which are carved more than 58,000 names of Americans who sacrificed their lives or are missing in action because of that tragic war. The man moved slowly along the wall, stopping now and then to run his fingers over some of the names. Tears were streaming down his face as he touched one he recognized. The wall is a place of gathered memories and a silent chorus that begs visitors to make peace, not war. The name that Thomas gave to Jesus is carved into our hearts at our baptism. We often need to rub the fingers of our Christian memory over it, recognizing with gratitude the peacemaking sacrifice of Jesus that is our salvation. We also need to recognize that Christ still shows himself to us in the wounds of the suffering members of his body: ourselves, and our sisters and brothers, known and unknown.

Today, when priests are in short supply or absent in many places, the first call is still to "gather the people," for our individual faith needs the support and witness of a community. From the beginning, meeting together was vital for the early Christians. In today's reading from Acts, the apostles are gathered in the Portico of Solomon in the Temple; some joined them, others did not dare to do so. Nothing is easy and ideal, nothing is without tension. The apostles touched the wounds of the people who were brought to them, those sick in mind and body, and the flood of suffering humanity flowed from the Temple into the surrounding streets. It is "in the streets," outside the holy places, that most sufferers are still found. In the power of the Spirit of Jesus, the apostles did what Jesus did in the days of his flesh, and Peter has a special mention. One of the three apostles who had been overshadowed by God's glory on the mount of Jesus' transfiguration, he is now the instrument of that same glory when his shadow falls on the sick to transform them into health. In the personal and communal life of Christians there will always be the rhythm of wounding and healing, pain and joy, failure and success.

The second reading proclaims the revelation (Greek *apokalypsis*) of the First and the Last, the Living One, to John (not the apostle, but the one often called the "seer") who had been exiled to the Roman penal colony of Patmos. He had been banished for preaching the word of God and giving witness to Jesus, both imperial offenses, and so he introduces himself as a brother who is in solidarity with those who are also suffering and patiently enduring for their faith, possibly under the persecution of the megalomaniac Diocletian in the last decade of the first century.

John's vision, on the Lord's Day, is described like the commissioning of a prophet. The language of the Book of Revelation (or the Apocalypse of John) is highly symbolic and veiled, but it is also the language of prophetic mission in the name of Jesus Christ, not just private revelation. Twice John is told to write down what he sees and hears so that others may be strengthened in their faith. He is possessed by the voice and the Spirit, and he describes his vision in words that recall Daniel's son of man (Dan 7:9-14), for it is to Jesus that now belongs the universal glory and kingship which makes him the hub of human history and the center of human longing.[2]

Clothed like the Jewish high priest (Exod 30:7), Jesus moves among the seven golden lamp stands, the number "seven" indicating the fullness of his dominion over the whole church. Jesus is not only ministering in the sanctuary of heaven, but in the midst of his church on earth. As a protective yet challenging High Priest, he will tend the divine light that burns in the temple of living stones until the end of time. In Jesus is our supreme confidence because, risen from the dead, he now holds the keys that give him the authority to unlock the prison of death for all who believe in him. This is our Easter faith; this is the everlasting love of God dwelling among us, moving in the Church; and for this we give thanks with the responsorial Psalm 118: "O give thanks to the Lord, for he is good; his steadfast love endures forever."

Third Sunday of Easter

• Acts 5:27-32, 40b-41 • Ps 30:2, 4-6, 11-13 • Rev 5:11-14 • John 21:1-19

John does not begin his Gospel with a call of the first disciples by the lakeside, nor does he even name them as fishermen. Instead, in John, the Sea of Tiberius (Lake of Galilee/Gennesaret) and the great haul of fish are placed in a postresurrection context. John 20:31 is considered by most commentators to be the end of the Gospel by that evangelist; the Good News we hear today is a part of the epilogue to John's Gospel, certainly inspired, but probably a "mosaic" created by a close disciple of John from various pieces of ecclesial tradition. It gives the early Christian communities a picture of some important aspects of life for *all* disciples after the "hour" of Jesus' death and resurrection: the primacy and mission of Peter, the place of the Beloved Disciple, the responsibility of all believers to be fishers of people.

Peter, the leader, has gone back to the everyday, the familiar way of being a fisherman, taking with him six other disciples. There is Thomas, who hovered between disbelief and belief until his experience with his wounded and risen Lord; Nathanael, the true Israelite without guile who had to decide whether anything good had really come out of Nazareth; James and John who had their own problems with status seeking; and two unnamed disciples, one of whom is later revealed as the Beloved Disciple. Into the shoes of the seventh unnamed disciple we may step, while still at times recognizing that we also walk in the footsteps of the others. These seven, the number of fullness, symbolize more than just a part of the apostolic group; they represent the whole community of believers down through the centuries who will encounter the risen Lord, be called by him to let down their nets into the sea of humanity, eat with him, profess their love for him, and follow him in many different ways.

The Gospel begins as a night scene of failure, with no fish caught. Then the sun rises, and the disciples are hailed from the shore by someone who calls them "Children." They are the "little children" of John 13:33 who are loved but still have much to learn. The stranger tells them to let down their nets, and emptiness is filled with a great catch. Then with the sun rising and the dawn of faith breaking, the disciple whom Jesus loves, who rested his head on the heart of Jesus, who stood his ground at the cross and holds the preeminent place of intimate contemplation giving him the keen eyes of faith, sees and proclaims with deference to Peter: "It is the Lord!" It is Peter, the model for pastoral leadership, but leadership that is also dependent on contemplative insight, who plunges into the water. Always eager and impetuous, he makes his way to Jesus. Again we are reminded that the way to the risen Lord is through the waters, through the baptism into which we are plunged.

When they come to the shore, the disciples are invited to breakfast at a charcoal fire on which bread and fish are cooking. As with an earlier feeding, the disciples, too, are to be involved in the preparation of this meal (John 6:5-13). Jesus tells them to bring some of the fish that they have just caught, and it is Peter, in his leadership role, who hauls the net, heavy with fish, from the water's edge. The word used for "haul" is the same word that John used to describe how the Father will "draw" people to Jesus (John 6:44), and how Jesus himself will "draw" others to himself when he is exalted on the cross (John 12:32). Such a "drawing" or "hauling" is the pastoral effort which Peter is to make as leader of the Church. Just as Jesus' seamless robe was undivided on Golgotha, so the net is described symbolically as unbroken, despite its great weight of fish. In the community of the drawn and saved for which Jesus prayed on the last night of his earthly life, the mission of achieving undivided unity must continue: "that they may be one" as Jesus and his Father are one (John 17:21-23).

The disciples share with Jesus a resurrection meal on the other side of death, which is where we now eat with him. This happens at a charcoal fire. The last time such a fire was mentioned, Peter was huddling beside it, denying Jesus (John 18:18, 25). More responsibility demands more love, so before what is to be a second spring of Peter's discipleship, Jesus takes him back into the winter of his failure. When Jesus asks Peter if he loves him, Peter humbly offers his love to Jesus. But he knows that he can no longer be brashly self-confident; he does not fully know himself, only Jesus can know him. Solemnly, in a three-times-repeated and pastoral dialogue of love, the broken covenant between Master and disciple is renewed. It is sealed with the Shepherd's gift of his flock to Peter, but the sheep and the lambs always remain "mine," says Jesus; no one else's authority is absolute. This dialogue of love and forgiveness must always be held in the memory of the Church, especially when the sheep and lambs have strayed.

The body of the Good Shepherd was ravaged in death for the sake of his sheep. So it will be for Peter as shepherd. The one who had so vigorously girded himself with his own clothes before he made his way through the water to Jesus is told by him that one day he will be bound by another and taken to death as the consequence of the love he is now professing. True to himself, Peter has a question! Looking over his shoulder at the Beloved Disciple, he says: "Lord, what about him?" We should not be surprised at Peter's question. Do we ourselves ever doubt the significance of our lives when compared to others? But comparison is not what discipleship is about; it can so easily lead to too harsh or too easy judgments of ourselves or others. Jesus replies to Peter: ". . . what is that to you? Follow me" (John 21:22). This is also what he says to all his disciples, calling them to fidelity to the different gifts of God, in our different places and lifestyles. What happened by the lake is happening to us.

The reading from the Acts of the Apostles is about the apostles as "repeat offenders" against the Sanhedrin. The high priest accuses them of disobedience and of laying the blame for Jesus' death on their council out of political motivation. But Peter replies that what they are doing by preaching and healing has nothing to do with politics and everything to do with obedience to God. Peter himself, he explains, is the leader of and witness to a movement toward God, in the power of the Holy Spirit, not a leader of a protest gang against the Sanhedrin. The intervention (cut from today's reading) of Gamaliel, a wise and respected member of the Sanhedrin, gives the apostles some breathing space. Gamaliel's advice is to wait and see how this movement goes. If it is of God it will succeed; if not, like so many other revolts, it will fail. On the other hand, the apostles are determined *not* to wait and see. After a flogging that they joyfully recognize as sharing in the sufferings of Jesus, they immediately return to proclaiming him in homes and in the Temple. As we recognize from Stephen to Oscar Romero and the thousands of known or unknown and unnamed martyrs, Christian discipleship will always be costly, especially when it demands discernment of the relationship between gospel obedience and civil disobedience.

John the seer gives us a vision of the liturgy of heaven celebrated around the sacrificed and glorified Lamb. An immense chorus of living creatures: angels, elders, animals are offering the Lamb a sevenfold praise. Perhaps the best "explanation" of this vision is not so much explanation but experience of artists and musicians like Jan Van Eyck's Ghent altarpiece, the *Adoration of the Mystic Lamb*, or Handel's No. 47 chorus from *The Messiah*. Surely the seer would have applauded Handel's reply to Lord Kinnoul when he congratulated the composer on his splendid "entertainment." Handel is reported to have said: "I should be sorry if I only entertained them; I wished to make them better." Our Sunday liturgy may seem a long way from John's vision of the liturgy of heaven, but his concern, too, is to "make us better" by proclaiming to us that the reality at the heart of our worship on earth, in the poorest slum or the richest cathedral, is part of the same cosmic praise, an overture to the symphony raised in heaven to the glory of God and the Lamb. One day, we hope to take our place in the full, eternal performance.

Fourth Sunday of Easter

• Acts 13:14, 43-52 • Ps 100:1-3, 5 • Rev 7:9, 14b-17 • John 10:27-30

In the western Indian state of Gujarat, many of the shepherds gather their various flocks together at night in one place. This enables the shepherds to share the night watches and more easily protect the sheep. At daybreak, each shepherd calls his sheep to take them to water and then move on. The call of each shepherd is different, and as the sheep hear it they disentangle themselves from the large flock and follow their own shepherd. This may not sound very surprising until we discover that as many as 5,000 sheep can be gathered in the one nighttime flock. Each shepherd is so familiar with his own sheep, and they with him, that when the sheep answer his voice, the shepherd recognizes the weak as needing extra care and notices and looks for the strays.

In today's Gospel, John describes Jesus as the Shepherd who gathers us into the flock of his community, aware of our weaknesses and strengths and our tendency to wander away from him, yet calling us by name and to life. We can say nothing more moving about human beings than that they call each other to life. It is the beautiful reality behind the fidelity of husband and wife or the steadfastness of friends; it is what helps relationships to endure through good times and bad. Yet all this is a faint echo of the creating word that God has whispered over the dust of each human person, a word that in its intimacy is unutterable by anyone except our Creator and the Son who was sent to make it flesh among us. In the Easter garden, the risen Jesus speaks the one most personal word to Mary Magdalene—her name, "Mary!" And she turns to him from whom she will never turn away, responding to the voice of the Shepherd with his name: "Rabbouni!" "My Teacher!"

Jesus is speaking in the portico of Solomon's Temple during the winter feast of the Dedication (Hannukah), a winter festival that commemorates God's deliverance of Israel from the Syrian tyrant, Antiochus Epiphanes, through the resistance of the Maccabees. After its profanation, the Temple was purified and rededicated in 164 B.C.E., and so this feast was one that remembered and renewed hope for deliverance from Israel's enemies. Jesus is not the powerful political leader that many were waiting for when Israel was again under occupation, a messiah who would save them from civil and religious tyranny. Jesus offers the people a different security: the safety of eternal life if they commit their lives into his hands and obey his voice. Jesus can do this because the Father has given him the flock for its safekeeping and shepherding. The Easter Triduum tells us how costly Jesus' care of his flock will be, but the body of the Shepherd that is ravaged in death is also raised in glory to know and name his sheep and call them into a share of that glory. With the responsorial Psalm 100 we profess our faith in this and recognize ourselves as belonging to God as his flock. That God's steadfast love endures for us forever, is most clearly revealed in the Christ who is both compassionate Shepherd and obedient Lamb.

The voice of the Shepherd is heard now in that of his disciples. This is the repeated message of the Acts of the Apostles. In Antioch in Psidia, Paul and Barnabas give voice to the good news of Jesus Christ, and we have a glimpse of what might have been: a great crowd united in listening and in worship. Jews, Jewish proselytes, and Gentile "God-fearers" like Cornelius (Acts 10:2); they all follow the two disciples and urge them to return the next Sabbath to speak more uncompromising words to them about Jesus and salvation. When that day comes almost the whole town turns out to listen.

But what puts an end to the spread of God's word in that place is still what does the same in our time and place. First of all, there is jealousy among some of the Jewish teachers because of the success of Paul and Barnabas and their warm reception by the synagogue (Acts 5:17). Changes in belief and values and the repercussions these have on the established order are often unacceptable to some, especially those who consider themselves the faithful elite. Paul quotes from the second Servant Song of Isaiah that proclaims that salvation will come to the Gentiles through the people of Israel. By using these words in the context of Psidian Antioch, Paul suggests that he, a Hebrew of Hebrews (Phil 3:5), is a servant light to the Antiochian communities. Simeon's sword of discernment (Luke 2:35) hangs over the city: many, but not all Gentiles joyfully accept Paul's message; some, but again not all of the Jews, reject it.

The other opposition to Paul came from politicking. As the seedbed in which to sow unrest, his opponents chose "devout women of high standing and leading men of the city," neither of which groups would welcome any disturbance of the settled ground of their faith and social status, and both of them no doubt flattered at being regarded as people of important influence. These stir up persecution against Paul and Barnabas, and the disciples leave the region. What drives them away is not fear, but prophetic protest at the lack of hospitality to the Word of God. They express this with the symbolic gesture of shaking the very dust of the place off their feet (Luke 9:5; 10:11). But what they leave behind is not only dust; they also leave a community of those who do believe and may have to face persecution. And so the Church moves on to new places, new people. In its human and religious diversity, its good points and bad, how far from the situation of Psidian Antioch are our own church communities?

John the seer envisages the "flock" of the Lamb as a vast, inclusive multitude of all nations and languages, who stand before the throne of God and the Lamb. In our earthly liturgy we have recently held palm branches, hailed our King, listened to the story of the Lamb who was slain for us but now stands as the Risen One, and rejoiced with the neophytes when they put on the white robes of their baptism. This glimpse of the liturgy of heaven affirms us in the meaning of it all: there will be spiritual warfare to be fought, robes to be washed in the blood of the Lamb, but also palms of victory to be won if we faithfully follow the Lamb through sorrow and persecution.

Into this dazzling scene of the inclusiveness of heaven, John the seer also incorporates the memories of the Jewish liturgy. The multitude of stars and the countless grains of the sand of the promises to Abraham will surely have their place. The immense gathering recalls the Jewish Feast of Tabernacles or Booths (1 Macc 13:51-52) when branches are carried as a sign of victory in battle, and temporary booths or tents are constructed on roofs or patios in memory of the fragile dwelling of the exodus generations and the protection of God who led them into the Promised Land. In the heavenly festival, God is now the tabernacle for his people, tenting over them to protect them from the fear of darkness, from hunger and thirst, from heat and cold that they will never suffer again. By the beautiful and paradoxical reversal of the Lamb who is Shepherd, leading his flock to the living waters, John tells us that what awaits us in heaven will be wonderful, unexpected joy beyond our imagination. But we need to be open to this joyful hope. What are the other values and visions that excite us more? What seems a more preferable and immediate way of quenching our thirst? Does heaven seem just an impossible dream? And can we be good shepherds to one another by following the example of the One who is both Lamb and Shepherd?

Fifth Sunday of Easter

• Acts 14:21-27 • Ps 145:8-13 • Rev 21:1-5a • John 13:31-33a, 34-35

Over the first verse of today's Gospel falls the shadow of Judas. The words about glory and love are spoken only after this chosen disciple has gone out into the night that is already within him. Jesus speaks gently to his own, to "my little children." In the five verses of this Gospel there are two words that are constantly repeated: "glory" and "love." Judas walks away from both. In the prologue to his Gospel, John proclaims that the glory of God was revealed in the descent of the Word into our humanity, "glory as of a father's only son, full of grace and truth" (John 1:14). Now as Jesus comes to his "hour," the love that will be his ultimate self-sacrifice becomes also his hour of glory, a new prologue to his ascent to the Father in the glory of the Resurrection. This is the life and love and glory that Jesus will share with his disciples.

This is the "hour" and this is the "today" in which past, present, and future flow together and are redefined as the reality in which all disciples, both at and beyond this gospel table, are to live Jesus' love command. This commandment is "new," not because the Old Testament was lacking in love but because, first, it is a commandment given with the authority of Jesus himself who loved his own to the end (John 13:1). Second, it is "new" because it is about the love that is to be practiced in the new Christian communities of Jesus' disciples. This does not mean that these communities will be elitist or exclusive, but is a recognition of the truth that Christian life and mission depend mainly on the witness of those who love one another as Jesus has loved, with the radical love that takes him to death and resurrection.

The loss of faith that so often results from the lack or distortion of this love is tragically evident in the past and present history of the Church. Sexual, physical, or psychological abuse by those named Christian—and especially those in whom great trust has been placed—denominational division and bickering, human rights ignored or violated: all these are failure in obedience to Jesus' command to love one another as he has loved us.

One of the significant New Testament words for resurrection is *anastasis*, "standing up." Jesus stood up for the insignificant, dispossessed, and disadvantaged people; he stood up against the lack of love in powerful people and places, both civil and religious, and he died because this is the way he lived. This is why God "stood up" for Jesus by raising him from the dead to the glory of his resurrection. In our parish communities we may have wonderful liturgies and eager ministers, but if there is also jealousy, possessiveness, status seeking, and more judgment passed than love given by both laity and clergy, if there are subtle policies of exclusion rather than inclusion, shadows fall over us. We become death-dealing individuals rather than life-giving communities.

In the reading from the Acts of the Apostles we are given a glimpse of what love in action was like in the early Church communities. In the two verses preceding the Lectionary portion, Paul had been attacked in Lystra by his Jewish opponents (Acts 14:19-20). They had stoned him, dragged him outside the city, and left him for dead. But Paul's disciples find him, surround him, and up he stands. Luke does not intend this as a scene of miraculous "resurrection," except in the important sense that Luke suggests; it is the protection and support of his disciples that gives Paul the strength to rise up and continue his apostolic mission in Derbe, despite his sufferings.

After some unspecified time, Paul and Barnabas make pastoral visits to a number of communities where they had been before, including Lystra. The aim of their visitation is to nurture these churches and put new heart into them by encouraging them to persevere in faithful discipleship despite many hardships. Paul's and Barnabas' own suffering and their perseverance in their faith and mission give great credibility to their leadership and a sense of solidarity with those they visit. There is also a need to stabilize the young communities with good local leadership, and so "elders" are appointed to each community, not by a quick pick but only after serious prayer and fasting and the commendation of these leaders to the Lord, whose work they are to continue after the departure of Paul and Barnabas. From the beginning, local leadership is seen as essential to the well-being and growth of the communities of disciples. The possible loss of first fervor would also have been a concern to Paul and Barnabas, just as it should be our concern for the newly baptized in our parishes. After the excitement and drama of the Easter Vigil, they too need to be surrounded by loving support as they continue their journey into the mysteries of faith.

When Paul and Barnabas return to Antioch, they announce to that church the good news that God has "opened a door of faith for the Gentiles" through their mission. This is hospitality in a deep Christian sense, and obedience to the love commandment of Jesus.

In the Book of Revelation, John unveils his vision to us little by little, lest we be blinded by its brilliant radiance or dismayed by its thick darkness. Now, near the close of the book, he believes that our eyes should be sufficiently adjusted to the light not to be blinded by the glory that will come at the end of time. The glory of God about which Jesus spoke at the Last Supper table is now stretched like a wedding canopy over the whole of creation. The marriage feast that is being celebrated is between the Lamb and all creation. These images, of course, are not to be interpreted literally; what we are in the midst of is magnificent, biblically inspired poetry and passion and prophecy, like that of Isaiah and Ezekiel.

As a bridegroom welcomes and takes home his bride, so God will welcome and dwell with all humanity in the new heaven and new earth. This is the greatest possible "newness," the final transformation by love. There is no more sea, that frightening reality which, for many ancient people including Israel, seemed untamable, and so was often used as a symbol of evil and chaos (Rev 13:1). The image of the holy city, Jerusalem, the center of Jewish life, belief, and worship, blends with that of Bride Israel. But it, too, is a new Jerusalem, where God now dwells not only as God-with-them for Israel (Ezek 37:27) but for the whole human race. In this new creation there is total openness and welcome; "people" have become "peoples." There will be no more tears or mourning, no more sadness or death, but only the final cosmic triumph of love that will transform the world as we know it.

This transforming love of the end time is among us "now," although "not yet" fully realized. The fine linen of the Bride's wedding gown is being woven in time by the righteous deeds of the saints, the followers of the

Lamb (Rev 19:7-7); the new Jerusalem is being raised, stone by stone, by those who are built into Christ, the once rejected cornerstone and now the foundation of the new and living temple of his body (1 Pet 2:5). And the tool for both the weaving and the building is love.

Sixth Sunday of Easter

• Acts 15:1-2, 22-29 • Ps 67:2-3, 5, 6, 8 • Rev 21:10-14, 22-23 • John 14:23-29

In today's Gospel Jesus continues to speak reassuring words about love. He knows the unspoken questions in the hearts of his disciples—not only those around the Last Supper table, but all those of future generations. How will we be able to do what we heard Jesus tell us last Sunday: love one another as he has loved us? "Those who love me will keep my word," says Jesus, and this word is what he has received from the Father who sent him. Obedience and love are bound together, not by any external law, but by the love that Jesus lived and now speaks to our hearts from the depths of his heart. He is in our hearts, to be loved freely, without compulsion. Jesus is present and loved when his disciples remember his words and release them from the past by allowing them to make a claim on their present and their future. The Liturgy of the Word and our personal reflective reading of Scripture (*lectio divina*) enable us to be claimed by the Word of God if we are open and hospitable to it, so that the Father, the Son, and the disciple are mutually "at home" with one another in that most joyous, indwelling space, which can only be created by love.

"Home" is something we all long for. One of the saddest cemeteries imaginable is on the edge of a large modern city. More than a hundred street kids are buried there under mounds of red earth. Nothing marks their graves, just a warning about snakes and a few rabbit burrows in a stretch of dry, cracked earth. These were children who knew little about love. They were homeless in life, unnamed and unclaimed in death, except, we pray, as God's children. Those with whom the Father and Son make their home live in love, are named as Christian, and will be claimed by Father, Son, and Holy Spirit in their death. Their "home-making" creates community on earth and in heaven.

Nostalgia for what life was like when Jesus was present in first-century Palestine imprisons us in the past. The new way of remembering him will be powerful, real, and yet invisible, as intangible but necessary a presence as the life-giving air we breathe. Jesus names this *Parakletos*, the Paraclete, the Holy Spirit. The word *parakletos* has been variously and richly translated as "encourager," "advocate," "counselor." The Holy Spirit is all of these for Jesus' disciples individually, and corporately as Church. The Spirit is both conservative and creative, the memory and future of the Church, enabling us to reach back to the memory of what Jesus said and did and bring this to that life which is constantly renewed with new understanding and experience of his mystery. In the *Dogmatic Constitution on Divine Revelation*, Vatican II speaks about the tradition that:

> . . . comes from the apostles and develops in the Church with the help of the Holy Spirit. For there is a growth in the understanding of the realities and the words which have been handed down. This happens through the contemplation and study made by believers, who treasure these things in their hearts (see Luke 2:19, 51) through a penetrating understanding of the spiritual realities which they experience, and through the preaching of those who have received through episcopal succession the sure gift of truth (art. 8).

Although the Church continues to move forward through the centuries, the Constitution continues, the fullness of truth will never be reached until the end of human history when Church gives way to kingdom.

On this night of gifts, Jesus next offers to his disciples the gift of peace. As with the new love commandment, this peace is also new; it is not sentimental, complacent, secure, or conflict free because it is "my own peace," says Jesus: a peace that comforts the afflicted and afflicts the comfortable. It is a gift given not in the context of cozy table talk, but on the cold eve of his death, when one friend has already become an enemy and left the companionship of the table, and Jesus is saying his last goodbyes to those who, with one exception, will fail to stand by him during his passion and death. He assures them that they should not be afraid, but find new courage in his peace. This peace is *shalom*, the right relationship that flows from our loving union with God through Jesus and the Holy Spirit. The "Go-Between God,"[3] as John Taylor calls the Holy Spirit, makes connections, establishes unlikely partnerships, and breaks down barriers between people—if we are open and welcoming to the Spirit's advocacy for this in us.

Jesus' life has been all about the God who sent him, not about himself, and in this sense he can say, "the Father is greater than I" (John 14:28). Jesus is leaving his disciples because of his obedient love of the Father that will take him through death into the glory of the resurrection that the Father will bestow upon him. Jesus and his Father will share this glory and love with his disciples through the Holy Spirit. These Last Supper words, therefore, are not about absence but about presence: the abiding presence of the Father and the Son with the community of disciples in the power of the Spirit, until the end of time. If the disciples' love is generous, not possessive, they will rejoice in the departure of Jesus for this is the accomplishment of his life's work. Tonight they only hear Jesus' words; when the risen Jesus again offers his peace and his Spirit-Breath moves over the chaos of their disillusionment and fears, they will understand (John 20:19-23).

The creative action of the Spirit is seen at work in the early church in the reading from Acts. The word of God had spread through the Gentile world with the speed of Pentecostal fire, but from the beginning the Church has never been a crucible in which all human differences are purified into the pure gold of total agreement about everything. The tensions and questions in this significant early Church event relate to the demands that are to be made of the new Gentile converts. Daniel Berrigan comments that: "Under the world-encompassing mission of Paul, the small, local, rather hide-bound Jewish community of Pentecost has been urged aboard ship and nudged into open sea . . . steering is by the stars. The daring course, the unknown, the wind of the Spirit is in the sails!"[4] And the church realizes that it must come to port in Jerusalem, drop anchor, and try to discern what future course to set.

The first Gentile converts had been "God-fearers" like Cornelius (Acts 10:2) or proselytes (Acts 13:43), people who had originally been attracted to the traditions of Judaism. But for those who had little or no such contact, the situation was very different, with Paul making no demands for Jewish observance from his Gentile converts. Some reactionary Christians from Judea then come to Antioch, teaching that circumcision was necessary for salvation, so Paul and Barnabas go up to Jerusalem, to the mother church, to take counsel with its leaders. In the twenty verses omitted in the Lectionary reading, the discernment process is described: personal experience is shared by Paul and Barnabas, the Scriptures are searched, and James adds his reflection on the word of God. From this conversation the outcome is communicated in a "pastoral letter" that is taken back to the churches in the provinces of Syria and Cilicia by Paul, Judas Barsabbas, and Silas. The decision is to lift the burdens from the Gentile Christians, not impose them. All that is asked is that new converts avoid idolatry and immorality, especially in the context of Jewish feasts. And this "has seemed good *to the Holy Spirit and to us.*" The Spirit is moving in the church, in human hearts, creating peace and proclaiming love. Moreover, no word is uttered about circumcision, and its inevitable male bias, so that women could now enter directly and personally into the Christian community without having to rely for their religious acceptance on the status and "patronage" of their closest and circumcised male relative. The promises of the gospel are being realized: the Holy Spirit is dwelling in the community and leading it forward to be an inclusive community where "there is no longer

Jew or Greek, . . . slave or free, . . . male or female, for all . . . are one in Christ Jesus" (Gal 3:28). Some of our contemporary conservatives could well "conserve" more of this process of decision making and inclusion.

But is this really possible or credible in our own world of racial, industrial, and domestic violence, and much religious indifference or intolerance? In his poem "God's Grandeur," Gerard Manley Hopkins marvels that although the world seems to have gone religiously stale and our humanity is smeared and smudged, it is not beyond the power of God to redeem and resurrect:

> Because the Holy Ghost over the bent
> World broods with warm breast and with ah! bright wings.[5]

One day, the Revelation reading assures us—when we have loved enough and made enough peace—our bent world will be transformed. To speak of this transformation, the seer uses the imagery of the holy city, the new Jerusalem. The city is bathed in the light of the glory of God and the Lamb. It is a city of reconciliation between Jews and Christians, for it has twelve gates inscribed with the names of the tribes of Israel and twelve foundation stones on which were written the names of the twelve apostles. There is no grand temple in the new Jerusalem, for God himself dwells there with the Lamb, not in a cultic setting, but in and with a wholly redeemed humankind (Rev 21:3). God tents over all creation; all is worship space, the divine is so all-pervasive that even the cosmos is transformed and there is no need of sun or moon. This vision is both future hope and present challenge to our world where everything is not beautiful, not good, not alive, not bright; where there is too much darkness in our hearts, too much of a culture of death, of privilege, of homelessness, of political and economic expediency. Again and again we need to go up the last high mountain of the Bible, guided by the Word of God and an angel, and contemplate the vision. There we can pray with the psalmist our thanksgiving for the final gracious blessing of God that will be revealed when God shines his face on us, and all the nations on earth revere him in the new and eternal Jerusalem.

The Ascension of the Lord

Seventh Sunday of Easter

• Acts 1:1-11 • Ps 47:2-3, 6-9 • Eph 1:17-23 • Luke 24:46-53

A contemporary sculpture of Jesus ascending into heaven shows him stretched between heaven and earth like a taut rubber band. One arm is stretched longingly to the heavens, while the other reaches down passionately to the earth, to the world that his Father and he loved so much (John 3:16-17). The sculptor has imaged what we all have experienced at some time when we have to say good-bye and return home without those we love: a sick parent, a son or daughter beginning college, soldiers departing for active service, the airport farewell to a dear friend after too short a visit. We have to leave each other, but it's hard to go. The aspect of the Easter mystery that we have come to call the Ascension is about not only Jesus' departure and homecoming, but also ours. Its integral place in the flow of Eastertide is emphasized, for example, by the transference (in most dioceses) of the feast from Thursday, the fortieth day of Easter, to the seventh Sunday of Easter. Also, we no longer extinguish the Easter candle on this day as if Easter is over and Pentecost begins. The fifty days from Easter Sunday to Pentecost are one great feast, on which the light of Easter extends the beams of its grace to all the seven weeks.

Many older icons of the Ascension show us only Jesus' feet dangling from a cloud with a little group of disciples huddling under them and gazing upward. We may think of these as the "under-standing" ones of future generations, who still need to gaze into the mystery of Christ for more wisdom. The feet are a sign that, just as triumphant rulers once inscribed the names of people that they had conquered on their footstools, so now all creation is inscribed under the feet of the victorious Christ: risen, ascended, and glorified.

In the readings for this feast we have two accounts of the Ascension: one at the end of Luke's Gospel, closing the period of his earthly ministry; the other at the beginning of the Acts of the Apostles (Part 2 of Luke's Good News) and the beginning of the Church's mission. Through the two accounts, Luke emphasizes the historical continuity of the mystery of the risen Christ. Jesus' departure is a continuing challenge to the disciples of the "in-between-time" of the Church. In the Gospel, the Ascension takes place on Easter Day; in Acts, it is forty days later. Again, there is symbolism in this number. Forty days recalls the experience of the two prophet ancestors who had spoken with Jesus on the mount of transfiguration. For forty days God instructed Moses in the law on Mount Sinai; for forty days Elijah journeyed to Sinai/Horeb before his encounter with God in the "thin" silence outside the cave. Forty is also a biblical number of transition to a new stage of salvation history: from desert wanderings to the land of Canaan; from Jesus' wilderness experience to his public ministry; from the earthly presence of Jesus to his presence in the Spirit in the community of believers.

For forty days the apostles are to be in the company of the risen Jesus, eat with him, and wait for the Holy Spirit, the promise of the Father, who will be given to them. They are to do this in Jerusalem, "the city built with the bricks of prophecy,"[6] and the end point of Jesus' earthly journey in Luke's Gospel. The earthly ministry of Jesus having been completed, in these "forty days" Jesus instructs his apostles about the beginning and continuing mission of the Church. It is to be in the power of the Holy Spirit, its members believing in his risen presence, eating at table, witnessing beyond Jerusalem to the ends of the earth, and gathering and waiting together in joyful expectation.

As children (and perhaps still as adults, if we take the time) we may have often been fascinated to watch the clouds and see how quickly they formed new shapes, new "pictures," especially on windy days. Above us there seemed to be a "becoming world" of surprises, where nothing was fixed or static. The cloud that is described as enveloping Jesus at his ascension wraps him in the glory of God and reveals, even as it hides, another aspect of the Beloved Son: that there is no place for his disciples to just "stand looking up toward heaven." The words of the two messengers, who by dress and words remind us of the two angels at the resurrection tomb, suggest that this is the wrong kind of waiting, a dawdling that will never harvest the fruits of Jesus' resurrection. The time for eyewitnessing is past; now is the time for proclamation. The Ascension points to the need for Pentecost and the driving, Spirit-filled passion that will make the disciples the witnesses of Jesus throughout the world until he comes again. In 2 Kings 2:9-10, Elisha is confirmed as Elijah's successor because Elisha sees Elijah ascending into heaven. He then takes up the prophet's mantle and passes over into his new mission. So the apostles are to take up the prophetic mission of their Master. Because of their apostolic tradition that has been handed down to us, we can sing the words of the enthronement Psalm 47 with assurance: "God goes up with shouts of joy. . . . God is king of all the earth," and in this faith we have courage to accept the responsibility to bear witness to its truth.

Luke concludes his Gospel by again opening his disciples' eyes and hearts to the Scriptures, as he had done at Emmaus. But now he goes further: in his name, they are commissioned to preach repentance and forgiveness of sins to all the nations. Luke does not name the Holy Spirit as he does in Acts, but speaks of sending them "what my Father promised." At the end, in Bethany, with uplifted hands Jesus bestows on his disciples the priestly blessing which, in the first chapter of this Gospel, had been nothing but a confused hand-flapping of the doubting and mute Zechariah (Luke 1:22). Before their ascending Lord, the disciples prostrate themselves with joy, and just as Luke's Gospel had begun in the Temple, so it ends there.

Now the praise of Simeon and Anna has been extended to the continuing worship and praise of the community of disciples.

The author of the Letter to the Ephesians acknowledges their faith and love about which he has heard, and prays for the continuing enlightenment of "the eyes of your heart" so that they will understand the hope that Jesus' call holds, the richness of the glories he has promised, and the power of the Spirit he will send. As we hear these words proclaimed, they become a present prayer for us, too. All creation is now under the feet of the victorious Lord Jesus, the head of the church "the fullness of him who fills all in all" (Eph 1: 23).

Hindu India has a magnificent image of God's relationship with creation: God "dances" creation, and the dancer and the dance are distinct but inseparable. The famous Indian poet Rabindranath Tagore (1861–1941) writes of this relationship in a way that might serve to remind us of the dynamism of the Ascension and its significance for the partners of the Dancer:

> Let the links of my shackles snap at every step of thy dance, O Lord of Dancing,
> and let my heart wake in the freedom of the eternal voice . . .
> Rebellious atoms are subdued into forms at thy dance time,
> the suns and planets—anklets of light—twirl around thy moving feet
> and, age after age, things struggle to wake from dark slumber
> through pain of life into consciousness.[7]

Pentecost Sunday

• Acts 2:1-11 • Ps 104:1, 24, 29-31, 34 • Rom 8:8-17 •John 14:14-16, 23b-26

As a baptized and listening people, drenched with word and water, we come to this culminating feast of the Easter season. This is too large an event, too big a mystery for Luke to describe with precision, so he gropes for comparisons. Unsettling, surging power and possibility are "like" a wind and "like" fire that fill the household of those who have gathered to await the Spirit whom Jesus has promised. The coming of the Spirit shakes the foundations of the household and, as Acts describes it, there is unleashed a new and unimaginable future for the men and women in it. In his Apostolic Letter, *The Spirit and the Bride*, commemorating the fortieth anniversary of Vatican II's *Constitution on the Sacred Liturgy*, John Paul II wrote that: "The Church's teaching must be able to 'dare.'"[8] Pentecost is an event that does exactly that. It is not just the "birthday of the Church"; it is the birth of "being Church," of daring to live the life of Christ into which we are born by baptism and in the power of his Spirit.

Pentecost sweeps up the dead bones of that first little Jerusalem community so that it comes alive, stands up, and goes forward to the ends of the earth with the good news of the risen Christ. Something is in the air that takes this community beyond complacency and despair, something that will keep blowing through every community of believers. The Spirit is not a gift to the proud achievers, then or now, but to those who pray, who wait obediently on the promise of the Father announced by Jesus, and who have discovered the passion, death, and resurrection of Jesus in their own frailty and aridity.

The backdrop to Luke's Pentecost drama is the Jewish Pentecost, the Feast of Weeks or Shavuot (Deut 16:9-12). Seven weeks after Passover and the ripening of the barley came the harvesting of the wheat and the offering in the Temple of sheaves, which were the first fruits of the crop, together with bread made from the first cuttings of the grain (Num 28:26). This earned for Pentecost its other two names: the Feast of the First Fruits or the Feast of the Harvest (Exod 34:22). As Israel became less of an agricultural society, its liturgical tradition developed the feast into a memorial of the giving of the covenant on Mount Sinai, described in Exodus as an event amid fire, clouds of smoke, and great quaking (Exod 19:16-18). The Hasidic rabbis say that Pentecost is remembered as the day of the *giving* of the Torah, not its receiving, for that must be done every day, everywhere.

Luke "inculturates" the Jewish experiences and memories into a new milieu: the mystery of Christ and his Spirit. The little shaken, burned, inspired Jewish community is the first fruits of the harvest that will soon come. On their tongues is the fire that proclaims the risen One in whom diverse peoples will be melted down into unity, and all false pride in race and culture destroyed. Babel is reversed, for immediately after the coming of the Spirit, the disciples go out to speak to the pilgrims who were thronging Jerusalem for the Jewish festival. No matter where the pilgrims had come from or what their mother tongue was, all hear the disciples in their own language.

For the contemporary church and society, there is still a great need to be able to hear what the other is saying and to communicate in a language that can be understood. Bishops need to listen to what their people are saying and avoid "church-speak" when they reply to them; the different generations need to make an effort to learn something of each other's language if they are to support one another; governments need honesty rather than the coded language of political subterfuge; and the media needs to speak without hysteria, cheap sensationalism, and costly untruths. We can all too easily rebuild Babel.

The Gospel we hear today begins with Jesus calling his disciples to obedience after he had just told them that he was going away (John 14:12). We know the great abyss that seems to open up when someone we love is about to leave us in death: a parent, a husband or wife, a lifelong friend. How will we manage without them? They will not be there to say, "Do you remember when . . . ?" or "What shall we do next?" And so we struggle for the faith that is so well expressed in one of the Prefaces for Christian Death: "Lord, for your faithful people life is changed, not ended" because an everlasting dwelling place has been prepared for us in heaven. In the freedom of death, those whom we love become more and more a part of our being, converting us, teaching us even more by their death than by their lives. Often this is because in and after the painful, deep love of the parting, this love gives us new eyes with which to see more clearly the meaning and significance of their life and their relationships. This is supremely true of Jesus' departure. He is asking his disciples to take a great risk: to be obedient and keep on loving him when it seems that he is abandoning them. If they show their fidelity to him by this obedient love, he and his Father will send them the gift of "another" Advocate. Jesus himself has been their encourager and comforter, their advocate before the Father (1 John 2:1). Now there will be "another," the Holy Spirit, who will be for them the love of Father and Son "at home" with them, dwelling intimately within the community of believers. Not dependent on physical presence, the Spirit is the enduring memory of Jesus' words and deeds and the one who urges the disciples to reveal and proclaim these to the world. The poetry of today's responsorial Psalm 104 praises God for the life-giving breath which not only brings us to physical life but also renews and "re-creates" that life through the Spirit of God.

Paul has no hesitation in writing to his Roman Christians the words that become a present reality for us as they are proclaimed in our assembly. The Spirit—the Spirit of God, the Spirit of Jesus—draws humanity into their life of communion and transformation. In the Christian, God is "at home"; made in God's image, the Christian is remade in the image of the Son, and there can be no greater human dignity than this. When we are joined to Christ and share his Spirit, we share in his Resurrection and his sonship, becoming children of God and able to call God by the name of "Abba, Father!", a name that is intimate to those who are no longer slaves but free children in the household of God. So daring are the claims that Paul makes that he summons two witnesses to testify to their truth: the Spirit of God and our own spirit. Then again comes the reminder: heirs to the inheritance of Christ we may be, but this means we must share in his sufferings if we are to share in his glory.

Notes

1. *General Norms for the Liturgical Year and Calendar,* no. 22.

2. Vatican II, *Pastoral Constitution on the Church in the Modern World,* art. 45.

3. John V. Taylor, *The Go-Between God* (London: SCM Press, 1972).

4. Daniel Berrigan, *Whereon to Stand: The Acts of the Apostles and Ourselves* (Baltimore, MD: Fortkamp Publishing Company, 1991) 160.

5. Gerard Manley Hopkins, "God's Grandeur," in *Poems of Gerard Manley Hopkins,* ed. W. H. Gardner and N. H. Mackenzie (Oxford: Oxford University Press, 1970).

6. Robert W. Wall, "The Acts of the Apostles" in *The New Interpreter's Bible,* vol. X (Nashville: Abingdon Press, 1995) 41.

7. Rabindranath Tagore, in *The Bible Through Asian Eyes,* ed. Masao Takenaka and Ron O'Grady (Kyoto: Pace Publishing in association with Asian Christian Art Association, 1991) 164.

8. John Paul II, Apostolic Letter, *The Spirit and the Bride,* article 14.

5

The Season of Ordinary Time

In the church year, Ordinary Time is not a dull, uneventful time. It is the continuous mining of the deep riches of the mysteries of Christ in an "ordered" way, Sunday after Sunday. The Lord's Day is to each week what Easter is to the whole liturgical year: the constant reminder that "Christ has died. Christ is risen. Christ will come again." It is also the "split time" of the weeks between the Baptism of the Lord and Ash Wednesday and the weeks after Pentecost. Having come down from the peaks of the seasons of Christmas and Easter, we continue to trek across the plains of thirty-four weeks, affirmed in our discipleship each Sunday by our "full, active and conscious participation"[1] in the Liturgy of the Word and the Eucharist.

Sunday after Sunday, therefore, we gather to keep the Easter fire burning in our hearts, to take the Easter bread in our hands and drink the Easter cup so that we may be more and more formed into the likeness of the risen Christ.

Luke's story of Jesus which we hear during this time is structured into three main sections: Jesus' ministry in Galilee (Luke 3:1–9:50), his journey from Galilee to Jerusalem (Luke 9:51–18:14), and his ministry in Judea (Luke 18:15–23:40). We hear what makes a faithful disciple, what is the cost of such discipleship, and how companionship with Jesus leads to Jerusalem and the suffering, death, and resurrection that are part of every disciple's life. The Lukan journey is signposted with Jesus' teaching: wonderful stories or parables, realistic warnings, daring challenges to reach out with compassion to the poor and disadvantaged. Along the way, Luke introduces us to other pilgrims and often surprising traveling companions who share conversations and ask questions of Jesus and one another. And into all this good news our Sunday assembly is invited as a community that seeks faith and commits itself to mission.

The first readings for the three-year cycle are chosen so that the assembly hears some of the most important passages of the Old Testament. Given the breadth of this choice, it is primarily governed by the principle of some correspondence with the Gospel: a thematic relationship or an explanatory background for the Gospel action that helps us to appreciate the significance of the salvation which comes to us in and through Jesus.

Unlike the first readings, the second semicontinuous readings in Year C are from the Letters of Paul, or those that bear his name but were probably written not by him but by one of his followers or someone in the "school of Paul." Passages from the Letter to the Hebrews are also read. The aim of these readings is to continue encouraging us to conform our lives to the paschal mystery of Christ that overflows into the weeks of Ordinary Time and appreciate the extraordinary comfort and challenge of this in our daily lives.

On the two Sundays following Pentecost, the church celebrates this "overflow" in a very conscious way with the Solemnities of the Most Holy Trinity and the Body and Blood of Christ. These two feasts that begin the second "split season" of Ordinary Time (after Pentecost Sunday) suggest what its weeks should be for us: the discovery of our true identity as a communion of believers who are offered the hospitality of life in God and the hospitality of the sacrificial meal at which we say "Yes" to what we are—the body of Christ in communion with one another in the broken bread and poured wine.

The Most Holy Trinity

• Prov 8:22-31 • Ps 8:4-9 • Rom 5:1-5 • John 16:12-15

The "Three" whom we celebrate today is never an "arithmetic" three. When we try to understand something of the mystery of the oneness of the Trinity, we often grasp at symbols, as does the Irish poet Patrick Kavanagh when he reflected on the poor farmers wrestling a sparse living from the soil in a bleak March spring. In the fleeting rays of the sun shining through bare trees, in the knowledge that the invisible sap was rising and that new leaves would bud from trees that seemed sealed in barrenness, he sees an image of the Father, the Holy Spirit and the Son.[2]

The church keeps this solemnity in order to shine some enlightening sun into the gap of our understanding of the deep wisdom of God, invisibly rising in our lives through the power of the Spirit, and enabling us to burst through death into the new life that the Son won for us from the sealed tomb. This is expressed in the mystery of communion and friendship of the One in Three Persons whom we call the Trinity. We mark our foreheads with the sign of the cross and name the Three Persons so often, but does anything of their mystery plow its significance into our hearts? At the beginning of our Christian lives, at baptism, we are named for them; at the beginning and end of each Eucharist we sign ourselves with their memory; when our bodies are signed in death, we hope they claim us; when we bless our children, we remember the creativity the Trinity shares with us. All these moments of naming the Trinity are occasions of life and love. When we are blessed "in the name of," we are incorporated into the personal history of the one named. The sign of the cross and the invocation of the Trinity, a prayer of gesture and words that we learned in childhood, are a simple yet profound statement that we belong to Father, Son, and Holy Spirit and are called to live in communion with them.

Because the Trinity is a community of wisdom-filled, love-oriented and Spirit-led communion, the readings for the feast seem to have been chosen to give us some insight into each of these dynamic aspects. In the Book of Proverbs, Wisdom is imaged as the feminine gift of God, a companion in offering the lavish hospitality of creation. There is no cosmic battle as in many of the ancient creation myths of other cultures, but only a joyful singing at the heart of the universe, like that which a craftswoman might croon with pleasure over the work of her hands. At play with the building blocks of creation, Wisdom is always in the presence of God who delights in her. In the last verse of the reading, humanity is singled out as the special joy in which Wisdom delights, and in her God and humankind are bonded. Love, delight, presence: these are the creative realities that later doctrinal formulation was to express about the Blessed Trinity.

The responsorial psalm, Psalm 8, is an ecstatic hymn of praise, the first such in the Psalter. It is the only psalm that directly addresses God throughout, and so is appropriate for this feast of deepest intimacy. In this cosmic work, humanity is not insignificant and lost in space; rather, men and women are drawn into creative co-responsibility with God for the stewardship of creation. Later biblical reflection on this psalm in the light of Christ saw him as the one crowned with honor and glory in his resurrection after what he had suffered. As the "pioneer" of our salvation, Christ draws us all into his mystery (Heb 2:5-9).

In the Letter to the Romans, it is again presence and love that Paul stresses. Access into the presence and life of God is by faith and through Jesus. God's love for us has been made known in the most tangible way through the incarnation of his Son. Therefore, we must go the same way as Jesus went to his glory: by suffering, patience, perseverance, and hope. Then the love of God will be poured into our hearts by the Holy Spirit.

In the short reading from John's Gospel, part of the Last Supper discourse, Jesus speaks about the Spirit, the great encourager, who will enable future communities of believers to have access to him and his Father after he is no longer with them in the flesh. For the Spirit there are no limitations of one place, one moment in history, one gathering of disciples. The Spirit gives the church a future and a hope. When Christian communities encounter new ecclesial, social, and global challenges, the Spirit enables past, present, and future to converge. The past and privileged words of Jesus will be remembered, but the Spirit will pluck the strings of memory so that a new melody is played, a new meaning sounds in the present context, and this song at the heart of the church will accompany disciples into the future.

The Spirit guides the teaching, interpretation, and witness of the church throughout the ages. It also places a great responsibility on those whose ministry is to spark a creative conversation between believers and the words of Jesus, especially those who, week after week, break open the Scriptures in the homily. Likewise, each member of the assembly has a responsibility to enter into that conversation with openness to the Spirit.

Theology has developed a word to describe the dynamic relationship between the Persons of the Trinity and the community of believers—*perichoresis*, or "dance." In this metaphorical language, the Trinity is a partnership of encircling and embracing, a graceful movement of loving attentiveness into which we are invited as partners who must, in our turn, draw others into the dance by our loving outreach to them. With the imagery of the dance we cannot think of God as solitary.

Theology, preaching, metaphor may all help toward some understanding of who and what we celebrate on this feast, but perhaps it is again the poet who has the insight to realize that it is only in the communion of death, when we are drawn into the community of those whom George Herbert calls the "unnumbered Three," that we will truly see and understand because it is only then, in death, that the dust we are will be transformed. No longer will it blow into our eyes to blind us but it will become a seeing dust that sparkles with a revelation of the mystery of the Three in our mutually unveiled presence.[3]

The Most Holy Body and Blood of Christ

• Gen 14:18-20 • Ps 110:1-4 • 1 Cor 11:23-26 • Luke 9:11b-17

In much the same way as for last week's feast of the Most Holy Trinity, the Lectionary readings for this feast illustrate later theological development of aspects of the Eucharist rather than a biblical event.[4]

The first reading is a difficult one for homilists, and for their listeners. The mysterious figure of Melchizedek, king of Salem (of "peace") and priest of the God the Most High, makes his one and only appearance in the Old Testament when he greets Abram after his battle with the coalition of five city-kings. Without any genealogy, and suggesting an eternal lineage, Melchizedek is a priest outside the chosen people who were descendants of Abram, and does explicitly what God had promised to Abram: he blesses him in the name of, or as a mediator of God Most High. And so Abram's story is inserted into the wider history of the blessing of "all the families of the earth" (Gen 12:3). Melchizedek brings bread and wine to refresh Abram after the battle, and no matter who the person, or what his origin, Abram acknowledges that Melchizedek's words are both a blessing for himself and the praise of Abram's own God. Abram responds to Melchizedek by offering to him the tithes of his spoils of war won from the kings, not from any political-military motivation, but only as a response to and acknowledgment of the blessing and protection of God spoken in the words of Melchizedek and the action of offering the bread and wine.

Later biblical reflection in the Letter to the Hebrews would develop the Melchizedek tradition in relation to the priesthood of Christ (Heb 7). He is our king of peace, the eternal mediator between humanity and God. His priesthood supersedes that of Aaron, since it derives from the authority of his indestructible life that is the fullest blessing and praise of God; and the bread and wine he offered are the signs of the new covenant. The memory of the Melchizedek/Christ tradition finds its way into the First Eucharistic Prayer when we pray for the acceptable reception of our gifts, blessed and transformed into the sacramental body and blood of Christ.

Paul received the last supper tradition "from the Lord"—not by word of mouth from Jesus, but through the witness of the faith community who are the body of Christ and whose lives speak of his presence. In this First Letter to the Corinthians, the importance of biblical and liturgical "remembering" is again stressed. The Eucharist is a "memorial" in which the past story of the institution of the Eucharist becomes a present reality for the worshiping community: a sharing in the broken bread and poured wine that are a participation in the death of the risen Christ and the pledge of the salvation yet to come when everything is transfigured, as is the eucharistic bread and wine, into the glory of the cosmic Christ. "Christ has died. Christ is risen. Christ will come again," we proclaim with faith and hope. To be shared, bread must be broken, wine must be poured. What Jesus does in communion with those he loves will be done brutally by the hands that break his body and spill his blood. His Last Supper action is a prophetic sign of the salvation he would accomplish for us by his passion and death. At every Eucharist we are a community of guests who are hosted into salvation by Jesus.

What we celebrate today is the hospitality of God in the gift of Jesus, shared with the world in his personal fullness, in his "body and blood." Luke's account of the feeding of the five thousand is situated in the part of his Gospel that focuses on mission (Luke 9:1-50), and it can be seen as symbolic of the outreach of the church. There is no special invitation to this Bethsaida meal, no house or dining hall in which to eat. Even though Jesus had planned a kind of ministry "debriefing" session with his apostles, everyone who had found out where they were and followed them is welcomed at Bethsaida, and Jesus teaches and heals them until late in the day. The Twelve tell Jesus to send the crowd away to find shelter and food, neither of which is available in the lonely place, but Jesus responds to them with the challenge: "You give them something to eat." Having just completed their first missionary field work of preaching, healing, and exorcising, the apostles are now called to partnership with Jesus in another apostolic mission: feeding the hungry crowds.

Jesus' command that the Twelve seat the crowd in a hundred groups of fifty each is an image of the local churches gathered as the church universal. Just as Jesus has taught the crowd throughout the day, so he will now teach his disciples something more about the kingdom in action when he takes, blesses, breaks, and gives the five loaves and two fishes into the hands of the disciples to give to the crowd.

Luke obviously wants his community, and all hearers of the Gospel, to connect this meal with the feeding traditions of Jesus' ancestors: the miraculous manna in the wilderness (Exod 16:15) and the story of Elisha who fed a smaller crowd with loaves of bread, some of which were left over (2 Kgs 4:42-44). Into this past, the present of the Gospel Bethsaida and all our eucharistic "Bethsaidas" are gathered.

The fragments of the meal are collected and fill twelve baskets. Such is the superabundant hospitality of God in Christ, that there will always be more than enough to feed the future Church of the Twelve when it gathers for its "Bethsaida" meal. But one thing is needed: hands to give the food to the people. The church, guided by the Spirit (about whom we have heard so much on the last two Sundays), needs a creative conversation with the words of Jesus at Bethsaida about the present shortage of ordained ministers to feed the hungry people of God and the right of the people to the have access to the Eucharist.

There are other "Bethsaida" questions this Gospel prompts us to raise: How ought we to celebrate Eucharist in a world wounded by so much injustice? Before Jesus fed the people, he taught and healed and exorcised. What are the paralyzing hungers of people who are physically starving, spiritually deprived, or psychologically damaged that we need to feed? What are the "demons" that need to be exorcised from ourselves and our communities so that our celebration of the Eucharist is not hypocritical?

Second Sunday in Ordinary Time

• Is 62:1-5 • Ps 96:1-3, 7-10 • 1 Cor 12:4-11 • John 2:1-11

The early Sundays of the church year are something of an "in-between time." Christmas is behind us and Lent is ahead, with the number of weeks before we reach that season varying from five to ten. As though the church is loath to leave behind the splendid light of Epiphany and begin to travel the way of everyday discipleship, this Sunday's Gospel is again an "epiphany," a manifestation of Jesus' glory, chosen not from Luke's but from John's Gospel. For the Eastern church, the showing to the Magi, the baptism of Jesus and the wedding feast of Cana were all celebrated at Epiphany as aspects of Jesus' manifestation. This tradition is preserved in the Western church by today's remembrance. By changing water into wine at the wedding feast in Cana of Galilee, Jesus gives the first of the Johannine signs that are to confirm his disciples' faith in him.

As Isaiah proclaims with the bridal imagery of the first reading, marriage is an image of God's relationship to the bride Israel, for marriage is always a privileged, opportune time. We might think of the last marriage we witnessed, the joy and celebration at the realization that here was the moment for the creation of a new reality of love and fruitfulness between a man and woman. Excitement and expectancy are always in the wedding air. Using this imagery, Isaiah suggests that the relationship of tender love between God and his people came out of a crisis that had caused Israel to lose face in the sight of the nations, yet God was faithful to his people. At Cana, another apparently smaller and domestic crisis of losing face looms, but with surprising and larger consequences that will point far beyond the solution to bad catering arrangements!

At Cana we meet Mary for the first time in John's Gospel, and we hear the first and last words that she speaks in this Gospel. Already there is a sense of separateness between the mother and the Son. They are at the same wedding, but come independently, Jesus being described as also invited with his disciples. John never refers to Jesus' mother by her personal name, nor does he do this when speaking of "the beloved disciple." Both the ideal woman disciple and the ideal man are described only by their relationship to Jesus. The mother of the Lord is the discerning one who notices that the wine has run out. She stands before Jesus in the privileged role of mother and presents him with the problem. Jesus' reply to her words have a note of rebuke as he calls her "Woman," not the expected response to one's own mother.

The mother is loved, but she is also an outsider—outside of Jesus' free, unique relationship to God, his Father (John 7:4; 8:19; 12:27). This pain will thrust through her most deeply when she is again named as "woman" on Golgotha and is the beloved and last gift from whom Jesus dispossesses himself before he hands over his breath to his Father. Then will be the "hour" that Jesus tells his mother has not yet come at Cana.

His mother is persevering, even in the pain of Jesus' response that amounts to telling her to keep out of it! How readily do we persevere in our discipleship in the face of what seems to be a rebuke to our faith? The mother's faith in the words of the Word goes beyond understanding. Not understanding, not hoping, but believing, "for the hope that is seen is not hope" (Rom 8:24), the mother speaks to the stewards, "Do whatever he tells you." We never hear her speak again in John's Gospel. Even on Golgotha, there is nothing more to be spoken out of her motherhood and discipleship. These words are enough for her, enough for John's community—and enough for us. In obedience to Jesus' words, the servants fill to the brim the six water jars used for the Jewish purificatory rites, then they draw and take the water-become-wine to the steward. The steward, who has not heard the words of Jesus or his mother, implies that it is the bridegroom who is responsible for this best wine. The Cana bridegroom is a shadowy, silent, and inactive presence, a foil for the next time a bridegroom is mentioned in John 3:29, when John the Baptist acclaims Jesus as the Bridegroom of his people, and himself as the best man who, according to cultural practice, presents the Bridegroom to the bride Israel, and then withdraws.

The purificatory jars at Cana numbered six, a symbolic number of incompleteness. At Jesus' "hour" there will be a seventh jar, when from the clay of his passion-fired humanity there will flow the wine of his blood, not only for purification but for exultant transformation.

> This wine-become-blood redeems and purifies his bride, the church, sanctifying and deifying her. It allows her to participate in the Lord's own death and transformation, and nourishes her with the life of the Resurrection. Accordingly, the wine of "the wedding of the Lamb" is the mystical image for the entire paschal feast of the Lord, the feast of the new and eternal covenant-making in the loving blood of the Lamb.[5]

It is this mystery of word and wine, this paschal celebration, which we celebrate at every Sunday Eucharist. We are now the wedding guests waiting to be filled with the sacramental wine.

The "humble jars" of the members of Paul's Corinthian church have been filled with many gifts by the outpouring of the Spirit. In the diversity of these gifts there is unity: unity of service of the Body of Christ. Paul's letter is a call to respect for, not passing judgment on, those who differ from us in the great "families of peoples" which the responsorial Psalm 96:7 acclaims. As a great shout of joy and praise, this psalm is also placed on our lips as an acclamation of the three readings: of joy at God's faithful and re-creative love for his people, of praise for the signs of the coming of the kingdom in the Spirit's gifts to each of God's people, of exultation at the beginning of Jesus' ministry and the new wine of the messianic feast he has poured out for us, which we share in a special way at our eucharistic celebration.

Third Sunday in Ordinary Time

• Neh 8:2-4a, 5-6, 8-10 • Ps 19:8-10, 15 • 1 Cor 12:12-30 • Luke 1:1-4; 4:14-21

"Today" is an important word for Luke. Already in his Gospel we have heard it sung by the angels at Jesus' birth, and as he begins his public ministry in his home synagogue, Jesus himself proclaims a year of salvation as a "today" event (Luke 4:21). "Today" is a time line that stretches in Luke's Gospel from the angels' song at Jesus' birth, through the healing of bodies (Luke 5:26) and souls (Luke 19:5,9), on into betrayal by friends (Luke 22:61) and his last forgiving moments on the cross (Luke 23:43). Announced in our liturgy "today," it is a powerful reminder of Christ's presence among us to transform, to liberate, to forgive, and to save us. As Anselm Grün says, "Luke's theology of 'today' shows us a way of bridging the deep ditch of history and experiencing the event of Jesus today as salvation and redemption."[6]

As we begin to journey with Luke through the semicontinuous Gospel readings of Year C, it is appropriate that the first four verses are read to remind us of Luke's purpose in writing his two-part good news, the Gospel and Acts of the Apostles. In the latter, it is the church that is committed to doing in the power of the Spirit of Jesus what he himself did in the days of his flesh. Theophilus, who is addressed in verse 3, was probably a significant Christian and a patron of Luke. "God-lover" though he may be, there is always more truth to be discovered, a greater commitment to be made, a new excitement about the tradition that has been handed down by those who were both eyewitnesses and servants of the word. Luke is not one of these, but he is respectful of what he has received from them. Using his own human gifts and guided by the Holy Spirit, he is eager to record, order, and interpret the Jesus tradition for the sake of his patron and the wider community of believers. "Today" we are among those believers, gathered into the Liturgy of the Word, into the presence of Christ.

The various roles of believers in the church assembly, especially those of the laity, can be a focus of much contemporary debate. In the first reading from the Book of Nehemiah, we hear a graphic description of the people who gather to hear Ezra read the Mosaic teaching (Torah) to them. It is Jerusalem of the mid-fifth century b.c.e. The people have returned from exile and have rebuilt the Temple under the leadership of Nehemiah the governor, and Ezra the priest. It is at the initiative of the people themselves (v. 1) that Ezra calls them together and reads to them what is probably part of Deuteronomy—for six hours! They are truly an inclusive community—men, women and children—which indicates the importance of the occasion. Perhaps it is out of consideration for the present day lector that the names of those who stood with Ezra are omitted, but what is lost is the realization that thirteen laymen are named (v. 4) and stand prominently at the reading bench in solidarity with the priest. Thirteen Levites, priestly assistants at the Temple, moved among the people, perhaps translating, certainly interpreting into contemporary practicalities the text that Ezra was reading to them. The crowd were probably descendants of those taken into exile and so may not have understood the Hebrew in which the Law was written and read. Two and a half millennia later, interpretation that enables us to hear the Word of God, identify with it, and respond to it in our own time is still a challenge for those who minister to faith communities. The response of the people to whom Ezra reads the Word of God is anything but passive! They stand to acclaim the Word, raise hands, bow down, prostrate themselves, and weep. Perhaps the last reaction is because they realize they have been unfaithful to what they hear, but Nehemiah (another layman), Ezra, and the Levites call the assembly to joy and celebration and feasting rather than tears, "for the joy of the Lord is your strength" (v. 10). It still remains true that we only really understand God's word when, personally and communally, it calls us not only to tears but also to paschal joy.

In the Gospel reading we have another Jewish assembly, another taking and reading of the scroll, another reaction to the Word of God when, as any adult male Jew can be, Jesus is called up to the reading desk in the Nazareth synagogue. The people are expectant: here is the hometown boy made good, with a teaching reputation already established throughout Galilee. They think they know him, but Jesus is *the* Messiah, *the* anointed One, with the fullness of the Spirit upon him. Born, baptized, proved the faithful Israelite par excellence in the wilderness, Jesus speaks forth as *the* prophet the words of Isaiah as a summary of his mission that he is about to begin. The prophet, he proclaims, is called to announce good news to the poor—their liberty, healing, freedom from all oppression—as in the Jubilee year of release described in Leviticus 25 and Deuteronomy 15. Whether such a year was ever actually celebrated in Israel is uncertain, but it persisted as a symbol of the possibilities of a new era of empowerment of the disadvantaged.

Then comes the climax, the moment of interpretation of the Word of God: "Today this scripture has been fulfilled in your hearing," says Jesus (Luke 4:21). That Jesus is the Word in our human flesh is what we have so recently celebrated in the festivities of Christmas. In the weeks of Ordinary Time, what will the "Amen! Amen!" and "So be it" that we heard in the first reading mean for us in our lives? Will the tears and joy of Ezra's and Nehemiah's community, the amazement of the Nazareth synagogue in response to the Word of God, be reflected in our responses to what we hear proclaimed in the Liturgy of the Word? (Next Sunday we will hear how fickle and fleeting the response to Jesus can be.) How well do we remember the excitement and hopes of the Third Millennium and the Great Jubilee? As people baptized into prophecy, have we become less urgent in advocating that our politicians continue (after some great initiatives) to remit debts of the poorest nations or adopt compassionate policies toward those detained as asylum seekers? What local church initiatives for justice and peace will keep Jubilee dreams alive through the decades of the Third Millennium? Could we be described, like Theophilus, to be "God-seekers"? What local church initiatives for justice and peace keep Jubilee dreams alive? And what do we do as individuals to be "good news" to the poor?

We all have different gifts, writes Paul to his Corinthian church; we will, consequently, all do things differently. But we are all one in the Body of Christ. At every Eucharist we make our sacramental response to this as we hold out our hands to receive communion, saying "Amen" not only to the Body of Christ in the consecrated bread, but also our "Amen" to what *we* are. Baptized into Christ, we are all members of his body, no matter what our gifts or roles; and we are all, therefore, called into solidarity in suffering and in joy. There is no place for personal or ecclesial competition or resentment, no place for attitudes of superiority or inferiority. What does this mean for us—beyond the liturgical moment? Word and sacrament are meant to permeate our daily lives and be for us, in the ordinary and everyday, the "spirit and life" that we acclaim in the responsorial psalm.

Fourth Sunday in Ordinary Time

• Jer 1:4-5, 17-19 • Ps 71:1-6, 15-17 • 1 Cor 12:31–13:13 • Luke 4:21-30

On January 27, 1980, only two months before he was murdered, Archbishop Oscar Romero referred to the Gospel that we hear today:

> In the most sublime homily ever given, Christ closes the book and says, "These things have been fulfilled today." That is what a homily is: saying that God's word is not a reading about times past, but a living and spiritual word that is being fulfilled here today. Hence our effort to apply God's eternal message to people's concrete circumstances.[7]

Romero did this and died for it because he was doing what we hear Jesus doing in his hometown synagogue at Nazareth: helping the people to understand the "today" implications of the biblical word. Last Sunday, the Gospel proclaimed how Jesus as the prophet, the forth-teller, was approved by the people—but not for long! This week we hear how the implications of what he said begins to dawn on them, and how their provincialism begins to assert itself. Here is someone they have known (or think they have known) from childhood, the boy who has Joseph for his father. Luke's communities, however, have heard the proclamation of Jesus' beloved sonship of the Father at his baptism (Luke 3:22) and his genealogy that ends with the proclamation "son of God" (Luke 3:39). The Nazareth assembly would like to own Jesus, make him conform to their expectations, perhaps do good for their businesses by enticing the crowds to Nazareth for some of the miracle working he has done in Capernaum. But he is the free prophet, bound by nothing but the compassion for the poor that he has announced. Accepted or not in his own country, it must be enough that he has spoken out.

The animosity that Jesus will encounter throughout his life, the opposition that will lead him to that terrible mission of martyrdom, seems to be concertinaed into this event as the Lukan sign of what is to come. Jesus dares to confront the synagogue assembly with the memory of God's grace shown to those beyond the community of Israel by referring to two other prophets: Elijah and Elisha. For the poor widow of Zarephath, a Gentile, Elijah miraculously replenished her meager store of oil and grain during a famine (1 Kgs 17:8-16); when commanded by Elisha to wash in the waters of the Jordan, the Syrian leper, Naaman, was healed (2 Kgs 5:9-14). None of us likes to lose an argument by having our own traditions used against us, especially those we have strenuously defended. When Jesus tries to make the people face the truth and consequences of their own Scriptures—and his ministry—this unwelcome reproach to their consciences enrages them.

They choose, as religious communities may so often do, to have a selective memory about their tradition. On this occasion, the crowd drives Jesus beyond the city walls to a hill from which they can either throw him down or stone him. But Jesus passed through their midst and "kept on walking." Where he is walking is to another hill, another angry crowd, to be thrown down onto a cross and lifted high. If today's Christian communities are closed or divided, Jesus will pass again through their midst and walk away.

When Jesus searched the Scriptures, discerning his response to his Father, it is not hard to imagine that he may have often turned to Jeremiah who, of all the prophets, suffers the most in his own prophetic role but continues to be aware of God's call to do battle on behalf of the oppressed and distressed. The call of Jeremiah that we hear in today's first reading begins with verses of profound intimacy: of God's choice of Jeremiah before he was conceived, of God's consecrating touch on his flesh while he was still being formed in the womb. Nothing, this suggests, nothing but prophecy was to be the life of Jeremiah. The Lectionary omits the next twelve verses, and the images that close the call of Jeremiah are very different. As an adult, God will make the prophet like a fortified city, an iron pillar, a bronze wall, because he will have to resist attack from those who oppose the truth of the Word of God that he pronounces. Jeremiah will have to "gird up his loins" (we might say "roll up our sleeves") to get ready for unencumbered hard work, and even for the battle, which prophesying will be. This will be a battle not only with the establishment, the institutions, with kings and princes, but also with his own people. Jeremiah will even struggle painfully with God as he tries to be obedient to his prophetic calling. This calling will take Jeremiah's words to the nations beyond Israel (Jer 46–51). Yet the closing words of the reading are a wonderful promise that still echoes over the valleys and mountains, the low and high points of the personal and communal history of those touched by God. Into our Sunday assembly of the baptized, those Words of God also echo: "I am with you, to deliver you." True prophets know that theirs can never be an overconfident, self-reliant, and untroubled life. As a prophetic people by our baptism, that is something we also need to realize.

With the words of Psalm 71, we respond with a song of praise for God who is for us a strong refuge, a rock on whom we build our lives. Even though, like the psalmist, we may be many years from the womb, this God is still our hope.

What makes possible every fidelity, to God and to one another, is love—the greatest of all the spiritual gifts, and the one that we are all called not only to receive but also to give. This is the simple yet profoundly demanding message of Paul to the Corinthian church. Prophecy, wisdom, generosity, even martyrdom are as nothing unless they are born of love. Paul gives us an "examination of conscience" about our love, one on which we could well reflect on more occasions than the weddings at which it is so often a reading. About the fifteen ways in which we may succeed or fail to love, Dianne Bergant comments:

> By stating what love is not, Paul is also suggesting what his hearers or readers really are: jealous, pompous, rude, quick-tempered. By stating what love is, he is intimating that his hearers or readers could be patient, kind, and forbearing.[8]

We are all a mixture of the potential to love or disregard love. Our strength for loving lies in God's promise: "I am with you to, deliver you." This promise became incarnate in Jesus, Immanuel, "God-with-us." When and how is our response to this promise as fickle as the assembly in the Nazareth synagogue or as steadfast as the prophet Jeremiah?

Fifth Sunday in Ordinary Time

• Isa 6:1-2a, 3-8 • Ps 138:1-5, 7-8 • 1 Cor 15:1-11 • Luke 5:1-11

As we started to journey through Ordinary Time, we met Jesus beginning his public ministry. Today we hear his call to his first disciples to follow him and companion him in this ministry. In all three of the readings for this Sunday there is a story of a call: different people, in different circumstances, with different social and religious status, yet all are touched by the divine initiative. Isaiah, perhaps daydreaming, was in the Jerusalem Temple; Paul, certainly persecuting, was on the road to Damascus; the fishermen, at the lake of Gennesaret (the Sea of Galilee), were washing their nets.

In the Gospel, Jesus is standing on the lakeside with a crowd pressing around him to hear the Word of God. Significantly, Peter and his companions are not part of this crowd. They are tending to their nets after an unprofitable night's fishing. Then Jesus himself becomes a "fisherman" for, as Proverbs 20:5 says, "The purposes in the human mind are like deep water, but the intelligent will draw them out." He gets into Simon's boat, hauls this probably nonplussed man in with him, and puts out a short way from the shore to continue teaching the crowd. After that, Jesus addresses his words to Simon only, telling him to launch out into the deep and put down his nets for a catch. Something that Simon Peter had heard as he sat with Jesus must have made an impression, for he responds to Jesus as "Master," and although he cannot resist reminding Jesus that their nets were empty the night before, in obedience to Jesus' words he casts them into the water.

Then a great reversal happens, as it does so often in the Gospels and as it will for all those who are obedient to Jesus. Empty nets become full to the breaking point, and Peter's personal encounter with Jesus leads to the call of James and John to help with the catch; emptiness becomes fullness in not only one boat but two. Peter is as overwhelmed as the boats. He falls down at Jesus' feet, now calling him "Lord," the post-resurrection title that Luke throws back into this early episode so that those who hear this narrative will recognize the presence of the risen One throughout the whole of his Gospel. Peter begs Jesus to leave him because he is a sinner. We may admire this as Peter's humble profession of his unworthiness to associate with Jesus. But if we read our own experiences, could there not also be a fear of the deep waters that Peter might be letting himself into, waters that would be less troubled if Jesus just went away and left the fishermen to their nets, empty or full? Are there times when we have said to God, "Why me?" when being asked to cope with this commitment, this vocation, this suffering? One day a young woman who had just given birth to a child with Down Syndrome, said in tears to her mother, "Why me?" Her mother replied, "Why? Because of all my eight children, you are the one I would choose—and God has chosen—to be the mother of this child who needs so much love."

This was a "holy interruption" to the lives of Peter, James, and John. Jesus calls them into new depths to become "catchers of people," men who will "net" others for the kingdom. This will mean dispossession of their identity as ordinary fishermen, of their business and boats. Dispossession is an important theme in Luke's Gospel, and the first disciples whom Jesus called were those who had to leave something behind. It will mean suffering, but in the company of Jesus and with faith in him there is no need for fear.

In his Apostolic Letter for the dawn of the Third Millennium, John Paul II reminded the baptized people of God, we who have met Jesus in the waters, of this section of Luke's Gospel: *Duc in altum!* (Put out into the deep!)[9] These words ring out for us today, and they invite us to remember the past with gratitude, to live the present with enthusiasm, and to look forward to the future with confidence: "Jesus Christ is the same, yesterday and today and for ever" (Heb 13:8). Now well-launched into the Third Millennium, how are we measuring up to this challenge?

There is a great external contrast between the call of the first disciples and Isaiah's call in the first reading. In 742 B.C.E., the year of the death of King Uzziah, there was political unrest in both the northern (Israel) and southern (Judah) kingdoms. Isaiah is in the Jerusalem Temple, a place with which he seems very familiar. There is the smell of incense, not fish, and Isaiah encounters God not in the itinerant Preacher surrounded by the Galilean crowd, but in the vision of God enthroned in majesty and surrounded by the heavenly attendants, the flaming seraphim. God's presence is transcendent and immense, with glory that not only fills the whole Temple but also extends to the whole earth. At the chorus, "Holy, holy, holy," the Temple is shaken and Isaiah too trembles with fearful awe. Like Peter, Isaiah professes his sinfulness. The Lord of hosts remains silent, but one of the seraphim (Hebrew "burning ones"), who is on fire with the glory of God, takes a hot coal from the altar brazier and touches the lips of Isaiah. From now on, Isaiah's lips will be purified for speaking the prophetic Word of the Lord. Only then does God speak the question which is a quest for a messenger: "Whom shall I send and who will go for me?"; only then does Isaiah give a free response, accepting the dangerous role of a prophet of God: "Here I am, send me."

At every Eucharist, we echo the chorus of the seraphim, "Holy, holy, holy," as we acclaim the glory of God that comes down on our altar as the sacramental Body of Christ. Do we sing or say this as "burning" ones, on fire with love and enthusiasm for this fearful wonder, or as mechanics of repetition? At our baptism, our ears and mouths were touched more gently than Isaiah's, as this prayer was said: "The Lord Jesus made the deaf to hear and the dumb to speak. May he soon touch your ears to receive his word, and your mouth to proclaim his faith, to the praise and glory of God the Father." Throughout our lives, in good times and bad, in the strength of our prophetic baptismal calling, we struggle to respond: "Here I am, send me."

It was when Paul was fully occupied in the daily persecution of the followers of the Way (Acts 9:1-19) that he met Christ. His is a wonderful and consoling witness to the truth that it is not only the most discerning, the most devoted, the most regular frequenters of the holy place upon whom the choice of God falls. In his First Letter to the Corinthians, Paul gives us one of the earliest creedal statements: Christ died, was buried, and rose to life for our salvation. He describes himself as a premature infant, thrust into the life of an apostle when no one expected it, and after the risen Lord had appeared to Peter (Cephas), James, and the other apostles and believers. Like Isaiah, Peter, James, and John, Paul proclaims that it is only the grace of God that has turned his life around and made him one who faithfully carries on his ministry of preaching the good news he has received.

Isaiah, Paul, and Peter all recognize and confess their sinfulness and weakness, and empty themselves of power and control. When we do this, there is room for God to enter into our depths. When we decrease in self-importance and risk being open to God's initiative then, in the words of the psalmist, God answers us, and out of steadfast love and faithfulness, increases the strength of our souls (Ps 138:2-3).

Sixth Sunday in Ordinary Time

• Jer 17:5-8 • Ps 1:1-4, 6 • 1 Cor 15:12, 16-20 • Luke 6:17, 20-26

Today's Liturgy of the Word confronts us with the questions: Where is my life grounded? What nourishes it? What does it mean to be happy or unhappy? Jeremiah hangs his answer on two images. The first is that of a desert shrub in a parched salt pan, a dead tree in dead earth; the second is a tree that someone has taken the trouble to transplant (from the desert) to a place near a running stream so that its roots can reach deep into the life-giving water. Not only does this tree survive the harshest summer drought, but it also bears abundant fruit and stabilizes the earth around it. "Transplanted" into our own lives this image bears witness that, if we sink ourselves deeply and trustfully into the ever-flowing stream of God's grace, we will survive the heat and dryness of those days when all that we are, all that we do, seems to be turning into dust; we will be "happy" people or (as this word may be translated in both the Hebrew and Greek) we will be "blessed." Disconnected from God, we become like withered scrub. Our choice is for life or death.

When we respond to Jeremiah's words with Psalm 1, the parallelism is very obvious. Many commentators suggest that the passage from Jeremiah was itself "transplanted" by editors of the Book of Psalms as the first "entry" psalm into the way of God's wisdom and truth. What keeps us on this way is delight in God's Word and the constant savoring of its richness in prayer and reading. There is a stark choice to be made: to choose to be like a stable, well-rooted tree; a person blessed by God; or to become insubstantial and unstable straw people, easily blown away from God.

In baptism, our lives are plunged into the life-giving stream of Christ's death and resurrection, "transplanted" into a new creation in him. At the baptism of adults, especially those we have accompanied through the Rite of Christian Initiation of Adults (RCIA), this uprooting from their former lives and planting in the new life of Christ and his faith community is much more obvious—above all at the Easter Vigil. But wherever and whenever a baptism is celebrated, the choice is made, on behalf of the child or by the adult and in solidarity with the faith community: the choice to renounce sin and commit one's life to God, the same choice as Jeremiah's or the psalmist's—for life or death.

This is no insignificant choice, Paul tells his Corinthians. It is a choice with consequences that extend throughout our lives and into and beyond our death. Christ is the tree whose first fruits are a promise of the quality of what is yet to be harvested by all who remain faithful to him, a promise of a future that cannot be extinguished even by death. We are all "works in progress," "unfinished" disciples until, with and in Christ, we attain the resurrection from the dead, that mystery into which we must thrust our roots if our faith is not to be what Paul calls "fruitless."

Luke's Beatitudes are part of a sermon on the plain, not on a mountain as was Matthew's chosen setting. It is not geography that governs each evangelist's choice, but theology and the particular challenge each emphasizes for different communities. Luke's setting reflects Jesus' very down-to-earth ground rules for inclusion in the kingdom of God. The Lukan Beatitudes are less spiritualized than Matthew's and, consequently, have more concrete social implications. Jesus is surrounded by the twelve apostles whom he has just chosen from among his many disciples, together with a crowd who are attentive to his words and hopeful of his healing. His words are as direct and as challenging as they were in the Nazareth synagogue. In the tradition of prophet and psalmist, Jesus also offers the choice of two ways: a life of blessings or a life of woes, happiness or unhappiness. His words put down the standards of his society and raise up those of the kingdom of God. Jesus is indulging in neither scare tactics nor praise for complacent satisfaction with one's social status, so how do we "transplant" these words into our own lives and society two thousand years later?

For Luke, the poor were not just the poor in spirit (Matt 5:3); they were the economically impoverished, the people on the margins, pushed there by a society that did not take seriously the covenant responsibility to which Moses and the prophets had called them. The poor are specially loved by God, not so much because of what they are, but because of what God is—the compassionate defender of the weak and powerless (Deut 10:18; Amos 2:6-7). As the liberation theologian Gustavo Gutierrez wrote:

> God has a preferential love for the poor not because they are necessarily better than others, morally or religiously, but simply because they are living in an inhuman situation that is contrary to God's will. The ultimate basis for the privileged position of the poor is not in the poor themselves but in God, in the graciousness and universality of God's agapeic love.[10]

As individuals, church, governments, our justice re-presents God's justice to the world. The poor, hungry, weeping, and persecuted people are those for whom the church calls us to make a special option, one that will have both personal and political consequences. In *Economic Justice for All: Pastoral Letter on Catholic Social Teaching and the US Economy*, there is a finely balanced statement of what this means:

Decisions (for the poor) must be judged in the light of what they do *for* the poor, what they do *to* the poor, and what they enable the poor to do *for themselves* (Par. 24).

Our option for the poor is to be preferential not exclusive, respectful not denigrating, enabling not patronizing.

Since the poor do not need to be told that they are poor, it seems that Luke has very much in mind the audience of affluent, comfortable, and self-satisfied Christians in his communities. To make sure that poverty is not romanticized, Jesus speaks the next two beatitudes to the hungry and weeping. Jesus and the early church, in his Spirit, will provide for the hungry (Luke 9:17; 16:21; Acts 6:1-4), and tears are more precious in God's sight than derisive laughter (Luke 7:32, 38). Discipleship is not to be domesticated; it may demand the high price of hatred, exclusion, scorn, and eviction from the places of the privileged. It is the struggle for justice when, for example, low income housing estates are gentrified or when those who fear a drop in their land value protest about group homes for people with disabilities being built in their "neighborhood" (the term that, ironically, is often used). When governments ignore the potential impact of climate change on the small land holdings of subsistence farmers, when their social welfare budget is insignificant when compared to the money spent on war, and when we—as citizens not only of our own nations but also of the kingdom of God—do nothing to advocate justice, then our ears need to be dug out by the "woes" of Jesus (Ps 40:6).

Seventh Sunday in Ordinary Time

• 1 Sam 26:2, 7-9, 12-13, 22-23 • Ps 103:1-4, 8, 10, 12-13 • 1 Cor 15:45-49
• Luke 6:27-38

Shortly after the 1989 murder in San Salvador of the six Jesuits and their housekeeper and her daughter, the theologian Jon Sobrino, S.J., spoke in London about the tragedy. As a member of the same community, he would also have been killed except for the fact that he was lecturing elsewhere on that tragic day. During his talk he described his experience at a celebration of All Saints' Day in a Salvadoran refuge. Around the altar were cards with the names of deceased family members and friends of those in the refuge. As they were not allowed to go to the cemetery to put flowers on the graves, they had painted flowers around the names. One card with no flowers read: "Our dead enemies." At the conclusion of the Eucharist, an old man explained to Jon: "As we are Christians, you know, we believe that our enemies should be on the altar, too. They are our brothers, in spite of the fact that they kill and murder us."

To love our enemies is surely hard, unreasonable, yet it is also the most radical obedience that Jesus asks of his disciples as he continues his Sermon on the Plain. To love our enemies who victimize us makes us no longer victims; we become free people whose behavior is determined by no one else—except the Christ of whom we are disciples.

Viktor Frankl, the Viennese Jewish psychiatrist imprisoned in the Nazi death camps, wrote about "the last of human freedoms" the ability "to choose one's attitude to a given set of circumstances."[11] It was this ultimate freedom that had helped him and others to survive even the most inhuman of situations. To love and not hate, to bless and not curse, to be generous and not demanding, to be compassionate and not self-centered—the choice is always there. For Christians, the strength to make such a choice depends on neither psychiatric theory nor theology (although both can support it); it is as simple and demanding as the words of the old Salvadoran refugee: "As we are Christians. . . ."

This is the good news that, paradoxically, seems such "bad news." "Bad" because it goes against our spontaneous inclination to give as good as we get from those who are our enemies, and we all have them! It is good news "to you that listen" because it is the word of Jesus. It is not hypothetical morality, but realistic Christian challenge to people who know what it is like to be slapped down, psychologically if not physically, whose generosity can be abused and who find it difficult to extend love beyond friends, admirers, or benefactors.

The following story is told of Rabbi Hillel who began to teach around 30 B.C.E. A man had approached Hillel's contentious and impatient contemporary, Rabbi Shammai, and said to him, "Accept me as a convert on the condition that you teach me the whole Law while I stand on one foot." Then Shammai drove him away with the rod that he held in his hand. Whereupon he went to Hillel, who welcomed him and said to him, "What is hateful to you, do not do to anyone else. That is the whole Law; all the rest is its interpretation. Go and learn!"[12] This "Golden Rule" was one strand of Jewish tradition (see Lev 19:18; Tob 4:15), known to Jesus, as it was to Hillel. And Jesus does interpret it for us. Love of enemies has nothing to do with self-interest, the rule of "You scratch my back and I'll scratch yours!" The only motivation for this love is our kinship with God as daughters and sons, kinship with a God who is compassionate. "Compassion" is a most privileged Gospel word. In Jesus' mother tongue it derives from the word for "wombs." It is like the womb-love that a mother has for her child, fiercely protective and lavishly loving. That the Lukan Jesus chooses to describe his Father's love as this mother love is not only a startling reinterpretation of what the "Fatherhood" of God means, but also a challenge to what it means to be a daughter or son of such a Father. The responsorial Psalm 103 calls us to remember the compassion and love of God who forgives and removes our sins. Our gratitude to God for this should urge us to try to be worthy sons and daughters of God, likewise compassionate and forgiving of others.

The story of David's encounter with Saul in the first reading is also a story of forgiveness of an enemy. Consumed with jealously, King Saul had turned against David and with three thousand men is pursuing him. David, with one companion, Abishai, comes across Saul and his contingent asleep in their camp. This deep sleep "from the Lord" is a providential intervention of God (Gen 2:21; 15:12) on behalf of David, the already anointed successor of Saul (1 Sam 16:12-13). Seeing Saul's spear stuck in the ground as a marker of royal rank and territory, Abishai is ready to seize it and kill the king. But David will not permit such indignity to the one who, even if he is David's enemy, is also still, in public, the anointed king. David entrusts to God Saul's life, as well as his own, and refuses to take advantage of Saul. He simply takes the spear and a water pitcher as evidence of his presence and nonviolence toward Saul. When Saul awakes, David calls to him across the valley, and shows him the spear. By not using it to kill Saul, David shames the king with enemy love. This event witnesses to a biblical truth that has relevance for our own times and for the warnings about our enemies and "axis of evil": the truth that there are ways other than opportunist violence to negotiate with our enemies.

Paul reminds us that there is always a struggle going on in us between the "dust" of the first Adam and the glory of the Christ, the Second Adam, who has risen from the dust of the grave. In the resurrection of Jesus, God has given us the ultimate expression of that compassion and love which for us is a consecration of our humanity that surpasses anything that the singer of Psalm 103, today's responsorial psalm, was able to imagine. Our human dust is capable of holy compassion and forgiveness. When the Nazi death camp of Ravensbrück was liberated, a prayer was found next to the body of a dead child, scribbled painfully on a scrap of dirty paper:

> O Lord, remember not only the men and women of good will, but also those of ill will. But do not remember all the suffering they have inflicted upon us; remember the fruits we brought, thanks to this suffering, our comradeship, our loyalty, our humility, the courage, the generosity, the greatness of heart which has grown out of this; and when they come to judgment, let all the faults which we have borne be their forgiveness. Amen.[13]

Eighth Sunday in Ordinary Time

• Sir 27:4-7 • Ps 92:2-3, 13-16 • 1 Cor 15:54-58 • Luke 6:39-45

"Look, I just want to say this for your own good. . . ." Do these or
similar words press the "BEWARE" button for us? The answer probably depends on those speaking and the tone in which they speak. If we recognize
them as people of good heart and great integrity, we will be willing to
listen to constructive criticism; if we sense destructive superiority and self-
righteousness in their words, we do not want them as our teachers. What
Jesus teaches, he lives, and in today's continuation of the Sermon on the
Plain he is the wisdom teacher who voices his expectation of this same integrity in his disciples. If we are blind to our own shortcomings, yet judgmental about those of our sisters and brothers, we have no right to guide
them with our advice; we will only succeed in dragging them down into
the metaphorical "ditch" rather than helping them out of their difficulties.
The church, the community of disciples, can contain such blind guides and
ditches, as both Luke and we ourselves know.

The good teacher, the wise parent, often makes a point by exaggeration,
as does Jesus in some of his parables, including the mini-parables in this
reading. To have a log of wood in our own eye does not make us a very efficient speck-remover for someone else's eye. Smug superiority distorts our
vision of ourselves and our neighbor. Some of us would have no trouble
winning a black belt for innuendo and faint praise, so quick are we on the
offensive against others, and even faster on the defensive about ourselves.

Using the familiar biblical image of a tree whose quality is judged by the
good or bad fruit it produces, Jesus teaches his listeners that the quality of
people is judged by their actions. There is more involved here than "spiritual
eye surgery" to get rid of the judgmental log that blinds us. It is a matter of
the biblical heart, that deepest personal reality, the storehouse of our dreams
and desires. Good will be drawn from the good-hearted person, evil from the
heart that is morally diseased. One of the surest indicators of good or bad
people is their words: words that are honest and match their deeds, as did
Jesus' words, or words that are a sadly hypocritical script for playacting.

The mass media and politicians are a source of many words in contemporary society. A prominent lawyer and social justice advocate speaking on
the topic of "Honesty Matters" commented that tact is kind, diplomacy is
useful, euphemism is harmless and sometimes entertaining but, by contrast, "doublespeak" is dishonest and dangerous.[14]

With regard to this "doublespeak," we need the wisdom and discernment
of which Jesus speaks. Recent history has many examples of "doublespeak"

that may be so familiar to our ears that our hearts no longer have a Christian reaction. "The final solution" meant the genocide of six million Jews; the "courtesy fence" around an asylum seekers' detention center is not electrified but "energized" (with 9,000 volts); "collateral damage" in war means the killing of innocent civilians; the "management unit" is a solitary confinement block. We need to take the pulse of our newspapers, TV, and governments to make a Christian diagnosis of such language and its reporters.

The reading from the Book of Sirach endorses the importance of speech. When, to make his gospel point, Jesus used images of blind and seeing people, logs and splinters and trees, he was following the wisdom tradition to which Sirach belongs. In this biblical wisdom book, there are also images from daily life: agriculture, pottery, horticulture, which help his audience reflect on their ordinary life experiences and then move from that to their relations with God and one another.

If these are rubbish, they will be sifted out and discarded; firing in the pottery kiln can either crack or shatter the potter's work, or it can bring out the unexpected beauty of the glaze and make the fragile clay durable. Just so, a person's conversation can be the kiln of creativity or destruction. There are more trees around, too, an orchard of them this time, planted in this text to serve once again as a metaphor of the quality of the fruit borne by our words.

Our words can be used to praise and give thanks to God for his love as we do in the responsorial Psalm 92. And here are the trees again! Worshiping in the house of the Lord and planted in God's fidelity, the faithful person is like a fertile palm, or as enduring in their love of God as a great Lebanon cedar. Designated as a "Sabbath song," this psalm is an appropriate response for us as we gather as a Sunday community of faith and worship in God's house and as a temple of living stones.

In the closing verses of his magnificent fifteenth chapter of the First Letter to the Corinthians, Paul writes of the final harvest that will be gathered by those who keep on laboring at the Lord's work. It will be the harvest of immortality and imperishability that flows from the resurrection of Christ who rose fresh-flowered from the tomb with the eternal dew of Easter morning on his face.

Ninth Sunday in Ordinary Time

• 1 Kings 8:41-43 • Ps 117:1-2 • Gal 1:1-2, 6-10 • Luke 7:1-10

On the next three Sundays, Luke gives us three cameos of very different people for whom Jesus is life and hope. Having finished the Sermon on the

Plain, Jesus, the Messiah of the word, shows himself to be also the Messiah of the deed. This is the integrity he also asks of his disciples. Today we meet the Roman centurion stationed in Capernaum, whose portrait in the Gospel we can gaze upon as a model for Gentile believers. By this, Luke was foreshadowing the mission to the Gentiles that unfolds in the Acts of the Apostles, and laying the foundations of this mission in the ministry of Jesus himself. For future generations, down to our own, it affirms all those believers who, like the centurion, have not seen Jesus but have come to believe in this presence through and in his life-giving word (John 20:29). Such faith is not "secondhand" nor disadvantaged, nor just a comforting and nostalgic panacea.

What are the qualities of this Gentile commander of soldiers that are relevant for us? He is a compassionate man, concerned about others, not standing on his dignity nor jealously guarding his status and authority as one in the service of either Herod Antipas, the tetrarch of Galilee, or Pontius Pilate, the procurator of Judea. The centurion's first concern is for his slave who was ill to the point of death. But his approach to Jesus shows that he is also one of those people who can build bridges over distances between social and religious groups. Not only is he a strong leader and compassionate for the weak, he is also a man of goodwill in a situation of tension between Jews, the Roman occupying force, and nonmilitary Gentiles. In the centurion are embodied the precious values of respect and friendship rather than animosity. The representatives of the local Jewish board willingly come to seek Jesus' healing on behalf of the centurion, testifying to his friendship and its practical expression in his generous patronage that enabled them to build their synagogue.

Jesus willingly goes with this deputation, but then another group meets Jesus: friends of the centurion and presumably Gentiles. The centurion, a man accustomed to his military words commanding attention and obedience, sends by these friends a very different word to Jesus who is addressed by them as "Lord" (*kyrie*). On Gentile lips, this could be just a humble, courteous greeting; in the ears of future Gentile Christians, it would sound the religious faith in Jesus that they had accepted. Underlying the centurion's wish not to put Jesus to any "trouble" is his sensitivity to Jewish religious observance that he knows would consider Jesus as made ritually "unclean" by entering a Gentile house. Through his friends, the centurion also makes a profession of faith in the healing power of Jesus' word. He is a man accustomed to being in authority and commanding others, yet he recognizes in Jesus an authority over life and death that is so much greater than his own. As a commanding officer he might send his soldiers into death, but he cannot bring them out into life.

That Jesus never comes into contact with the centurion is significant for those of us who, in another time and place, believe in him and the power of his word that can cross far geographical and many generational gaps. The word of Jesus is not just an utterance of the past, but the presence of God in our midst to create and sustain our faith in the present and the future. To the crowd, Jesus praises the faith of this "outsider" that surpasses the faith of so many in Israel. The messengers add nothing to either the words they speak on the centurion's behalf or to Jesus' words to the crowd, but their silent return to the centurion's house is loud with what seems to be also their own unexpressed faith that is affirmed when "they found the slave in good health."

It is the request of the Gentile centurion that the church puts on our Christian lips at every communion rite. Gathered around the altar as friends of God, attentive to the Word of God, and believing in the sacramental word that transforms and heals, the worshiping community is a sign of the reign of God. But every Eucharist is also a challenge to break down the walls around our community and, like Jesus, welcome the outsiders and strangers, the "centurions" of our present times. As Timothy Radcliffe, O.P., writes:

> Every Eucharist is the sacrament of our home in the Lord, and yet breaks down the little home that we have made. We must throw down the walls that we build to keep out strangers. This is the necessary paradox of being both Roman and Catholic, both a particular historical community and the sacrament of a community which transcends us and stretches out to embrace all of humanity. It is a tension that will mark every Eucharist until the Kingdom, when the sacraments will cease and the Church will be no more.[15]

There could be no better reminder of this than the words of the pagan centurion on our lips just before we eat the sacramental bread of healing and hope.

The first reading that the Lectionary twins with today's Gospel is part of Solomon's prayer at the dedication of the Jerusalem temple, for which building he had been responsible. Solomon prays for the "strangers" in the land, not those non-Israelites who were permanent residents, but those who were there on a temporary basis, usually for diplomatic or military reasons, and who would eventually return to their own nations. Solomon's prayer welcomes those who have heard of the name (the person) of Israel's God, and have come to the place that symbolized the heart of Israel's faith in the divine presence. Solomon's extraordinary prayer has nothing to do with conversion of these pagans; it is a prayer to God who is the liberating

God of all the nations, and not the exclusive property of any one building or people. Solomon hopes that through the temple hospitality offered to the outsiders, these will return home to their own distant lands to spread the fame of the God of Israel.

The responsorial psalm, Psalm 117, the shortest psalm in the Psalter, is a call to the foreign nations to praise God for his strong and faithful love, a call to which so many generations later, the Roman centurion will respond.

This Sunday we begin to read Paul's Letter to the church of Galatia, a part of what is modern-day Turkey around the main city of Ancyra (today's Ankara). Paul reminds the churches in this region that he has been called to be an apostle by Jesus Christ and by God the Father who raised Jesus from the dead. His apostleship is founded, therefore, on the death and resurrection of Jesus, and this is the Good News, the Gospel, which Paul preaches to his communities. He is disappointed and astonished that some of the Galatians have listened to other Jewish Christian preachers who have come among them saying that, as Christians, they must also submit to the Jewish rite of circumcision. Paul sees this as confusing the Galatians by implying that God is not free to work outside of the prescriptions of the Jewish law. Paul recognizes these preachers as "troublemakers" who distort Gospel teaching. And they have not been absent from our more recent history; for example, from the German non-Confessing church of the 1930s, the Dutch Reformed Afrikaaners of the apartheid years in South Africa, or the arrogant opponents of Vatican II who manipulate the Christian message to fit their own theological viewpoints. We ourselves can sometimes distort or rationalize the demands of the Gospel by longing for the applause of others, the choice of the familiar, the comfortable, the self-justifying interpretation of the Gospel. As we wrestle with this tough, honest lesson in the following weeks, we are summoned to accept the hard grace of approval by no one but Jesus Christ.

Tenth Sunday in Ordinary Time

• 1 Kgs 17:17-24 • Ps 30:2, 4-6, 11-13 • Gal 1:11-19 • Luke 7:11-17

When a son or daughter dies before a parent, the grief is often deeper because such a death seems a reversal of human expectations. The first and Gospel readings today recount such sadness. Death dispossesses both the widow of Zarephath and the widow of Nain of an only child. Their grief and vulnerability, therefore, is even more poignant and devastating because given the patriarchal structures prevailing in the society of both the Old and New Testaments, a woman was dependent on the men in her life for

any social status. Without support of father, husband, or son she was rele-
gated to the margins, to belonging with the poorest of the poor (*anawim*).
The way a society treats its weakest members is still today a "litmus test" of
its moral health; it was certainly this for the people of God. When they for-
got that "You shall not abuse the widow or orphan" (Ex 22:22), it was the
prophets who reminded them of their responsibility in the strongest words
(e.g., Isa 1:17; Jer 7:6; Ezek 22:7). In his letter, James writes that true religion, "pure and undefiled before God the Father, is this: to care for orphans
and widows in their distress, and to keep oneself unstained by the world"
(Jas 1:27)—a significant conjunction.

The widow of the first reading had, in return for Elijah's miraculous befriending of her in the famine (1 Kgs 17:8-16), offered Elijah the hospitality
of her Sidonian home. But when tragedy strikes in the death of her son, her
faith in Elijah wavers. She accuses him of bringing down upon her, a pagan,
the displeasure of his God because of what must be regarded as her sinfulness. Elijah immediately takes the child from her and tenderly carries him
to the prophet's upper room. There he calls upon God in honest, almost ac-
cusing prayer, lays the child's body upon the bed and shares his prophetic
breath with him. Three times Elijah does this before God, the universal
giver of life, is revealed as the liberator from death whose power is not con-
strained by boundaries of nationality or religion. It is God's word on the
prophet's lips, God's spirit/breath that, through the prophet, enlivens the
child. And Elijah descends with this only son in his arms and gives him
back to his mother. Then her wavering faith is restored, faith not only in
Elijah, but also in the God who puts his breath and the words of truth into
the prophet's mouth.

As hearers of the Word, we are called to reflect: Who is our God? The
God of our wavering faith? The inclusive God of all the nations? The God
whose spirit/breath we share? The God of the prophets who speak out for
the vulnerable and dispossessed? The God who is all this, in and among us,
in Jesus Christ?

For the first time in Luke's Gospel, death retreats before the authority of
Jesus when he raises the widow of Nain's son. Neither mother nor son is
given a name; no initial approach is made by anyone to Jesus; what happens
to disrupt the death march is wholly at Jesus' initiative. He and his followers
are heading one way into the town, the poor funeral procession crowd is
going in the opposite direction, to the burial place, which religious taboos
dictated must be outside the city. The Lord (named by Luke for the first
time with this post-resurrection title) interrupts the processions. The woman's tears are her silent cry, a cry to which Jesus responds. This is echoed

today in so many parts of our world by women like the Argentinian Mothers (and Grandmothers) of the Plaza de Mayo who marched in silent protest every Thursday, demanding by their presence to know the fate of the 30,000 sons, brothers, and husbands who had disappeared in the "dirty war" of the 1970s. When the government collapsed, the action of these powerless women was recognized as a contribution to the new life that was brought forth from political death.

Jesus' compassion and the widow's tears both well up from deep "womb-love." For Jesus, this love is the sustaining mercy of God for the poor, those to whom, at the beginning of his mission in the Nazareth synagogue, he had announced that he would bring good news. Jesus had reminded that self-satisfied and closed community about the hospitality of God to the widow of Zarephath (Luke 4:24-26). Now he is about to make that hospitality take flesh in Nain as he welcomes another widow's son back to life. Disregarding any law except that of compassion, Jesus touches the bier on which lies the body wrapped in a bundle of rags. He has no need for the three-times-repeated symbolic action of Elisha; no need to pray three times to God for the life of the dead son. It is Jesus' own powerful words, "Young man, I say to you, arise!" and his own simple touch of the bier which make the shroud of death become the swaddling bands for the miracle of a child newly born into life and able to speak words that we are left only to imagine. As Jesus, like Elijah, gives the warming son back to his mother, perhaps we may be permitted to wander for a moment into John's Gospel, and look to a far and cold horizon when he, another only son, would again say the words, "Mother, here is your son" (John 19:26).

The mother, threatened with social destitution, and her son have both been given a future by the words and action of Jesus. As prophets always do, Jesus disrupts the status quo, but in the most radical way: disrupts death with life, and the people hail him as a prophet. Through those who had witnessed this miracle, the word about him spreads beyond Nain to Judea and the neighboring region. What is the word that we are called to spread about Jesus after we have listened to these readings and left the liturgical space? It is the word of faith in Jesus who is the resurrection and the life, a word that urges us to stop and speak to and touch those who are considered "untouchable," those about whom contemporary society (and even the church) lists many taboos. Perhaps it is right that the widow and her son are anonymous, because we need to give contemporary names to today's "untouchables," to the marginalized, the destitute, the hopeless. Every day there are "deaths" from which the words of Christ in our mouths can bring life: when we forgive; when we stand up for justice for the disadvantaged; when we accept to be given to others for their nurturing in marriage, community, and friendship; when we interrupt where we are heading, even for a moment, for a gracious phone call or attentive listening to another. In baptism we were raised to life in Christ, became prophets in him. It is the integrity of our words and deeds, filled with the Spirit of Jesus, that will enable others to recognize that God has truly visited his people.

In his Letter to the Galatians, Paul recognizes himself as the instrument of God's powerful grace. Through Jesus Christ, he had been called from the "death" of being a zealous persecutor of Christ and Christians into the new life of an apostle and preacher to the nations. Paul has his strong Jewish memories of the prophets Isaiah (Is 49:1) and Jeremiah (Jer 1:4-5) and the prophetic vocation for which they were destined. He writes of his own calling, too, while he was still in his mother's womb, but proclaims that his spiritual birth was induced only by the revelation of Jesus Christ. Paul continues to confront the Jewish Christian missionaries of the circumcision faction who were undermining the faith of the Galatians and tempting them into the false security of ritual observances and customs and away from the gospel that Paul preached. This gospel was not of human origin nor from human teachers, but from God's revelation in Jesus Christ. Only later did Paul have limited contact with the Jerusalem church: with Cephas (Peter) and with James. From being a persecutor of the Christians, Paul himself became the persecuted, a possibility for anyone who eventually stands with outsiders to oppose those who consider themselves the elite insiders.

The responsorial Psalm 30 is a grateful song of rescue from the grave, of night tears transformed into dawn joy, of mourning become dancing, and all this through the loving mercy of God. It is also the psalm with which we respond at the Easter Vigil to the final victory over death in the resurrection of Jesus himself. As a eucharistic community, we join the chorus of thanksgiving, the pledge of praise to our God forever.

Eleventh Sunday in Ordinary Time

2 Sam 12:7-10, 13 • Ps 32:1-2, 5, 7, 11 • Gal 2:16, 19-21 • Luke 7:36–8:3

Our contemporary mass media is so full of the bad news about politicians, clergy, executives who are guilty of using their power and status to abuse trust and manipulate others—from children to shareholders—that the story of David and Bathsheba could have a familiar ring. Less familiar, unfortunately, is the simple and contrite response of David: "I have sinned against the Lord." To put today's reading in proper perspective we need to read 1 Samuel 11:2–12:6. It is a story of the king's lust for Bathsheba, his arrogant misuse of his royal power to seduce her, and his successful planning to murder her husband, Uriah the Hittite, a mercenary in David's own army, by having him placed in the most vulnerable front line of battle. But it is also a story of David's painful realization that, king though he may be, he has no control over Bathsheba's pregnancy, Uriah's strong moral principles, or God's just anger. It is a story of tragedy and repentance bravely told and not hidden by the biblical author as part of the history of God's people. It is certainly not the "Romeo and Juliet" of the Hebrew Bible, nor the Hollywood rescue by royal true love of a so-called abused wife (e.g., *David and Bathsheba*, Twentieth Century Fox, 1951)!

David was God's chosen and anointed one whose lineage was to be blessed, but he was also and especially accountable to God. When gift becomes grab, privilege becomes possessiveness, this hero of God falls, not in battle as did Uriah, but into a moral abyss. This is the temptation of all who live with power, both individuals and institutions. It is the temptation that has seduced the church, as John Paul II confessed to the world at the turn of the new millennium. On March 12, 2000, in St. Peter's Basilica, he did what many of the bishops had wanted done in the *Pastoral Constitution on the Church in the Modern World* (art. 43). He stood before the bar of history and confessed, specifically and publicly, some of the most serious sins of the Church: against truth, against the unity of the body of the Christ, against the Jews, against the rights of and respect for people and cultures, against the dignity of women, and against the fundamental human rights.[16]

The consequences of David's sin, and our own, are not only personal, they are also social. In his lineage were sown the seeds of death, rebellion, and incest that would undermine the Davidic monarchy. But when confronted with this truth by the prophet Nathan, David's repentance is immediate and wholehearted. This is why the liturgy put on our lips today the words of the penitential responsorial Psalm 32.

The Gospel is also about love, forgiveness, and the relationship between a woman and men. Into the Pharisee's meal and male companionship, where Jesus is an invited guest, comes an uninvited woman who is known publicly in the city as a sinner. This need not mean unmistakably that she is a prostitute. However, if the service of her woman's body, which she offers to Jesus, is seen as an extraordinary reversal of her "hospitality trade" with other men, the incident is more remarkable for its moving witness to the woman's love. If we consider the mini-parable which is at the heart of this Gospel narrative, it would seem that the woman had already met Jesus and witnessed or experienced his forgiving love, yet in the eyes of those gathered at table she is still a sinner. She is the foot washer of Luke's Gospel who uses her woman's body in the service of Jesus: her tears are the water, her unbraided hair is the towel with which she bathes and dries his feet; her lips and precious ointment anoint them. We might speculate that the money for her alabaster jar of expensive and perfumed ointment had probably been earned by her trade, but now she spends it on Jesus. Forgiveness is never earned, but is the free gift of God in Christ to which this anonymous woman responds. Known as a public sinner, she now wants to be known in public (and we are part of the "public") as a servant disciple of Jesus. She is a boundary crosser of social and religious taboos as she breaks into this "men only" meal.

Simon the Pharisee, who had invited Jesus, is affronted by the actions of the woman and passes a wordless judgment on her. To him, she is a sinner who defiles the one she touches. Simon has to be converted from his harsh misunderstanding to acceptance of the woman. Ironically, it is because Jesus *is* a prophet that he can see the truth and read the hearts of both the woman and Simon. By means of a mini-parable about two debtors, Jesus contrasts the behavior of Simon and the woman. In Aramaic, the word for "debt" also means "sin" (Luke 11:4). With this word play, Jesus contrasts the debt/sin of Simon's failure in hospitality with the sin/debt of the woman. In a culture where hospitality was of such great importance, Simon had deliberately snubbed Jesus by offering no water for his feet, no kiss, no oil. Socially, therefore, he is in debt to Jesus. He has also sinned against love by his judgmental attitude toward the woman. She, in contrast, has offered to the body of Christ exactly the service that Simon refused. Although Simon has misjudged the woman's actions, as a Pharisee he cannot fail to understand Jesus' parable that acclaims love as the free, unmerited gift of God in Christ. If the woman violated socioreligious boundaries, so does Jesus when he does the almost unthinkable: criticizes the begrudging and belittling hospitality of his host. Yet Jesus does not offer this criticism directly to Simon but as he, the reader of hearts, turns away from him and toward the woman. Among (or within?) themselves the other guests begin to query the identity of Jesus. Their queries and Simon's further response is left hanging. The woman is told to go in peace, saved by her faith. Where did she go? Did she find a welcoming community who would accept her as a forgiven sinner who loved Jesus? Do we go out from dining with Jesus at the Eucharist to offer hospitality or judgment to a sister or brother? It is for us, whom God has loved and forgiven, who listen to this Gospel, to write the next episode in our own hearts and with our own servant discipleship.

In today's church, women continue to minister out of their resources: personal, pastoral, and theological. In so doing they may often have to cross boundaries, transform taboos, and incur unjust judgments in church and society. If, like the woman of this Sunday's Gospel, they are impelled by love of Jesus, they too can go on in peace, saved by faith.

For Paul, the loving self-giving of Christ "who loved me and gave himself for me" has made Paul a new person with a new life that is caught up into this mystery. It is not just a momentary "high" experience, but an ongoing faithfulness that is ready to risk "crucifixion" with Christ: the dangerous and painful surrender of so much of what Paul had held dear, especially the security of the Mosaic teaching and the exclusivity of his ethnic heritage. But so complete is his radical transformation through faith in Christ that his old way of life is over and he can say with poetic passion: "it is no longer I that live, but it is Christ who lives in me." It is the transformation that Christ also makes possible for us.

Twelfth Sunday in Ordinary Time

• Zech 12:10-11; 13:1 • Ps 63:2-6, 8-9 • Gal 3:26-29 • Luke 9:18-24

Unlike Mark and Matthew, Luke does not set Jesus' first passion prediction and the following instruction on true discipleship in Caesarea Philippi, but in the landscape of prayer: "One day when Jesus was praying alone, with only his disciples near him. . . ." For Luke, prayer is both the privileged place of encounter with God and a witness to Jesus' relationship with his Father. It is prayer that, at the baptism of Jesus, tears open the heavens to reveal the identity of Jesus as the Beloved Son in whom God is well pleased. It is the prayer of Jesus that leads us this Sunday into a narrative about who Jesus is and who he is considered to be by other people, including the disciples. Prayer marks crucial, decisive, or turning points in Jesus' mystery and mission. The "one day" of this Sunday's Gospel is also our "today." Gathered as a praying and eucharistic community listening to the words of Jesus, we are faced with the same question as Jesus put to his disciples: "But who do you say that I am?"

How many times in a discussion group have we prefaced our answer to a question with: "They say . . ."? If the group has a good facilitator, we are encouraged to change our contribution to an "I" response which is much more personally honest, much less escapist behind the screen of the anonymous and ubiquitous "they." Like us, the disciples are very ready to respond with what others say about Jesus. In the flow of Luke's ninth chapter the disciples had just been on their first mission: exorcising, healing, preaching with the power and authority given them by Jesus. They had been involved in the miraculous feeding of the five thousand and, suggests Luke, Herod's queries about the identity of Jesus were well known. Then comes Jesus' second question. Forget the comfortable reference point of the crowds: "But who do *you* say that I am?" The question is direct, personal, demanding. It is a question that we, as disciples of Jesus, also have to answer and live out the consequences of our answer—not just on "one day," but repeatedly, continually, especially in our everyday. Like the disciples, our answers will be embedded in our own experiences, in what others say about their experiences, and in the way that we, as Christians, interpret such experiences. It is almost possible to hear the squirming silence that follows Jesus' direct question. Then Peter takes a deep breath and answers, naming him "the Messiah of God," his single voice a witness to the need for a personal response to Jesus. Peter speaks out of his own religious and political hopes, but his understanding has a long way to go—as far as Calvary, and until that journey is completed, and the crucified One has risen from the dead, the full truth about him cannot be spoken because it has not been experienced. Discipleship must continue to grow in its perception of Jesus. Discipleship that is content with earlier and immature perceptions runs the risk of becoming ossified, of drying out and disintegrating.

Jesus responds to Peter with a reference to himself as "the Son of Man," a title that recalls the Book of the Prophet Daniel and the mysterious figure who stands in solidarity with, and is even identified with, those who suffer and are ultimately vindicated by God (Dan 7:13-14, 27). Suffering, rejection, death will happen to him and to all who keep following him, says Jesus. Sacrificial living is not masochism, not a death wish; the cross is not sought, but it will happen. For many tragedies in our lives we have no responsibility, but we are responsible for the attitude we take to this suffering: bitterness or compassion, despair or hope, selfishness or generosity. Luke stresses that this is *daily* acceptance of the cross, a readiness for continuous sacrificial living for others day after day, and not just in times of major crises. Discipleship is to be distanced from the fervor of the moment and from what, in Luke's narrative, had just preceded this first passion prediction: the physical satisfaction of 5,000 full stomachs, talk of political aspirations, and the drama of miracles. In the Gospel, to save one's *psyche*, one's "life," means that like Jesus we must give away the self that turns inward, that is self-serving and self-regarding.

At an ecumenical Good Friday Way of the Cross, about a thousand people were following a bare wooden cross around a local park. One father had a toddler hoisted on his shoulders and another four-year-old by the hand. Not having her brother's good view over the crowd, her piping voice asked, "Daddy, where are we going?" "We're following Jesus' cross," replied her father. Did he wonder at that moment what his words would mean for his children and himself in the future? The unexpected cross is so often just around the corner, but hidden by the "crowd" of the present moment. We need to be ready for "third day" risks and surprises, rather than for any security except that which the responsorial Psalm 63 proclaims:

> . . . for you (O God) have been my help,
> and in the shadow of your wings I sing for joy.
> My soul clings to you;
> your right hand upholds me.

In the sixth century B.C.E., the prophet Zechariah, whom we hear in the first reading, had no knowledge of the mystery of Christ, but as the New Testament authors searched for the best language and memories with which to proclaim Christ's mystery, they often transplanted the words of the prophets into a Christian context. Zechariah speaks of the pierced body of a loved and righteous one, perhaps King Josiah, who fell on the plains of Megiddo (2 Chr 35:20-27), or some other royal figure, and the people's mourning over him. Yet over those who do mourn the sinfulness that has put the pierced one to death, God will pour out a spirit of kindness and mercy that changes judgment of sin into the forgiveness that will renew the people of Jerusalem. Zechariah's words remind us of descriptions of the crucified and pierced body of Jesus (John 19:37) and the vision of the risen firstborn from the dead (Rev 1:7) from whom the breath was sent forth and the water and blood flowed over the world in the greatest act of God's saving mercy.

Our new birth in the Firstborn, and the radical inclusivity that results from this, is described by Paul. One most precious grain of sand, one unique star, one descendant of Abraham, Jesus the Christ, shares his inheritance with all who "put on" his way of life through baptism. This is nothing external, but a clothing in Christ in the depths of our personhood. There should be no more divisions, no more privileges—social, sexual, ecclesial, national, or political—because by baptism we are all one in Christ. And yet perhaps in our contemporary church there is no more dry or weary land (see the first verse of the responsorial psalm) than the lack of inclusivity; nothing for which we should thirst more than for the healing of relationships that divide us from our baptismal unity.

Thirteenth Sunday in Ordinary Time

• 1 Kgs 19:16b, 19-21 • Ps 16:1-2, 5, 7-11 • Gal 5:1, 13-18 • Luke 9:51-62

This week the Gospel takes a decisive turn as Jesus resolutely sets his face toward Jerusalem, and what is often called the "journey" section of Luke begins: the journey of Jesus to his passion, death, and resurrection, and the journey of every community of disciples that is called to accompany him. Immediately he is met with opposition from the Samaritans through whose villages he was traveling. Regarded by observant Jews as despicable Jews who were hybrid religious half-castes, the Samaritans were well known for their resistance to and competitiveness with everything associated with Jerusalem. Immediate, too, is the response of James and John who, with inflated ideas of their own powers, suggest a simple solution: call down upon them the "fire from heaven" to burn them up! But Jesus exorcises the brothers of their demons of violence as he would no doubt wish to rebuke present political leaders for whom violence and the distortion of the "fire from heaven" of sophisticated modern warfare is the immediate response to oppositions, real or imagined. The Lukan Jesus challenged those who were resisting the universal preaching of the Gospel, in this instance, to enemy Samaria. At home and abroad, true Christian discipleship calls us to work for the healing of historical, cultural, and religious divisions, and replace such hostility with hospitality. How responsible are church leaders, as well as politicians, about this challenge? Closer to home, about whom are we hesitant or opposed to taking the Gospel?

The road that Jesus takes to Jerusalem is signposted with encounters, events, stopping places along the way, without any logical or geographical progression. This serves to universalize the way of discipleship, because this has nothing to do with map reading or chronology, and everything to do with following Jesus in our own time and place. To help us along the way, Luke describes three encounters with would-be disciples. We hear the request, we listen to Jesus' response, but we learn nothing of the outcome of the meetings. It is as though Jesus is saying to us by this narrative silence: Listen to the answer your own life makes.

The first would-be disciple takes the initiative in approaching Jesus. He seems to be brashly confident, the enthusiast who needs to be tested for staying power, for readiness to be a powerless, homeless, and dispossessed disciple of a rejected Son of Man. Into Jesus' reply is woven the suggestion that in Roman-occupied Palestine everyone is at home except the true Israel. The "foxes" referred to are not just burrowing animals, but people like "that fox," Herod Antipas (Luke 13:32), who have dug themselves into politically secure positions. The "birds of the air" were an apocalyptic symbol for the "roosting" Gentiles, the Romans who had disinherited Israel, and now lord it over them. If you want to follow me, says Jesus, be prepared to be a powerless and dispossessed follower of a rejected Son of Man.

In the second encounter, it is Jesus who takes the initiative in calling the person to follow. We probably have a sneaking sympathy for this one who seems to make a very human and religious request of Jesus: "Let me go and bury my father first." But there is a cultural context to these words that persists even to the present in some Middle Eastern communities, and which throws a very different light on Jesus' demand, as the following contemporary incident shows. A group of young Lebanese men in their twenties were discussing their plans for migration. One of them had already booked his passage, but the other two questioned him seriously: "Aren't you going to bury your father first?" Now the man's father was a hale and hearty fifty-year-old, in no apparent danger of death. What was at stake was the cultural expectation that the son would postpone his immigration until his father did die and release him from his familial duties. In Jesus' invitation was the urgent and present call not to delay, not to put off the "today" demands of the reign of God. For all who answer the Gospel call, there will be some contradiction of cultural expectations, some necessary reordering of priorities in our relationships. "Leave the dead to bury the dead," is Luke's literary device of exaggeration to emphasize the priority of Jesus' call. In no way does it deny the love for our parents that is explicitly commanded by God.

The third would-be disciple wants to follow Jesus, but on condition that he is allowed to "first say farewell to those at home." This seems a reasonable request, especially in the light of the first reading that describes how Elijah gave Elisha permission to go and say good-bye. But the following of Jesus has to be unswerving; not even this detour is allowed. The mini-parable of the plow explains further what is also Luke's literary device of exaggeration. The light Palestinian plow was guided with one hand, usually the left, while the plowman's other hand carried a stick with which to goad the oxen that pulled the plow. To make a furrow that was straight and of the right depth, to lift the plow over rocks that might shatter it, demanded great concentration and dexterity. To take one's eyes off the plow for a moment could spell disaster. So it is with his disciples, says Jesus. The eyes of our heart must be fixed on the reign of God with unwavering commitment so that the field of this world may be well plowed and made ready for God's harvesting.

Like James and John, the Elijah of Mount Carmel had been a "fire happy" prophet on Mount Carmel (1 Kgs 18:19-40), but the first reading recounts the new plan God had for Elijah in the exercise of his ministry. It will be less flamboyant, one that dispossesses Elijah of his inflated ideas about himself as the only true prophet in Israel (1 Kgs 18:4), and accepts that another, Elisha, will assume prophetic authority. After Elisha's family farewell, Elijah throws his mantle over him. This is a significant and symbolic gesture, for the last mention of Elijah's mantle was when he hid his face in it at the door of the cave as he recognized God's presence to him on

Mount Horeb (Sinai). Elisha is now to be God's prophet, always aware of God's presence. Elijah had experienced the closeness of God in the "thin silence" of the calm that came after the storm of his slaughter of the false prophets of Baal and his consequent terrified flight from their supporter, Queen Jezebel. When the mantle of God's presence falls upon Elisha, he too turns away from his former way of life. He burns his plow and sacrifices his team of twelve oxen in the flames, cutting himself off from his substantial livelihood and leaving himself with nothing to fall back on should this prophetic business not work out. In a touching (or pacifying?) gesture, Elisha gives his workers a good severance meal of roasted oxen!

In his Letter to the Galatians, Paul sends out a clarion call to his communities that summons them to fidelity to the freedom that Christ has won for them, the freedom that acknowledges that "It is no longer I who live, but it is Christ who lives in me" (Gal 2:20). This does not mean rugged individualism. The Spirit of Jesus leads disciples to the formation of communities that are one in him, with all the barriers of nation, race, social class, and gender broken down. In Jonathan Swift's *Gulliver's Travels*[17] there is a graphic description of Gulliver finding himself held captive by the tiny ropes with which the Lilliputians had diligently crisscrossed his body while he was asleep. This is a provocative image of the way in which we can choose to limit our Christian freedom. As Paul suggests, it is the small self-indulgences, the hurtful word that "chews up" a brother or sister, the chilling silence that ignores them that, tiny cord by tiny cord, makes us captive to what is opposed to the Spirit.

Fourteenth Sunday in Ordinary Time

• Isa 66:10-14c • Ps 66:1-7, 16, 20 • Gal 6:14-18 • Luke 10:1-12, 17-20

A consequence of following Jesus is a readiness to be sent on the mission of Jesus with the conviction that there is a world waiting to be made ready for his return at what we call his Second Coming or *parousia*. There will, therefore, be no end to this mission until that final visitation.

From twelve on mission to seventy (or seventy-two in the Greek version) is quite an increase, but these numbers are symbolic of a deeper meaning than an indication of a successful vocation drive. With the memory of the Twelve tribes of Israel, the Twelve now represent the mission to the Jewish people. Against the backdrop of Genesis 10 and the Hebrew listing of the seventy Gentile nations (seventy-two), this number symbolizes the missionary mandate to proclaim the Gospel throughout the world, a harvesting responsibility to which every disciple is called in diverse ways.

There is also the memory of the seventy elders chosen by Moses, to whom he delegated authority to assist him in the governance of the people (Num 11:16-17), exercising "collaborative leadership," as we would say today. Yet their authority, as with all ecclesial authority, is not to be a sign of the glory of those who exercise it but a witness to the coming reign of God. Two by two they go out, not to chaperone one another, but to validate their witness according to Jewish law that required the evidence of at least two witnesses for credibility.

"Mission statements" are the order of the day for communities of all kinds such as parishes, religious congregations, businesses, caring facilities, or volunteer organizations. Luke presents today's Gospel as the early church's "mission statement" and a practical handbook for its implementation. Our society is different; travel, communication, economics, multiculturalism and multifaith contacts have changed greatly from a generation ago, let alone almost two millennia. So what relevance has this Gospel for today? How can we distill the essence of its truth so that it can inform our mission today?

First, the world needs the mission of Christians because there is a plentiful harvest waiting to be reaped. Second, prayer to "the Lord of the harvest" is essential for the empowering of the harvesters. Third, because it is Jesus who sends us on mission, we can go in confidence in his active protection. This is not to discount the fourth missionary principle: the reminder that there are "wolves" to be confronted on the way—personal, communal, and structural realities that will try to hunt down and consume those who proclaim the Gospel. Every generation of Christians needs the gift of discernment so that we can name and recognize these "wolves." In confronting them, Jesus calls us to be courageous "lambs," sincere and vulnerable like himself, rather than calculating and self-serving, choosing nonviolence as the way of resistance.

Fifth, in our mobile society we know that to travel well is to travel lightly. When the goal of our journey is the reign of God, money, possessions (or perhaps possessiveness), or concern with status can be hindering baggage. "Carry nothing" is again a device of exaggeration that would have been understood by Luke's communities as emphasizing the urgency of the mission. The same is true for the sixth warning to "Salute no one," not a recommendation for brash impoliteness, but a condemnation of social dalliance and time-consuming gossip.

Whether accepted or rejected, the precious gift of Christ's healing peace, not a false or conventional greeting, is to be offered to the household that the missionaries visit. This seventh instruction puts into the disciples' mouths Jesus' own resurrection greeting of Easter eve, "Peace be with you" (Luke 24:36), to be freely accepted or rejected. The seventh guideline also requires disciples to avoid social climbing or drifting around looking for more congenial situations or compatible companions.

Hospitality that is graciously accepted and allows the host to dictate the "menu" not only at meals but also in the broader cultural context of the table of life, is the eighth principle. Good missionaries do not impose their own cultural expectations on others, but are nourished by whatever is offered by the host, both personal and social. This does not deny efforts to try to dismantle social barriers, and the mention of the curing of the sick reminds us that this is a work of loving service that speaks a universal language of care and respect for suffering humanity, no matter what a person's culture or social status. Accepted (v. 9) or rejected (v. 11), the message is the same: "The kingdom of God has come near to you." And so the ninth missionary principle is the realistic expectation of failure, of being resisted and rejected as Jesus was. Luke describes a simple ritual of dismissal, wiping off the dust of the place that has not accepted the good news of the kingdom, but there is to be no harsh judgment, no calling down of fire as James and John offered to do for the Samaritans, only to be "exorcised" of this suggestion by Jesus who himself knew rejection and simply moved on to another town (Luke 9:54-55).

The tenth and last principle of the missionary charter is that, no matter what, we persevere in our proclamation of the reign of God by our words, our relationships, and our rituals. The closing mention of Sodom is not in reference to any sexual immorality, but to the great sin of the denial of hospitality to God's messengers (Gen 13:13). This is what disciples of Jesus are. Those who deny them a welcome will be judged by what they reject—the reign of God.

When the seventy return, rejoicing at the success of their mission, Jesus makes neither too much nor too little of it. Above all, there should be no triumphalism, because all the gifts and talents of disciples are the gifts of God, given in the name (person) of Jesus, who calls us and sends us out to put them at the service of the world that it may become the kingdom, a cosmos obediently under the reign of God, not Satan. Jesus has a vision of the cosmic future of the new creation, and Luke will write in the Acts of the Apostles of the protective presence of God against dangerous "snakes and scorpions" (Acts 28:3-5; Deut 8:15). These are symbolic of more than wildlife; they are everything that will threaten disciples in hazardous places as they go on mission to establish the new creation. The reward of their mission will be that their names will be written in heaven in the book of life (Phil 4:3).

What Christians can and should boast about, writes Paul in his closing words to the church of Galatia, is the cross of our Lord Jesus Christ. It is through this that we become new women and men, both personally and as a people of God. One of the most moving rituals of the RCIA (Rite of Christian Initiation of Adults) is when the catechumens are presented with the cross, the Christian symbol of salvation. Before any physical representation is given (and when the ritual is well done), the presider makes the sign of the cross on the body of the catechumens from head to foot, smothering them with its mystery. These are the marks of Jesus that all the baptized carry, the "stigmata" of the cross, the suffering—spiritual, physical, psychological—that will come into all our lives in so many different ways. Paul speaks about the stigmata on his body, the signs of his physical suffering as an apostle who suffered scourgings, stoning, and other physical afflictions that bore external witness to the Gospel of the cross (2 Cor 11:23-25; Acts 14:19). Neither this suffering, nor the wound of circumcision, nor being an uncircumcised Gentile, is important. All that matters is that through the cross we are made new in Christ. Painful, too, was Paul's spiritual distress, the battering of his ministry by the opposing Jewish Christian missionaries and their undermining of the faith of his beloved Galatian church, yet he ends this letter on a note of reconciliation with and blessing of those whom he names as "brothers and sisters" united in the grace of Jesus Christ.

In the reading from Isaiah we have a joyful acclamation of a restored Jerusalem compared to a comforting mother who embraces her repentant children and provides nourishment for them. Then there is a dramatic switch in imagery, and instead of the fondling city we have one of the beautiful feminine image of God as a nursing mother (Isa 66:12). She, too, is described with full breasts, wide lap, and arms ready to gather into an embrace of everlasting love and forgiveness all those who come back to her. For those who may be too accustomed to thinking of God in male terms, this is an image of a tender, protective, and playful God who welcomes us into new insights about her love for all her sons and daughters.

Fifteenth Sunday in Ordinary Time

• Deut 30:10-14 • Ps 69:14, 17, 30-31, 33-34, 36-37 • Col 1:15-20 • Luke 10:35-37

What we have come to call the parable of the Good Samaritan is told in the context of a meeting between two teachers: the Jewish lawyer and the Jewish Jesus. It is a "shocking" story, intended to make us think about alternatives in our relationships with God and one another. It is introduced with the lawyer's determined effort to justify himself with regard to the two great commandments: love of God and love of neighbor. Self-justification is centered on "I" and "my": "What shall I do to inherit eternal life?" he asks, and Jesus responds with two questions of his own: "What is written in the law? What do you read there?" The lawyer is quick to answer; he has all the right and holy words, can quote his source documents perfectly, and adopts the faultless theological stance of Deuteronomy 6:4-5 and Leviticus 19:17-18. But Jesus urges him from right answering to right living: "Do this and you will live." But the lawyer continues to seek after self-justification rather than truth, responding: "And who is *my* neighbor?" Everything is in reference to himself. But discipleship does not start with myself, with asking whom I shall or shall not love or what are the boundaries of my responsibility? At the end of the parable, Jesus will ask the lawyer another question that banishes self from center stage: "Which of these three, do you think, was a neighbor to the man who fell into the hands of the robbers?" This is how our commitment to Jesus is to be defined: from the perspective of the half-dead, the fallen, the wounded, the abandoned ones, the person with whom every other character in the parable comes into either negative or positive contact.

And so we meet the wounded traveler. The two most important indicators of social or racial identity in first-century Palestine were speech and dress. Stripped naked and half-dead, these clues were unavailable. The wounded man is simply, profoundly, a human being in great need and, as such, is typical of Jesus' concern for the powerless, the marginalized, the anonymous people with no status. Toward such people Jesus always acts as a free man, with no barriers to his compassion.

Not so the priest and Levite, the "professional religious" of the parable. The priest seems to take a definite detour around the wounded one as "he passed by on the other side." Rather than obedience to the Old Testament command to love one's neighbor as oneself (Lev 19:18), the priest opts for man-made legalisms and rule book. According to that, even to approach an injured or possibly dead person would render him, as a priest, ritually unclean. He would be unable to rejoin his family and community, share the latest Jerusalem news, and would be forced to return shamefully to the Temple he had just left to take his place for the prescribed number of days in an outer court with other breakers of the law. So "likewise" the Levite, with a little less religious status, a little more ritual freedom, but perhaps with a minor official's determination to guard what he has. He edges up a bit closer, sees, and also passes by.

Then comes the shocking entry of the third traveler as Jesus introduces a Samaritan, a "corrupted" and despised Jew, into the parable. The Samaritan is the one who came and saw and did compassion. In the New Testament, "compassion" is a remarkable verb; one *does* compassion. It is used only in reference to Jesus or (in Luke's Gospel) by him in this parable and that of the Prodigal Son. In Hebrew, "compassion" derives from the word for "womb," and in Greek it has the sense of the gut feeling that embraces the situation of another. The implication of these Gospel references is that we can be compassionate only in Jesus, who makes flesh the creating, sustaining, and birthing love of God. This is what the Samaritan does. He does not pass by; he touches, supports, nurtures the wounded man, recognizing him as nothing but—and this is everything—an abused and wounded human being. For him the Samaritan does compassion, which is also a work of justice because it announces that another's hurt or dignity is to be taken seriously; that it is not human to pass by, no matter what boundaries of race, ethnicity, culture, or prejudice have to be crossed.

While the priest and Levite hurry on to Jericho for their religious services, the Samaritan serves the abandoned man by bandaging his wounds and pouring out a libation of oil and wine on the "altar" of his broken body.

Jesus prefaces the entry of his three characters by saying, "Now by chance. . . ." None of them knew what would happen on the road, but their responses indicate the degree to which each traveler was ready and willing to serve another's pain when such an occasion arose. Only the despised Samaritan had within him the personal resources that enabled him to do compassion in an unexpected, unplanned-for moment.

David Jenkins had dreamed for years of catching the perfect wave, so in 1999 he decided to go to the island of Nilas off Sumatra. "By chance" when he got there, along with the waves he found hundreds of people suffering from serious but treatable illnesses. The next year he founded SurfAid, and in the devastating 2005 earthquake, "surfies" were among the first unexpected people to minister to the wounded on Nilas.

To go on to Jericho or back to Jerusalem to find a lodging for himself and the half-dead traveler was a further act of brave compassion. Palestinian inns hardly offered five-star accommodation, especially if you arrived with a battered body slung over your donkey's back! Jesus' listeners might well imagine that the morning after the Samaritan's vigil with the patient there could be a thankless awakening when the traveler found himself ministered to by a Samaritan. After all, how would we feel about being helped by someone whose sexual, racial, political, or social status we find extremely distasteful? And are we ourselves ready for the sometime thankless responses after long nights of our ministries?

The innkeeper is told to take care of the man and given the resources to do so until the Samaritan returns, when the innkeeper will be repaid for anything that he has spent on the care of the wounded one. In this sense, Jesus is telling us, as well as the lawyer, that we are all innkeepers, entrusted by Jesus with the care of the wounded, asked to respond to the prophetic call that sounds through the centuries. Jesus shouts most loudly at us—"It is mercy I want, not sacrifice" (e.g., Hos 6:6)—until his return at the end of human history when we will be repaid for our compassion, or lack of it.

Which of the three, Jesus asks the lawyer, was a neighbor to the one who fell among thieves? The answer is inescapable: "The one who showed him mercy." Back comes Jesus' response to all who travel not only from Jerusalem to Jericho, but on his Way: "Go and do likewise" with the humility to recognize that we are sometimes each one of the four characters in the parable. Do we ever admit that we are wounded travelers in need of another's compassion? When are we too self-centered or legalistic or frightened to get our hands dirty by touching another's physical, psychological, or social wounds? When do we do justice to our shared humanity that often seems "unlovely," and recognize the Christ who:

> . . . plays in ten thousand places,
> Lovely in limbs and lovely in eyes not his,
> To the Father through the features of men's faces. . . ?[18]

The first reading is from what is structured as Moses' farewell speech in the Book of Deuteronomy (ca. 600–700 B.C.E.), the "seconding" or affirmation of the Mosaic teaching. The people who had suffered exile and the destruction of the Temple, who stood at the threshold of a return and rebuilding of their lives and faith, are encouraged to come back to God with courage and obedience. We do not have to reach for the stars or cross the seas to find the word of God. Its geography is the human heart for loving, and the mouth for proclaiming.

In the magnificent hymn to Christ in the Letter to the Colossians, we are reminded that everything in the cosmos is created and reconciled to God through him. In his encyclical, *Ecclesia de Eucharistia* (April 17, 2003), John Paul II wrote of the cosmic mystery of the Eucharist which:

> is always in some way celebrated *on the altar of the world*. It unites heaven and earth. It embraces and permeates creation. . . . Truly this is the *mysterium fidei* which is accomplished in the Eucharist: the world which came forth from God the Creator now returns to him redeemed by Christ. (Intro., #8)

This is the mystery of cosmic transformation in which we participate at every Eucharist.

Sixteenth Sunday in Ordinary Time

• Gen 18:1-10a • Ps 15:2-5 • Col 1:24-28 • Luke 10:38-42

We have become accustomed to paintings of Luke's Martha and Mary showing them at table. Martha is usually fussing around Jesus with bread or bowls, while Mary sits, unmoving, at his feet. Yet there is another extraordinary painting by the master Fra Angelico, painted around 1450 in Cell 34 of what is now the Museum of St. Mark in Florence. It is entitled "Agony in the Garden." Christ kneels, tended by an angel; the three male disciples are sound asleep, and in the bottom right foreground in an open building sit the two sisters of Bethany. Mary is reading a book, and Martha prays in much the same pose as Jesus. This is a different, alert Martha, much more in touch with Jesus' agony than is her sister. So how are we to read Luke's account, in its own Gospel terms, and not with John's very different narrative about Martha and Mary? Can we rescue it from the resentment felt by many hospitable and hardworking women toward the "luxurious and contemplative?"[19] We need to rinse our eyes when we approach this text so that we can see more unity than division in its good news.

Jesus and his companions are on their journey, and it is hardly possible that Jesus left them outside the door and presented himself as a privileged solo guest to the house at Bethany. Quite a crowd enters! Martha emerges as the dominant sister: the house is described as her home; she is the one who "receives" (with the sense of "welcomes") him; Mary is her sister. What distracts Martha is her service, her *diakonia*, a word that in the early church had a much broader meaning than only domestic duties (Acts 6:4 and the apostles' *diakonia* of the Word). She complains that Mary's silent sitting at Jesus' feet is no help to her ministry. She, Martha, has been left to cope on her own. Rather like the lawyer in last week's parable, Martha is indulging in self-justification. In response, Jesus admonishes the one who criticizes and defends the criticized. Mary has chosen the better part on this occasion, but for both the sisters it is only a *part* of the service of Jesus, not the whole picture; nor is the service of Jesus constant or unwavering by either sister, as Fra Angelico suggests. Only both sisters, together, can accommodate Jesus in the way he should be welcomed.

Teresa of Avila writes explicitly about this unity rather than separation of Martha and Mary:

> Believe me, Martha and Mary must be together to accommodate the Lord and keep him with them for ever, otherwise he will be served poorly and remain without food. How could Mary who always sat at his feet have offered him food if her sister had not jumped in? And his food is our gathering souls, that they may be saved and praise him in eternity.[20]

And this from a mystic! We do not have to divide the world between competing poets, prophets, and pragmatists, nor do we need to choose once and for all between contemplation and action. Rather, what will unite us is to welcome them all, to respect our differences, or to accept that we may be sometimes one and sometimes the other.

Some medieval legends describe Martha and Mary as traveling together to France, where Martha became a dragon slayer. And yet Mary was there too, teaching and preaching as an active servant of the word she had once heard at Jesus' feet. Many of the women in our own times who have been to the forefront in slaying political "dragons" are also women of prayer, like, for example, the "Women in Black." This movement began in 1988 with Israeli and Palestinian women united in keeping weekly public and prayerful vigils at the Western Wall in Jerusalem to protest against the Israeli occupation of the West Bank and Gaza. Since then the movement has spread worldwide to different situations and places of prayer as a peaceful protest about social injustices. Many people, especially the young, are eager for both social action and service to the disadvantaged, while also searching for a spirituality that is contemplative but does not retreat into introspection. A wonderful example of this is the Sant' Egidio Community, a lay community founded in Rome in 1968 by university students, and now comprising over 50,000 members in more than seventy countries and four continents. Its solidarity with and ministry to the poor, efforts for peace and ecumenism, are founded on personal and communal prayer. Every week in three Roman churches, hundreds gather with members of the community for Evening Prayer and the sharing of the Word. To divide and divorce the Martha and Mary in each of us is a real temptation. Both are needed to keep vigil and to be present to Christ when he is again in agony in our suffering brothers and sisters.

The welcome of the three-to-become-one at Abraham's and Sarah's tent at the Oak of Mamre is a wonderful event of hospitality. Abraham is ready to be disturbed, even from his siesta at the hottest time of the day, for in the Middle East hospitality offered or refused could be a matter of life or death. At Mamre, what begins as human hospitality to strangers becomes hospitality to God, a truth that echoes through both Testaments (see Heb 13:1-2). Abraham greets the strangers with courtesy and eagerness—with washing of feet, bowing, running, hastening, hurrying. The self-effacing offer of a "little bread" brings Sarah into the picture to do much more than "a little"! Having orchestrated the efforts of Sarah and their servant, Abraham presents the meal to the guests. He then receives from the strangers the promise of a son within the next twelve months. Unfortunately, the compilers of the

Lectionary chose to end the reading at this point, and so we miss not only the account of Sarah with her ear glued to the tent flap and her incredulous postmenopausal response to what she overheard, but also the question: "Is anything too wonderful for the Lord?" to which Abraham is silent and Sarah protests about her cynicism over the promised birth of the son. The child will be named for her laughter, "Isaac" ("He who laughs"), and at his birth the laughter will become God-given joy (Gen 21:6). Hospitality to strangers, be it at Mamre or Emmaus (Luke 24:13-35) or in our own home, community, church, or nation, enables hope to break out of hopelessness, new life out of dead "wombs" for, now as then, the God for whom nothing is too wonderful is welcomed.

The hope that Paul speaks of in the Letter to the Colossians is the mystery of Christ among us. And if Christ is among us as our hope of glory, so will his sufferings be, for we cannot have one without the other. Christ's sufferings are "lacking" insofar as they continue in the bodies of the members of Christ, and for this reason Paul welcomes his sufferings. Through them he will become a more effective servant in his revelation of the mystery of Christ. This is the constant tradition of the church that so many Christians live out quietly, obscurely, gracefully; and in their living and dying, they continue to reveal to us the mystery of Christ, present among them too as "their hope of glory."

The psalmist of Psalm 15 reflects on those who will enjoy the hospitality of God's Temple, the tenting place of God's special presence on Mount Zion. The context of the psalm was probably a rite of entrance conducted by a priest for those who wished to be admitted to the Temple. It says nothing about ritual purity or legalisms. The criteria for entering into the holy place were relationships of justice toward other people: honesty, integrity, the refusal to belittle or slander one's neighbor, and the rejection of bribery. The person who was present to a brother or sister in this way would enjoy the hospitality of God in the holy place. As we enter into the holy place of our Sunday eucharistic assembly, do we measure up to the criteria expected of those whom God will receive as his guests?

Seventeenth Sunday in Ordinary Time

• Gen 18:20-32 • Ps 138:1-3, 7-8 • Col 2:12-14 • Luke 11:1-13

In the Jewish Talmud there is found the tradition that in each generation there will be "thirty-six just ones," because of whose presence God does not destroy the world. These people are humble, ordinary, unassuming, and this tradition was the inspiration of André Schwartz-Bart's moving novel, *The Last of the Just*. It ends with the death of Ernie Levy, one of the just, and his wife, Golda, in a Nazi gas chamber. The old love poem, "Hear, O Israel, the Lord is our God, the Lord is one," rings in their ears as the gas jabs at their throats and lungs with needles of fire. The author wonders, then, about the other six million "Ernie Levys" who died in the *Shoah*, the "catastrophe" of the Nazi era.[21] No doubt we all know unobtrusive just ones whose attitude to their suffering is helping, as Jewish tradition expresses it, to "repair the world" (*tikkun olam*). As Christians would say, the sufferer is united with the suffering of Christ for the salvation of the world, even though this may not be how such sufferers would know how to, or want to, express their attitudes.

Behind the Talmud stands the long memory of what we hear in today's first reading: the advocacy of Abraham, the just man who is so intimate with God that he can stand before God and plead for the population of the city of Sodom. This is an event that is much more than a scene of Bedouin bargaining. Abraham, the just, intercedes not for his own people, but for foreigners, for he is the one in whom "all the families of the earth shall be blessed" (Gen 12:3). We might ask ourselves how often we intercede for the inhabitants of our contemporary "Sodoms": those whose ethical, sexual, personal stances we find distasteful, disillusioning, or destructive? Abraham's justice and his role as intercessor flow from his intimate relationship with God who is the Just One of all the earth (v. 25). If we read forward into Genesis 19, we discover that the sin of Sodom was the brutal lack of hospitality to strangers, and the social chaos that resulted. This is an indication of what is—or should be—the strong sense of the "corporate responsibility" of the people of God in Judaism, and in Christianity our sense of the Body of Christ. God is described as coming down to judge what is the actual situation in Sodom, and Abraham stands before him as a participant in the divine discernment. He speaks not just as an advocate but, above all, as a friend. Only a friend of God can speak to God with the courteous but blunt, persistent directness and intimacy that Abraham models, and which is also so characteristic of the psalmists. (Perhaps the image of Tevye in *Fiddler on the Roof* comes to mind.) Abraham goes from advocating that God will spare the city if there are fifty just men, down to ten; he does not dare to take his pleading lower than that. It will be many centuries later that *one* Just Man saves not only a city but all humanity.

Why do we pray? It is not to impose our will on God, but to ask God to make us available to the divine will and to share our concerns with God, to place these under God's loving judgment. It is, therefore, not an effort to change God, but to change ourselves. Of all the evangelists, it is Luke who speaks most about prayer. His Gospel begins (Luke 1:10) and ends (Luke 24:53) in the context of prayer. At significant moments in his life, Jesus prays, and it is his example that leads the disciples to ask him: "Lord, teach us to pray, as John taught his disciples" (Luke 5:33). The Lukan version of Jesus' response is direct, shorter, more simple than Matthew's (Matt 6:9-13), and expresses the deepest reality of Jesus' own relationship with his God, into which he wants his disciples to be drawn. The words are no magic formula, but help us to realize the personal reality of the One to whom we pray.

Our familiarity with the Lord's Prayer may blunt our appreciation of its radical, even subversive, teaching about prayer. It is to be the prayer of a community that is conscious both of its intimate relationship with God and its presence in and responsibility for the world. In both Testaments God is "Father," a metaphor vastly different from that of the powerful Roman emperor, the "father of the homeland," or the authoritarian father of the family social unit. Especially in the Gospels, God is the *Abba* of Jesus, in loving, faithful, and intimate relationship with the Beloved Son. The kingdom for which disciples pray is not a kingdom of political power, but one that belongs to the poor, the liberated, excluded women, forgiven sinners. That we may be changed, we pray for bread, forgiveness, and deliverance. Given Luke's emphasis on hospitality, "the bread we need" from day to day is probably a request for this basic necessity that should be shared with the poor. We also need to be nourished with one another's forgiveness, because God will never starve us of forgiveness, and God's behavior must be the norm for his sons and daughters. To live in this way will save us in the time of trial. The only other time that Luke uses the same word for "trial" or temptation is again in the context of prayer in Gethsemane, when he urges the disciples, who slept while Jesus prayed, to "Get up and pray that you may not come into the time of trial" (Luke 22:46).

The Lord's Prayer is no magic formula. It is an instruction about the Father to whom Jesus and his disciples pray. Jesus affirms what should be the quality of our prayer by telling two parables, both of which describe situations to which the response to "Just suppose" would be "Never!" What is described in the parable of the Friend at Midnight concerns three friends: the one who arrives unexpectedly, the host, and the one to whom the latter goes to ask for bread because he has run out of his own supply. To fail in hospitality by not being able to offer the barest sustenance to a friend and guest would be shameful, and if the third friend did not unbolt his door and help out, his shame would be the talk of his neighbors who no doubt would hear the midnight disturbance! If we are in an enduring relationship as prayerful "friends" with God we can be assured that God will be hospitable to us in our need.

In the first parable, a neighbor deals with a neighbor; in the second, a father deals with his son. Jesus is assuring his listeners that those who keep on asking, seeking, knocking will be answered, will find, will be welcomed. Impossible to imagine that a loving parent is going to trick a child by handing over a flat white stone instead of bread, a water snake instead of a small edible fish, or a scorpion which has rolled itself into an egg-like ball! How much more generous, therefore, will God be in providing good things for his children. And the greatest of these gifts will be the Holy Spirit. Rabbi Dov Baer, a great Polish storyteller, used to say that a person is like a *shofar*, the ram's horn, which is sounded at the Jewish New Year as a ritual of awakening. The *shofar* sounds only when the breath is blown through it. So we are summoned to prayer when the Spirit/Breath of God blows through us. Nowhere should this be more of a reality for Christians than in the assembly gathered as "Eucharist," that is as "thanksgiving," during which we always recite the Lord's Prayer with confidence.

In baptism, says Paul to the Colossians, we enter into the death and resurrection of Christ not historically, but by sacramental identification with him. Christ is the Just One who forgives our debt of sin. Our thanksgiving and faith in this give new significance to the response we make with Psalm 138: "Lord, on the day I called for help, you answered me," words which we transplant from the original song of thanksgiving to express our gratitude for the faithfulness and love shown us by God in Jesus Christ. The reason for a criminal's sentencing was nailed to his cross, but our guilt has been ripped off and replaced by a sentence of life through the triumph of the risen Christ over death.

Eighteenth Sunday in Ordinary Time

• Eccl 1:2; 2:21-23 • Ps 90:3-6, 12-14, 17 • Col 3:1-5, 9-11 • Luke 12:13-21

Failures in big business enterprises, ups and down on the stock exchange, court cases about disputed family inheritances, such economic issues hit the headlines in our mass media and often intrude tragically into the lives of hardworking, hard-saving people. When the annual lists of the world's richest individuals and nations are published, the discrepancy between the top and bottom rungs of the economic ladder may raise our eyebrows if not, unfortunately, our consciences. It is often said that it would profit us if we read the Scriptures with a Bible in one hand and the daily newspaper in the other, discerning how the words and deeds announced by both are related. The Gospel we hear this week begins with a question to Jesus from a man in the crowd who tries to draw him into an inheritance dispute with his brother.

The Mosaic teaching of Numbers and Deuteronomy is clear (Num 27:1-11; Deut 21:15-17), and Jesus rejects the role of an interpreter, only cautioning his questioner about greed. Nor does Jesus refer to the tough words like that of the Preacher (Qoheleth) that we hear in the first reading from the wisdom Book of Ecclesiastes. Only once every three years do we hear this sobering voice proclaim: "Vanity of vanities. All is vanity!" "Vanity" in Hebrew can mean "vapor," a transitory, fleeting breath—and material wealth is like this. Jesus chooses to make his point as a storyteller, putting imaginative flesh on wisdom teaching with the parable of the Rich Fool.

The man is introduced as already rich, with a surplus harvest. He has no appreciation that this blessing is from God, nor of the Jewish religious tradition and human prudence that demanded that he make provision for himself and his whole community in case of any famine which might follow years of plenty. His "retirement plan" is a self-centered recital of "I will, I will, I will," well-punctuated by references to "my." The rich man considers that he owns everything: crops, barns, grains, and even his own soul. In a culture where a transaction at a street stall involved long and animated discussion between buyer and seller, the inappropriateness of such self-talk would not be lost on Jesus' audience. Likewise, it was expected that important decisions would be made in community, but for this man there is no one with whom he can or wants to talk—no family, cronies, advisers. His calculated option is to make and live in an isolated and alienating vacuum. This cannot be the option of Jesus' disciples.

Ironically, the parable uses the prophetic language of "pulling down" and "building up" (Jer 1:10), but in a sadly cheapened context. The rich man is the opposite of the courageous prophet who does this in the name of and for the purposes of God. Tithes and offerings were set aside in landowners' barns for collection by the priests and Levites, but for this man, barns are just for hoarding for himself. For the early Christians, the storage barns of the community were to be the mouths of the poor and responses such as the collection for the poor of Jerusalem (Rom 15:25-28). A contemporary and tragic irony persists with the silos that are stocked with nuclear "abundance" or "deterrence" while many of those living almost in their destructive shadows are hungry and disadvantaged. Closer to home, perhaps our Christian families, parishes, or communities need to have annual "discipleship garage sales" to dispose of our surplus and give the profits to those in need.

The rich man's final speech is again a speech made to himself, to his "soul," the life principle of his deliberately lonely self. As he relaxes into his own company, satisfied to "eat, drink and be merry" for many years, the voice of God thunders into his monologue to announce that there are no more years, not even a tomorrow ahead for this fool. It is as though the man has been self-hypnotized into a kind of practical atheism, and has forgotten that even his own life is a gift on loan from God. When Luke writes that this very night his soul will be "required" of him, he uses the word for calling in a loan. It is no longer an earthly inheritance that is at issue, as at the beginning of the reading, but a heavenly one. The text also suggests that this foolish man has so isolated himself that he will die without heirs of either family or friends, "for whose will his wealth be then?" The parable ends without any response from the rich man. That is left to each one of us, and our decision whether or not to be rich and generous toward God and our brothers and sisters.

There is a rabbinic story about two brothers with very different attitudes from the one who questions Jesus about an inheritance dispute, or from the rich fool. A man had two sons, one rich and one poor. The rich son had no children, while his poorer brother was blessed with many sons and daughters. On the death of their father, they each received half of his land as their inheritance. But the rich son was worried, saying to himself, "I am rich, with bread enough and to spare, while my brother and his family are poor, with scarcely enough to eat, although they trust in God's providence. I will move the landmark that indicates the boundary of our properties so that my brother will have more land than me, and so the prospect of more crops to harvest." The poor brother, too, could not sleep, saying to himself, "Here I am, surrounded by the riches of a wife and children, while my brother daily faces the shame and sorrow of having no children. He deserves to have more of our inherited land to compensate him for his great poverty." The next night, the two brothers arose, and each went to move the landmark. There they met, embracing one another with tears. And there, on that spot, was built the holy temple of Jerusalem. Still today, wherever sisters and brothers love and share, there is holy ground; there God is worshiped and praised.[22]

With the responsorial Psalm 90 we acknowledge that life is short, and that only God can give us the wisdom to live it to the full. From our human experience, we know how quickly the years slip by, how those whom we love are swept away from us in death. It is especially when we are distressed by our own or others' fragile and time-bound humanity that we need a relationship that is a steadfast refuge. It is an eternally loving God who offers us that. This psalm was the inspiration for Isaac Watts' much loved hymn, "O God, our help in ages past, our hope for years to come," frequently sung at the funeral of our loved ones.

Through baptism, proclaims the Letter to the Colossians, our refuge is so secure that it is as though we are hidden with Christ in God. We are therefore to set our hearts on what is above, not in the spatial sense, but in the sense of where our priorities lie. In Paul's list of what a Christian is to avoid, he makes a special mention of greed, which can become a kind of idolatry when, like the rich fool of the parable, money becomes the center of our worship. In baptism, we have been stripped naked, descended into the waters, and ascended with Christ. A powerful witness of infant baptism by full immersion is that, like the little child, we have nothing, have done nothing, to deserve to be clothed with the grace of God made known to us in Jesus Christ. Death discloses the final poverty of the rich fool; our fidelity to our baptismal dying and rising with Christ will reveal our riches.

Nineteenth Sunday in Ordinary Time

• Wis 18:6-9 • Ps 33:1, 12, 18-22 • Heb 11:1-2, 8-19 • Luke 12:32-48

> "The poet's eye, in a fine frenzy rolling,
> doth glance from heaven to earth, from earth to heaven."

So remarks Theseus in *A Midsummer Night's Dream* (Act V, sc.1). Luke's poetical biblical eye seems to do just that in today's Gospel. He recognizes that life on earth is busy, often worrying, and that our stress levels can be high. But then he rolls his eyes to heaven and the vision of the kingdom which it has pleased God to give us. In its light, worry and fear are put into the correct perspective. This Sunday, Jesus wants us to glance at a building that is very different from that of the rich fool's barn about which we heard last week. Today the eyes of our hearts are directed to that treasure house which is full of emptiness on earth, but well stocked and secure in heaven because of what we have shared with the poor and disadvantaged. Although most of our computer spell-checks announce "almsgiving" as "unknown/incorrect word," the Gospel check is much more knowledgeable.

Jesus' command to "Sell your possessions and give alms" cannot today be considered solely as an individual response. It also lays upon our global village an international obligation to restore life and hope to the peoples and nations of the world who are burdened by impossible monetary debts and sanctions, land confiscation, and rape of their tiny share of our planet earth. Humanity as a whole should emerge as winner from globalization, not through anarchist and violent protests, but through agreements of loving justice and peace. Meetings of the G8 often provoke symbolic demonstrations on behalf of the poor: the human chain of more than 70,000 links of young and old, people of many different ethnic origins and political allegiances, those with strong religious faith and those with none, that encircled the International Convention Centre in Birmingham, UK, in 1998 is one example. The white-clothed band of 225,000 people who ringed Edinburgh imploring G8 leaders to "Make Poverty History" at the 2005 Gleneagles meeting; the global reach of the Live 8 concerts—these all are symbolic actions waiting for translation into sufficient political action.

The sayings and parables of today's Gospel are stitched together with the themes of vigilance, preparedness, and fidelity. Christians are to be "girded," ready for action. The biblical memory behind the parable's action is the Passover from Egypt when the Hebrews had to be girded, clothed, and belted up suitably so that they would be ready for their escape into freedom (Exod 12:11). The early church lived in expectation of Christ's return during the great Easter Night, yet unfolding history showed that the watch for the parousia would be long.

In the first parable, addressed to disciples in general, the faithful servants are eagerly awaiting their master's return from a "wedding banquet," a favorite biblical image of the end time. This Lectionary selection may seem to be more appropriate to Advent, but the positioning of it in both the middle of Luke's Gospel and halfway through the journey to Jerusalem reminds us to be alert at all times so that we may recognize the Lord when he comes. He comes in those we meet, in the circumstances of our daily lives, and in the signs of our times. In a very real sense, every hour is an hour of the Lord's coming and knocking, and our response to this will either prepare for or hinder its final fulfillment.

For those who open the doors of their hearts to Jesus, the parable has a dramatic reversal of roles: the Master will be our "God-in-an-apron" who serves his watchful servants. The hospitality of God, incarnate in Jesus, serves us at every eucharistic table. At each Eucharist, too, we have some form of the "anamnesis," the "not-forgetting" prayer that recalls the death and resurrection of Jesus and the need to be "ready to greet him when he comes again" (Third Eucharistic Prayer). It is a reminder, too, that one Eucharist will be our last, that our life and world history will both end. Then we will go to meet the ascended and risen One who stands in the heavens waiting for and waiting on those who have lived a lifestyle of ready welcome to him, especially as he comes to us in the poor and marginalized. The Lord's arrival will be as unexpected as a night thief, and the Eucharist is the sacrament of vigilant hope that nourishes and strengthens us for such eager service.

Whereas the first part of the Gospel was lovingly addressed to the whole Christian community, Jesus' "little flock," the second parable is told in response to Peter's question, and is more specifically directed at the leaders of that flock. Jesus has gifted them with a share of his authority over the household of God's people, but they still remain servants of the Master. A leader's authority, therefore, is an authority of service. If a steward becomes drunk with power and status, abusing physically or psychologically the members of the household (Luke typically mentions both sexes), he will earn the great displeasure of the Master at his return. There is no dispensation from the demands of discipleship for the church's leaders. As Augustine told his people: "For you I am a bishop; with you I am a Christian"—and a Christian of whom even more will be expected because of the gifts with which a leader is entrusted. This Gospel throws into tragic relief the shadows cast over the church by the sexual abuse, financial misappropriation, or lavish lifestyles of some of its leaders. The punishing word that is translated in some lectionaries as "cut off" (*dichotomein*), literally means "to cut in two" and, in the context of the parable, is a fittingly ironic and symbolic statement about the fate of one who lives a double, "divided life."

In well lit, electrically powered societies, there is an almost universal availability of light. When there is a power failure, we suddenly realize our vulnerability as we stumble around looking for the matches and candles, which millions of our sisters and brothers have to rely on every day in places where there is no generation of electricity, or what there is may be highly unreliable and beyond the economic means of most people. Perhaps it is only when we camp under the night skies, away from the perpetual day of our cities, with only the sky and stars above us, that we have some feeling of the vastness of the cosmic mystery of night. The first reading from the Book of Wisdom recalls the night coming of God to rescue his people from the Egyptians. It is an example of how, in the biblical "night," love, fear, and hope erupt into human history as exodus, prophetic dreams and visions, birth, death, and resurrection, and what is yet to come—the return of the Master. One day the Master will return for us in the "Passover" of our own death, and at the end of human history Jesus will return to give to the Father the whole of the created universe as the new heaven and new earth.

In the Letter to the Hebrews, the author reminds us of people who traveled through the night of hopeful faith, risking everything on a promise. Out of a long roll call of such Old Testament heroes, the Lectionary reading selects Abraham and Sarah for our special attention. Faith was the one great possession they took with them when, obedient to God's word, they set out for a land they did not know, but trusted that God would show them. For these aged travelers to believe in the promise of descendants when Sarah was well past childbearing age was a witness to their extraordinary faith in their promise-making God. Abraham endures the heartbreak of the call to sacrifice Isaac, the child of the promise, and the joy of receiving him back from God, newborn as it were, from Abraham's obedience. But for the great believers of the Old Testament, the horizon of their hope was always ahead of them. Only when the most tender mercy of God, in the person of Christ, rose like the dawn over that dark horizon, would our surest hope be revealed. In our assembly today, we who are also the children of Abraham, our father in the faith, sing with the psalmist: "May your love be upon us, O Lord, as we place all our hope in you."

Twentieth Sunday in Ordinary Time

• Jer 38:4-6, 8-10 • Ps 40:2-4, 18 • Heb 12:1-4 • Luke 12:49-53

The Jewish heritage of Jesus is full of the imagery of elusive, purifying fire. "I AM" speaks out of it; the pillar of God's fiery presence leads the Hebrews through the desert nights, sparks out on Sinai, burns in Temple lamp stands of pure gold, licks up the waters of Carmel, and anoints the lips of prophets. In the fullness of time, the holy fire takes flesh in Jesus, the Earth Firelighter of this Sunday's Gospel. Perhaps we are never more conscious of this than when we gather in the darkness around the Easter fire. The leaping flames celebrate the fulfillment of Jesus' strong desire and determination to engulf the earth with the fire of his Spirit after he has suffered the "baptism by fire" of his passion and death.

Those who follow Jesus will not only be warmed and enlightened by him; inevitably, they will also feel the painful heat of their association. Sadly, some aspects of even the most intimate relationships of family and friendship may be scorched, or even totally destroyed. Earlier in Luke's Gospel (Luke 3:16-17) that uncompromising precursor, John the Baptist, had spoken of a baptism that would be greater than his purificatory rite: a baptism with the fire of the Holy Spirit that the Messiah would enkindle. Those whose lives were husks, empty of any repentance or commitment to the Coming One, would not be harvested into the kingdom, but would be burned in "unquenchable fire." Read in context, what John is speaking about so strongly are issues of social justice: sharing with the disadvantaged, nonviolence, and economic integrity. From the time he had announced his mission in the Nazareth synagogue, this was also the burning social commitment of Jesus (Luke 4:16-21). A fire that was familiar to the inhabitants of Jerusalem was the regular garbage being burned in the Valley of Hinnon (Gehenna) just outside the city. But there is another and blessed fire that is to be lit from the person of Jesus himself, who burns with a wild love for the world. This is emphasized by the personal repetition: "I have come," "I wish," "I have a baptism," "I am here," "I tell you." For Jesus to speak of himself in the first person in the Synoptic Gospels is extremely rare. It is an indication of the urgency that he wishes to communicate to his listeners. The adult Jesus who is speaking was the child whose birth was announced as heralding peace (Luke 2:14), but was also recognized by Simeon as a source of division (Luke 2:34). The two are not incompatible. Jesus' peace is not a warm, fuzzy glow, a comfortable satisfaction with the status quo. It is a burning decisiveness that results from the self-discovery and discernment that Jesus experienced in the wilderness—that fierce place of temptation and commitment. Out of the wilderness he was driven on mission by the power of the Spirit, ready to live, suffer, and die for his God (Luke 3:1-14) and the salvation of the world. This mission has nothing to do with the *pax Romana* (or the *pax Americana*). Those who follow Jesus share his experience by becoming part of it. In this Gospel text, it is significant that it is not extraordinary, dramatic suffering that Jesus speaks about so passionately, but the intimate, painful divisions and misunderstanding that the choice of discipleship can cause in families. A close and faithful relationship to Jesus will influence all our other relationships in terms of values and priorities.

In the first reading, we see Jeremiah almost as a "rear vision" mirror image of Jesus. The Lectionary enables us to look back to the early seventh century B.C.E. and reflect on the prophet's situation, noticing similarities with what will be the fate of Jesus. Jeremiah is resisting the false prophets who, in the royal circles where they try to curry favor, are talking loudly about peace when there was no prospect of it. King Zedekiah had earlier asked Jeremiah for a word of the Lord, to guide his decision making with regard to the onslaught of the Babylonians. The officials around the king do not like what they hear: Jeremiah's advice to surrender to Nebuchadnezzar rather than have Jerusalem burned and destroyed and the king himself, along with the women, grossly abused. (Read on to vv. 21-24.) The officials regard Jeremiah as a traitor, someone who could seriously undermine the morale of the army, and so they decide to bury alive this causer of divisions in a deep, muddy pit. King Zedekiah vacillates, wobbles through rejection and support of Jeremiah, and then backflips to allow his servant, Ebed-melech, to rescue Jeremiah from the pit. Why, we might wonder, with our later memories of a Roman centurion and the first African convert (Luke 23:47; Acts 8:27-40), did the Lectionary compilers cut out verse seven which tells us that Ebed-melech, a pagan Ethiopian and a eunuch, was the one who recognized the prophet's innocence? To disagree that "God is on our side," and to consider that those who speak out against involvement in war are "traitors" to the national cause, even when there are strong opposing religious and moral reasons for doing so, is still a present position taken by many in twenty-first century politics.

What God has done in the past, he will do in the present and the future—for Jeremiah, for Jesus, for each one òf us. This is the assurance that we sing in the chosen verses of Psalm 40. In a death-threatening situation, the psalmist cries out to God who, with loving care, "stoops down" to help the afflicted one. The pit and suffocating muddy clay were metaphors of death and, coming after the description of Jeremiah's rescue, have a correspondence with his punishment. So, too, does the "new song" of praise of God who rescues the afflicted one. The suffering servant, Jesus, "waited, waited for the Lord" for three days in the pit of death, but then was raised by God so that we might see and trust in that same God.

The Letter to the Hebrews completes today's liturgical montage, encouraging us in our marathon race of discipleship. A cloud of witnesses, those who have already reached the heavenly finishing line, cheers us on; and ahead is the great Pace Setter, Jesus, who ran through the flames of opposition and death to take the prize of resurrection. Runners in the Greco-Roman world ran naked so as to be as unencumbered as possible. In our modern Olympic Games, we watch the competitors persist despite the pain of bursting lungs and exhausted muscles; we continually see the evolution of new styles of swimsuits and track suits that offer the least resistance to water and wind. We are called to keep on running for the prize that Jesus has won for us through his death and resurrection, and to strip ourselves of the sinfulness that encumbers us. Watching our race, cheering us on, is a cloud of witnesses of those who have already successfully competed in life's marathon. Anyone who, at the Easter Vigil, has watched a parish's RCIA candidates prostrate themselves before the community and the fire of the paschal candle while the Litany of the Saints is sung over them and then seen them rise up with tears of joy on their faces, cannot doubt the hope that these elect place in the support of the cloud of parish witnesses. Like Jeremiah, there will often be times when we are "in the pits," sinking in the mud, unable to pull ourselves out of the quicksand of suffering and despair. It is then that we hope that we will be able to grasp the helping hand of our God, extended through a sister or brother, to draw us out and again set our feet on the Rock.

Twenty-first Sunday in Ordinary Time

• Isa 66:18-21 • Ps 117:1-2 • Heb 12:5-7, 11-13 • Luke 13:22-30

This Sunday's Gospel opens with a reminder that Jesus is still journeying to Jerusalem, answering questions and telling stories along the way to explain what is expected of a disciple. "Lord, will only a few be saved?" asks someone—no doubt with the unspoken hope "along with me!" The anonymity of the questioner drags us all into both the question and Jesus' reply. This reply is not a direct answer, but a parable about the effort that is needed to be saved. Central to the parable is the image of the narrow door. It is not a locked door, but one that requires disciples to give up self-indulgent ways and go into a spiritual training program that will slim us down and enable us to pass through this door into the kingdom. The media is full of stories of the demanding regime that athletes have to follow in their training. To squeeze into a sports team, especially as a representative of one's country, is a cause for celebration; to be citizens who squeeze into the kingdom of God (Phil 3:20) is an eternal joy beyond compare. It is in Jerusalem, where Jesus is heading to suffer, that the narrow door of salvation will be forced sufficiently wide for us by his crucified and risen body.

The Letter to the Hebrews maintains that for the spiritual olympiad, suffering is part of our training. The "encouragement" to which the author refers at the beginning of the reading is from Proverbs 3:11-12, and what follows is influenced by a reflection on parental discipline. The word translated as "discipline" (*paeidia*) means "instruction," with less emphasis on punitive connotations. There is certainly a punitive aspect to parental discipline, but this is born out of a parent's love and is for the sake of the child's own character development and ability to live in peace and goodness in adulthood. If human parents act like this, how much more will this be true of a loving God? The childhood discipline of our parents lasts only a few years, but we never outgrow God's loving instruction in our race toward the kingdom. At the end of the reading, therefore, the author returns to the imagery of athletics, reflecting imaginatively on the effort required by those who follow God's holy way (Isa 35:3) and God's "running track" (Prov 4:26). Although there is no unanimity among scholars about the time, place, or authorship of the Letter to the Hebrews, it would seem that it is addressed to a community experiencing tensions, with some of its members stumbling and faltering along the way that Christ had run before them (Heb 5:8; also see last week's reading). Some were even on the verge of dropping out of gathering as a community (Heb 10:25). Flagging disciples must never lose sight of Jesus and his endurance of the cross if they, too, are to endure in the face of hostility from without and lack of commitment from within themselves and their community. In an era when we are made privy to all the details of an injured sport hero's physical therapy routine ("punishing," as it is often described!), we need to reflect on our own routines for enduring the kingdom race as we strive to reach heaven.

The second image in the Gospel, the second door, is a locked one. The door to the kingdom of God will not remain open forever. There comes a time when for each one of us personally in death, and cosmically at the Second Coming of Christ, the door will be closed. Jesus, the risen Christ, is the Master of God's household who "rises" to shut the door. He will not open it to name-dropping or pleas of casual associates who by their protests only indicate how shallow their relationship with Jesus has been. In fact, says the Gospel, Jesus will be busy at the back door with those who are too ashamed to come to the front: the strangers, the beggars, those healed in their bodies and psyches, the abused women, the repentant sinners, and all those who may not have known much about God. But they were known by God as the last who deserved to be first in the kingdom. This is a scene of Gospel reversal, with graphic language to impress on Jesus' audience that those who expect to be the guests at the messianic banquet, who consider themselves holy, may be disappointed. They will have no place in the history of salvation, and will not sit at table with Abraham, Isaac, Jacob, and all the prophets; others will take their place. We should remember that these words of Jesus are admonitions rather than predictions. If we are honest with ourselves, especially our self-righteous selves, we will admit that we still find it rather scandalous and upsetting that "those people," with their contemporary name tags we choose to write and their categorizations we describe, might be invited into the feast—or at least have a more favored place at table than we do.

In his "Sermon on the Narrow Door," St. Augustine concludes with an image of heaven as a vast threshing floor:

> From this threshing floor will come enough wheat to fill the granary of heaven. Listen, my beloved, to what Scripture says: "I had a vision of a great multitude, which no one could count, from every nation, race, people and tongue" (Rev 7:9). This is the wheat-pile of the saints.[23]

In the last chapter of the Book of Isaiah, the Third Isaiah gives us a magnificent glimpse of "the others" in his extraordinary vision of the ingathering of the nations. These are not people who are returning exiles, nor captives of war. They are people from nations and lands mentioned in Genesis 10, the table of nations descended from Noah's sons rather than from the inhabitants of Babel. This radically imaginative text points beyond itself to the future crowds of peoples who will stream into the Temple and then out again to bring others to the worship of the God of Israel (Isa 2:2-4). All ethnic privilege and cultic laws are put aside. Nowhere else are the Gentiles described as so equal to and included in the worship of God's people that some of them are even consecrated as priests and Levites. Yet until the grandeur of what God accomplished in Jesus Christ was revealed to the world, even Isaiah could not visualize the magnitude of God's final purpose. How myopic can we be about the ingathering of nations in our own time and place? Too often hospitality to the nations becomes fear of job losses because of immigrants (something that is universally disproved by sociological studies); governments raise specters of terrorism that haunt attitudes to and policies about refugees and asylum seekers; our own culture and language is considered the preferred universal norm: and those who don't measure up would be better "back where they came from." Both Old and New Testaments do more than just hint at the surprises that may be in store for us when we do come to our final and heavenly home.

Such was the surprise for Ruby Turpin in Flannery O'Connor's short story, "Revelation." Ruby is a woman who considers herself a good Christian, but is actually a bigot and racist. Near the end of the story, Ruby is raging at God who, she believes, has let her down in an encounter with a mentally deranged college student. Sick of what she calls "trash," she accuses God of favoritism toward those she considers freaks and lunatics, and yells out at him to go and get some of these to keep him company in heaven if he likes them so much. God does just that! In her red-hot anger, Ruby has a vision of a bridge reaching up to heaven and on it are crowds of those whom she had considered so despicable. For the first time in their lives they were clean, clapping, dancing "trash," souls climbing upward into the star-studded sky with shouts of "Hallelujah." And Ruby eventually drinks from this cup of her wrath and pain and discovers that she is sweetened by this "trash."[24]

In its two verses, Psalm 117, the shortest psalm in the Psalter, puts on our lips a hymn of praise for the large inclusiveness of God's plan for the world. God is bound to all peoples and nations in steadfast love and fidelity. When we pray this psalm as a Christian community, we are united in praise of the inclusiveness that challenges us to overcome all divisions in the human family because: "The Lord is the goal of human history, the focal point of the longings of history and civilization, the center of the human race, the joy of every heart, and the answer to all its yearnings."[25]

Yet so often this vision is destroyed: by war, by self-interested factions and movements, small and large, political and personal, that define themselves in terms of division and competition. From such divisiveness, the church of progressives and conservatives is not immune. When we are more intent at all levels—national, social, ecclesial, and personal—on making friends rather than enemies, we will be true to what we sing with the psalmist and hear in this Sunday's readings.

Twenty-second Sunday in Ordinary Time

• Sir 3:17-18, 20, 28-29 • Ps 68:4-7, 10-11 • Heb 12:18-19, 22-24a • Luke 14:1, 7-14

Anyone who has ever had to juggle seating arrangements—from a family wedding to political conference dinners—knows the hazards! Where, with whom, do we sit people to avoid frosty silences, heated arguments, exhausting prattle, or offended sulking? In today's Gospel, Jesus lays down the rules for "gospel seating," Christian table etiquette, and the compilation of guest lists. He himself is the guest at a Sabbath meal hosted by a leading Pharisee. The Lectionary omits the preceding verses that describe how Jesus heals the man with dropsy and is watched with silent disapproval by the lawyers and Pharisees who are at table with him. This, then, is the charged atmosphere in which Jesus does not hesitate to tell his parables. Luke structures his narrative in such a way that the hostility of Jesus' opponents provokes sympathy in his followers.

In Palestinian society of the first century, honor and shame were powerful social influences. A guest was expected to show appreciation for the hospitality offered, no matter how meager it might be. To criticize the host's action or the circumstances of the meal would be considered shameful for both the host and the guest, so Jesus takes the more subtle approach of storytelling. His first parable rebukes the social competitiveness of those who jockey for the best seats at table. The fact that Luke calls Jesus' words "a parable," indicates that more than social commentary is at stake. Jesus is about to serve a gospel ethic to those who sit at table with him.

Jesus deliberately invites into the parable the lawyers and Pharisees whose motive for dining with Jesus seems to be more to "catch him in something he might say" (Luke 11:53-54) than to enjoy his companionship. "When you are invited," Jesus begins. Today, as a eucharistic assembly, we too are invited to the table and into the parable. Jesus describes how a guest at a wedding feast loses face when asked by the host to move to a lower place because someone more important has arrived. To presume self-importance is great foolishness. On the contrary, to be humble, and consequently free from the promotion push, is an honorable attitude, and is recognized as such by the host's invitation to take a more important place at the table. But the parable is more than a piece of conventional social wisdom. A wedding feast is frequently a biblical image of the heavenly banquet, and so we can hear this parable as a warning that it will be much more painful if, at the kingdom banquet, we find ourselves put down for those who had no such grandiose opinions of themselves. Those who are most distinguished in God's eyes because of their humble love may be the very ones whom we blindly consider to be of little worth. What we do "now" is preparing for our "not yet" reception in God's house. In our contemporary situation, it is not so much the grab for seats at a meal, but the 'wannabe' culture that, in so many contexts, tempts us to elbow others out as we try to climb the ladder of self-importance and success.

Yet we should not confuse attitudes of false humility and passive resignation with taking the lower place. Those at the top and bottom of the social ladder will only meet when the poor are empowered by advocacy, education, and just health and economic policies to climb up to a more equitable future, and the rich relinquish some of their privileges in order to go down and share with those in need.

To Christian ears, the mention of any table event also has eucharistic overtones. Paul had to confront the Corinthian church with their lack of equity at the supper that at one time preceded the Lord's Supper (Cor 11:17-34). Before the poor working members of the community, especially the slaves, could arrive, the rich and leisured had eaten the best food in the most comfortable places. This was unacceptable preparation for the communion of believers where social position, gender, or race were to be of no importance. Life and liturgy must always be an indivisible expression of each other in every age and every Christian community.

Much apparent generosity can be a generosity of obligation or an instance of "you scratch my back and I'll scratch yours." In his second parable, Jesus criticizes this attitude with regard to the compilation of "Christian guest lists." People with social status were accustomed to invite to a dinner those to whom they were indebted or those who might be useful to them in the future. Neither is a qualification for Jesus' invitations nor those of his disciples. It is the Word of God, not that of hosts who seek their own social advancement and prestige, that invites to Christian companionship. And as the Gospels show, it is usually the poor, the crippled, the blind who answer Jesus' invitation much more readily than the rich and powerful, although some of these may also be eager to sit with their disadvantaged sisters and brothers, and this at great cost to their social status and connections. Jesus ends this second parable by pronouncing a blessing on those who offer hospitality to the unwanted with no hope of any repayment from them in this life. These hosts of the poor will be welcomed into the lavish and eternal hospitality of God in the kingdom. In the responsorial psalm we name God as the father of the poor, the defender of widows, the shelter of the homeless, and the liberator of prisoners, who rains his loving mercy on those in most need. Is this the God who would feel at home in our Christian communities because we are welcoming signs of hope for the least regarded members of society and give visible expression of this inclusiveness at the eucharistic table?

These parables continue to raise questions for our contemporary church. Who is missing from our guest lists? Have we a eucharistic openness to people from different economic strata, different racial or ethnic origins, which is expressed in the appropriate inculturation of our liturgy? What about the divorced who still come to Mass but never to communion, or those who stay away yet long to belong? What is our attitude to those of different sexual orientations? How can we find our way to inclusive ecumenical table companionship, and do we even want it? The church is a pilgrim who has not yet arrived at all the answers, but must never lose sight of the questions.

The first reading from Sirach (Ecclesiasticus) reminds those who have some social standing as sages that they should be both wise and gentle in their behavior. It offers advice to a student from a wise teacher who seems to know from personal experience the temptation to intellectual pride and intolerance. By avoiding any kind of patronizing, truly wise people will always be humble enough to allow those with whom they deal to retain their human dignity. This is more than just practical advice for maintaining harmonious human relations. It is an attitude that is proper to scholars, says Sirach, because of the knowledge they should have gained of their own humanity and its limitations when compared to the all-embracing wisdom and love of God, the giver of all good gifts. On the other hand, pride can be a terminal illness, the best preventative medicine for which is a listening heart and an attentive ear that enables a person to be open to wisdom wherever it is found, and to honestly accept one's own strengths and weaknesses.

The Letter to the Hebrews reminds us that it is Jesus who has shown us the divine gentleness of the God that gathers us into the intimacy of "first-born" sons and daughters in the new Jerusalem. This is the inclusiveness of the city of God, of the communion of saints and angels, to which we look forward.

Twenty-third Sunday in Ordinary Time

• Wis 9:13-18b • Ps 90:3-6, 12-17 • Phlm 9-10, 12-17 • Luke 14:25-33

Jesus' audience is now no longer his table companions, but the great crowds who were following him along the way to Jerusalem. These people can be left in no doubt about where they are heading if they stay with Jesus. Jerusalem will be the place of suffering, death, and resurrection. So that no one is under any illusion, his first words are a Semitic expression of exaggeration, rather like we use when we really want to make a point, for example, about our annoyance with someone, saying: "I could murder her!" ("But I won't, really!") When Jesus calls for "hate" of parents and family, he is not discarding his love command, but using a word that exaggerates the choice one must make in establishing priorities. Commitment to Jesus will involve putting him first in all our relationships. Life experience teaches us that one important choice often excludes others: to marry means to put husband or wife before parents; to allow our children their freedom as adults means not keeping them dependent on us; a decision for a single lifestyle means forgoing marriage. But no matter what our human relationships, says Jesus, Christians have to yield first place to him.

We know how we can get into trouble by neglecting to read the small print on documents like our guarantees, book or CD club membership, or advertisements for apparently wonderful bargains! Jesus wants us to be quite sure that we understand the "small print" of the gospel demands on his disciples. There are three conditions that disciples must be clear about. The first is to prefer intimacy with Jesus to all other intimacies; the second is to accept the cross—not only that of the ordinary, painful suffering that is part of being human, becoming sick, dying—but also the cross of the persecution, ridicule, and conflict that may come with discipleship; and the third is to surrender possessions and possessiveness. To impress on his hearers the importance of these demands, Jesus tells two parables about two possible fools: one at work, the other at war.

The first foolish man is a landowner who decides to build a tower, probably a watchtower, on his property. He is a captive of his wild, momentary enthusiasms. He wants a tower; let there be a tower! But he has no finances to raise anything on the foundations and is ridiculed by the onlookers who scoff at his lack of foresight and planning. The other man is the king who engages in the serious business of war. He would be a fool not to weigh the possibilities of succeeding with a smaller army than his opponent and try to negotiate for peace rather than engage in war. As builder and king, both the men are people of some substance, so to fail in what they set out to do will be a cause of great shame. Jesus seems to suggest that it is disciples who have some material and social means at their disposal who need to consider the cost of discipleship most carefully, because they will pay a greater price in terms of social status and possessions if they give up these to follow him. With memories of the mission of the seventy (or seventy-two) disciples in Luke 10:1-12, some may be expected to be itinerant missionaries, leaving the security of home and family but finding a new security and sense of belonging in the household of the church.

In *The Cost of Discipleship*, Dietrich Bonhoeffer compared "costly grace" and "cheap grace." The latter is grace without the Cross, and so without Jesus Christ. As leader of the German Confessing Church, which confessed Jesus in opposition to the Nazis, Bonhoeffer "hated" his own life to the extent of being executed by them on April 5, 1945, only a few weeks before the end of World War II in Europe. In comparing these two "graces," Bonhoeffer writes of:

> . . . the person who hears the call to discipleship and wants to follow, but feels obliged to insist on his own terms to the level of human understanding. The disciple places himself at the Master's disposal, but at the same time retains the right to dictate his own terms. But then discipleship is no longer discipleship, but a program of our own to be arranged to suit ourselves, and to be judged in accordance with the standards of rational ethic.[26]

How ready are we to pay the cost of Christian discipleship in our own times by doing works of justice, by sacrificing reputation and advancement because we confess the needs of the disadvantaged? How can those who are disadvantaged be enabled to achieve self-advocacy and self-respect? Are there aspects of our lives in which we are wild enthusiasts for the Gospel—but with no staying power? Today's Gospel is a source of both encouragement and challenge.

In the Lectionary readings it is usually the first reading that is most closely and obviously related to the Gospel. Today, however, it is the second reading from the shortest of Paul's epistles (335 words), his Letter to Philemon, that reflects so much of the Gospel. Probably written from prison in the late 50s or early 60s, about two decades before Luke's Gospel, it is at the same time both the most personal of Paul's letters, addressed to Philemon, a leader of a house church, and a call to the wider church to be transformed by love and pastoral concern. Paul writes as "an old man now," and not only a prisoner of the Roman Empire but also of Jesus Christ who, with gospel paradox, is his greatest freedom. He writes about Onesimus, Philemon's runaway slave, who in some way has made contact with Paul and become a Christian through his influence, just as Philemon himself had. Paul reminds Philemon that both slave and free man are a new creation in Christ, and so old social conventions are to be demolished. It was not humanly possible for Paul to demolish the imperial structures of slavery, but he asks a radical response of Philemon at the personal level which would amount to a small social revolution in his house church and locality. Philemon should forgive Onesimus and receive him back into his household, not as a slave but as a beloved brother, because those baptized in Christ are a new family. Paul will feel sorrow at the departure of Onesimus who has become very dear to him, but he will sacrifice this friendship for the greater good of the transformation of both the master and the slave in their following of Christ. Onesimus, meaning "useful" in Greek, was a common name for slaves. In verse 11, which the Lectionary cuts out, Paul indulges in some theological word play. If his slave proved "useless" to Philemon because of his behavior, his conversion to Christ made him "useful" to both Paul in prison and as a witness to the transformation of relationships that Paul expects of Philemon when he welcomes Onesimus back as a brother in Christ.

Paul's words to Philemon alert us to the importance of individual and local church activity that advocates for and practices social justice, that is ready to defy social conventions, and that offers a ready forgiveness even to those who have wronged us in some way. The tone of the Letter also has something to say about the exercise of authority. Paul writes to Philemon with gospel persuasiveness and with the freedom of mature old age in the service of Christ, not with heavy-handed authority.

That human wisdom is limited, is the reminder of the first reading. It is hard enough to be intelligent and insightful about earthly things, given that our minds are so often teeming with anxieties and inconsistencies. How, then, could we possibly know anything of the mystery of God without the wisdom of God to guide us? The Welsh poet, R. S. Thomas, expresses this feeling of the distance between God and humanity in his poem "Via Negativa":

> . . . He keeps the interstices
> In our knowledge, the darkness
> Between stars. His are the echoes
> We follow, the footprints he has just
> Left. We put our hands in
> His side hoping to find
> It warm. We look at people
> And places as though he had looked
> At them, too; but miss the reflection.[27]

One day, as this poet and Christian minister also believed, Wisdom became incarnate and dwelt among us, left human footprints on our earth, was warmly touched by needy hands, and showed us the surest path to the life, the "wisdom of heart" for which we pray in the responsorial psalm.

Twenty-fourth Sunday in Ordinary Time

• Exod 32:7-11, 13-14 • Ps 51:3-4, 12-13, 17, 19 • 1 Tim 1:12-17 • Luke 15:1-32

The opening verses of the Gospel set the stage for the three-act drama in parables. The tax collectors and sinners seem to draw near to Jesus spontaneously while, more aloof, is the grumbling huddle of Pharisees and scribes whose main complaint is that Jesus eats with sinners. To share a meal was considered a way of celebrating shared life and solidarity, and so the outcast and marginalized were not the "unclean" company which Jesus' opponents wished to keep—and criticized him for keeping. But like the Woman Wisdom who searches out the poor and disregarded ones and invites them to her banquet (Prov 1:20-23; 8:1-5; 9:1-11), so Jesus invites his audience to feast on his wisdom through parables. Characteristically, these begin with the familiar and comfortable, and end with the unsettling demands of the reign of God that justify association with the poor, the marginalized and the sinners.

"Shepherd" was a familiar metaphor for God in the Old Testament (Ps 23; Ezek 34), but in first century Palestine, flesh and blood shepherds had come to be considered thieves who often trespassed on other people's lands to chase their sheep, and were also regarded as ritually unclean because of their work associated with handling animals. Yet it is with such rejected people that Jesus does associate from the time of his birth (Luke 2:8-20). Certainly the scribes and Pharisees would not like to see themselves as sharing life with such outcasts! To be invited into the parable with Jesus' question, "Which one of *you* . . . ?" would be, for the scribes and Pharisees, an invitation to an act of "scandalous" imagination.

A flock of a hundred sheep would either have been owned by a family clan of shepherds or by one prosperous owner who hired a number of shepherds to do his unpleasant work for him. In both these cases, the shepherd who lost the sheep would be answerable to others, for that loss that affects them all. The presumption is that the culpable shepherd would go in search of the 1 percent of the flock that was lost, leaving the other sheep in the care of his companions. It takes a great effort to find a lost, frightened sheep in difficult terrain. (When a sheep that had been lost for eight years recently and desperately staggered from hiding in the New Zealand highlands, Trek—so nicknamed—had to be shorn of his massive coat of wool by a master shearer!) In human terms, the parable reminds us that to allow ourselves to be found, untangled from our sins and carried home by the huge effort of a loving and shepherding God, is a necessary aspect of repentance. The gift of God's forgiveness, like any gift, is not gift until it is freely and gratefully accepted. The return of the shepherd with the sheep is a communal event of shared joy. Just so, says Jesus, does the community of heaven rejoice over the one sinner who is found and repents.

In the second parable about a lost coin, Jesus does not dare to openly and directly invite his male opponents to identify with the woman who has lost her coin! More subtly, though, he puts God into an apron, with a broom in her hand. Hers is a 10 percent loss that requires great and immediate energy. Using up the precious oil in her lamp, she sweeps the floor of her house, listening for a little drachma clink. The great joy of the "women's network" at finding the coin is again like the communal joy in heaven over the return of a sinner, without whom the kingdom community is impoverished. Women's reflections on and praying of this parable have recently suggested that we might also take the "coin" as a metaphor for the wealth of women's experiences that have fallen through the cracks of the church and for so long have been regarded as insignificant and uncelebrated. For any rediscovery of the wealth of this experience, there should be ecclesial rejoicing.

The third parable, usually called "The Prodigal Son," can be regarded as the Gospel in miniature, announcing as it does the compassionate love of God in Christ that forgives and welcomes home the sinner. The first-century Middle Eastern context of this parable is important. In that culture, a father might take the initiative to apportion his property to his children before his death, but even then they were not to use it until their father had died. "So he divided his property among them," continues Jesus. The word used for "property" is *bios*, with the more radical suggestion of "life" or "livelihood." It is the word "them" that often escapes our notice, yet it should alert us to the fact that the elder son also took his share of the inheritance without protest and without any attempt, as the elder, to be the expected go-between in the reconciliation of his father and brother.

In giving his sons their inheritance, the father makes his first gesture of radical, "foolish" love, and allows the younger boy the freedom to leave home. In so doing, the son had no intention of ending up in a pigsty, but that is where he eventually finds himself—starving and impoverished, both materially and spiritually. With all his inheritance squandered, enslaved by a Gentile boss, and looking after his pigs, he also makes himself ritually unclean and ostracized from his Jewish inheritance. So sitting down, he "came to himself." He proceeds to work it all out . . . *himself*: the initiative he will take to return home, the suggestion he will make to his father about being taken on as a hired, wage-earning hand and so able to work off the debt of his inheritance and repay his father. But coming home to himself will not save the son; coming home to the father will.

A second time the father shows his foolish, costly love. There is no cool, reserved reception of his son, but a running welcome, a kiss, a compassionate embrace that squeezes all the preconceived plans out of his son. All the boy can say is: "Father, I have sinned against heaven and before you; I am no longer worthy to be your son." And from their dead relationship, his father raises him to new life, newly clothed and feasted.

The late Henri Nouwen, who also reflected on and wrote movingly about this parable,[28] described his "homecoming" from academically successful but personally unsatisfying professorships at Harvard and Yale to his life with men and women with disabilities in the L'Arche Daybreak community in Canada.[29] With these wounded but loving and unpretentious people, Nouwen gradually learned to let go of his drive to do things and prove things. He was able to be his vulnerable, unadorned, and unmasked self, able to receive and give so much love. The parable of the Prodigal Son shows us an image of our Father who is also prodigal—a spendthrift with his love for each one of us, his unadorned and vulnerable children.

For the third time, the father is a foolish lover when, at the cost of being considered both rude and stupid, he ignores his guests in order to plead with his elder son to join in the communal rejoicing over the return of his brother. But he refuses to be reconciled; he, too, has to learn what it means to be a son. He describes himself as one who "has been working like a *slave* for you." He refuses to say "my brother," speaking only of "this son of yours."

Abruptly, we are left with the elder son on the threshold of choice: to accept or reject the father's love, to be reconciled or unreconciled with a brother or sister. Jesus invites us, today's listeners, to write the conclusion to the parable with our lives. And given the fact that the losing and finding in all three parables is a communal event, that the father's embrace is one of overwhelming compassion for the sinner, what are the implications for the church and the celebration of the sacrament of reconciliation?

In the first reading, God is also proclaimed as a God of generous mercy for the people who have been rescued from slavery in Egypt only to be "lost" in their impatient worship of the golden calf. By their disobedience and worship of this false idol, God's own sons and daughters are squandering their inheritance promised to the patriarchs. Moses pleads with God on their behalf, and God responds to Moses' unselfish entreaty with forgiving, compassionate love.

The First Letter to Timothy, written in Paul's name, again praises the inexhaustible mercy and forgiveness that was shown to Paul by Christ. The apostle is a living witness to God's concern for sinners that the parables proclaim. With the responsorial Psalm 51 we join our gratitude for the compassion and mercy of God to that of Moses, Paul, and the forgiven, welcomed sinners of all ages.

Twenty-fifth Sunday in Ordinary Time

• Amos 8:4-7 • Ps 113:1-2, 4-8 • 1 Tim 2:1-8 • Luke 16:1-13

Given the widening gap between rich and poor, continuing G8 discussions about attempts to help the world's most disadvantaged nations, and the frequent and irresponsible consumption of the world's natural resources by the rich global minority, it seems important to listen to what the Gospel has to say about money management. We must beware, however, of a simplistic transference of the ancient Middle Eastern social situation into our own times and places. God is certainly interested in contemporary issues of social justice, but acts through the Spirit who did not become incarnate in any one historical situation. Throughout the generations, the Spirit abides in the women and men who are baptized into Christ and who, in his Spirit, make the biblical word "living and active" (Heb 4:12) in their own days.

At first hearing, today's Gospel may make us feel uneasy—about the word of God. We are unfortunately familiar with wheeling and dealing money managers, but how appropriate is it for Luke to introduce us to one of them as "good news"? Through many of Jesus' parables, however, there is a parade of unpleasant, or at least dubious, characters who are used to shock us in various ways into reflection on kingdom values and attitudes: enemy Samaritans, unpopular tax collectors, bothersome widows. Stories of wise rogues and clever tricksters were common in Jewish folklore, and these and the "larrikin" traditions of some cultures may be a help in understanding their appeal, or at least in sympathizing with their ingenuity. Since "shrewd" is not a description of approval normally bestowed on disciples, the second half of today's parable acts as a clarification and corrective.

In last Sunday's Gospel we met a prodigal son; this week we meet a prodigal steward or business manager. Both squandered property. Whether the steward's wastefulness was because of negligence, incompetence, or malice, we are not told. Where he is efficient, however, is in the speedy formulation of a plan that will ensure his future now that he has been denounced. He thinks quickly and shrewdly. Without the physical strength to become a laborer or the humility to beg, he has to act before the news of his dismissal spreads throughout the village. So he decides to grant favors—debt reductions—and this, the debtors will presume, will be at his master's generous initiative, not the manager's. They would never imagine, rightly, that the manager would have such authority. The debtors gladly rewrite their promissory notes with the percentage cut offered them by the manager, and there is much consequent praise of both the master and his employee. The latter has now feathered his own reputation nest, and assured himself of receiving another debt, one of gratitude, which will result in making him welcome in the homes of those who have benefited from what the debtors mistakenly consider the manager's speedy and efficient carrying out of his employer's generous decision. When he hears of his manager's actions, the master can do nothing more than make the best of the situation. To renege on the debt reduction for which the debtors think he is responsible, to tell them that he did not authorize the remissions, and so admit that he had no control over his steward and that the remissions are null and void, would mean a shameful loss of face and honor, unthinkable in that culture.

So the master wryly praises his manager, not for his business ethics, but for his flair and roguish intelligence in a time of crisis. The "children of this age," those like the manager who are driven by material values and are knowledgeable about the way to save their own unethical skins, show themselves resourceful in social dealings. The barb of the parable is that the "children of light," those enlightened by Jesus and his Gospel proclamation, should be even more alert and enterprising, more ready to risk everything because they rely on the mercy and honor of their Master. "What will I do?" is a question for each of us as a disciple and trusty steward of the rich property of God's household, not only of the material resources that are to be shared with those in need, but especially of the mysteries of God (1 Cor 4:1). To some degree, we are all like the manager, a mix of the despicable and the commendable.

Probably none of us will ever feature in the list of the world's top billionaires but, says Jesus, it is the one who can be trusted with little things who can be trusted with the great, and so win a rich inheritance in the kingdom. It is all too easy to be irresponsible with and indifferent to the familiar, everyday tasks, lacking the manager's honest self-knowledge and harboring the illusion that we will be reliable and committed when the big demands come. But most of us in the near future will not have a stunning success on the stock market, launch a scheme for global economic recovery, or die a martyr's death. More likely, we will contribute to or disregard our parish planned giving; buy or resist purchasing what we don't really need; recycle our garbage or destroy a few more trees. The mundane is rich in opportunities for storing up treasure in heaven. If we are tainted with acquisitiveness, the best thing to do with our money is to give it away to those in need. Although we may not be introduced to them until we meet in the kingdom, our generous initiative will win us friends among the poor who are raised up, the hungry who are filled.

In Amos' time, about 760 B.C.E., the Northern Kingdom to which he was called to prophesy was enjoying an era of great economic prosperity. Those to whom Amos addressed his words considered the liturgies of Sabbath and festivals as nothing but unwelcome interruptions in the more important business of moneymaking. They swindled and exploited the poor, tampered with weights and measures, and imposed impossible debts on them. It is just as easy for us to be split-brain people, thinking (perhaps reluctantly) about religion at Sunday worship and eager to get back to business as soon as possible. Then we, too, inherit Amos' and Jesus' warning: "You cannot serve God and wealth." One or the other has to be the master and take precedence in our lives. When we respond to this reading with Psalm 113, we do a dangerous thing: we praise God as the one who befriends the poor, and admit that God's concerns must be realized in our own active responsibility for those in need today.

The dishonest manager wrote off a portion of what was owed by his master's debtors, but in the First Letter to Timothy we are reminded that Christ Jesus, in offering himself as "a ransom for all," canceled the debts of all humanity. He is the Steward of the inexhaustible, universal, and unconditional love of God that surpasses any human love. Every Eucharist is the greatest prayer of thanksgiving and praise for this salvation by Christ, a wondering worship of the constant love of the one mediator between humanity and divinity. United in the Spirit, in the liturgical assembly we pray in communion and for communion with everyone, everywhere, and for the whole created universe.

Twenty-sixth Sunday in Ordinary Time

• Amos 6:1a, 4-7 • Ps 146:7-10 • 1 Tim 6:11-16 • Luke 16:19-31

A story is told about St. Lawrence, the third-century Roman deacon, who was ordered by the city's prefect to hand over the valuables of the church to the civil authorities. Lawrence, however, had already sold these and distributed the proceeds to the poor, so at the appointed time he gathered many of these needy people and presented them to the Prefect, saying, "Here are the treasures of the church." The Prefect was not amused, and Lawrence was martyred.

Jesus is speaking to the Pharisees "who were lovers of money" (Luke 16:14) and were ridiculing Jesus over what he had said about idolizing wealth over the worship of God. This Sunday, poverty and wealth, the "haves" and the "have-nots" are given human faces in the parable about a beggar at the gate of a rich man who sits comfortably, securely, and blindly in his splendid dwelling. Likewise, the Lukan beatitude, "Blessed are you who are poor, for yours is the kingdom of God" (Luke 6:20), and the woe, "Woe to you who are rich, for you have received your consolation" (Luke 6:24), become narrative in this parable. The beggar is the only character in any of Jesus' parables who is given a personal name. He is called Lazarus, meaning "God has helped." The rich man is often referred to as "Dives," which is not used in the text and is simply the Latin for "rich man." In our society, it is usually the poor who are nameless while the mass media screams at us the names and faces of the rich, along with their often inconsequential doings. This is an early hint of the gospel paradox that Jesus will proclaim in this parable.

The rich man dresses sumptuously, even down to his linen underwear, and feasts abundantly every day. He fits perfectly Amos' description of the idle and corrupt rich about which the first reading is so scathing. In painful contrast, Lazarus lies outside his gates, ignored, clothed with sores and not much else, hungry for even a few crumbs from the rich man's table, but no one comes out to offer him anything. Obviously paralyzed, he at least seems to have a few friends who dump him in his begging place, but he can do little to get rid of his dog companions who rummage through garbage in hope of some scraps of food, and regard Lazarus and his sores as an adjunct to this garbage. That the dogs lick his sores would infect them still further, add to his human degradation, and make him doubly unclean in the religious ritual sense.

Then comes death to both Lazarus and the rich man—and the great reversal. It is revealed that Lazarus does have some wonderful friends, the angels, who carry him from his dumping place to the loving and intimate company of Abraham, the model of Old Testament hospitality, the hospitality that he never received from the rich man. The rich man is dismissed abruptly; dead and buried, he ends up in Hades. All of a sudden, stirred by self-interest, he does notice Lazarus, and even knows his name. No magnificent clothes and food and drink are available to the rich man; he is consumed by thirst and clothed in flames. But even in Hades, the rich man cannot throw off his pride, his total self-centeredness, and his indifference to any suffering except his own. During his life, he prepared his own sorry future, but he refuses to admit responsibility for this. He wants Lazarus to be his slave, his water carrier, and his messenger boy. Through the voice and character of Abraham in the parable, Jesus emphasizes that what we do in life has eternal implications. Lazarus says nothing. In his time of glory, at Abraham's side, he utters no words of spite or revenge. In every "Lazarus" who recognizes him- or herself as the one whom "God has helped," anger will have no place, but be silenced with gratitude for God's generosity.

The rich man and his five brothers could have crossed the gulf between the rich and the poor if they had listened to and obeyed what Moses and the prophets said about the care of the poor (e.g., Deut 10:16-19; Isa 58:6-7; Ps 41:1-3). Those who will not be converted on the basis of the Scripture will not be convinced by miraculous signs, "even if someone rises from the dead." If the rich man had recognized Lazarus as a "sixth brother" during his life and not been indifferent to him, there would not be the fixed gulf between them. The conclusion of the parable is a reminder that those who are attentive to the Scriptures, and to the Word of God in Jesus, the One risen from the dead, will also be attentive to the poor and their needs.

We listen to this parable in the assembly as brothers and sisters in the house of living stones, gathered together by the One who has risen from the dead and comes to us in his Word and sacrament. Is our liturgical celebration a secure and comfortable "gated" separation from the "poor" who are outside? Or is it a challenge to our welcome to and service of them? Do we ever try to put human faces on those who lie at the gates of our institutions and nations, or allow ourselves to be challenged by those who are covered with contemporary sores: the unemployed, people with disabilities, asylum seekers, abused women and children? (The last named are the most numerous "Lazaruses" in our world today.) When "the poor" are just an abstract concept, they continue to be separated by a great chasm from their more fortunate sisters and brothers. The success of human interest stories in our newspapers and on TV bears witness to the impact of faces and names.

We must try to bridge the chasm in whatever way we can: through personal generosity, individual and group advocacy, information that stirs the heart to outreach, ethical business investments, or responsible voting; we are called to respond to the Word of God in *this* life. Like the rich man and his five brothers, no signs, no miracles, not even the Word of God, can break into and convert our hearts if we are determined to lock out the disadvantaged from our lives, because in them our poor brother Jesus still sits begging at our gates.

The concern of the prophet Amos is the sprawling, bawling, and idle rich, the so-called beautiful people of Israel in the eighth century B.C.E. who live lives of luxury at other people's expense and have no sense of responsibility for anyone except themselves. In this reading, Amos directs the word of God to the comfortable rich. The greed of the rich will lead to social breakdown, exile, and ruin. As Paul VI was to write many centuries later in his 1967 encyclical, *On the Development of Peoples*:

We must repeat that the superfluous wealth of wealthier nations should be placed at the disposal of poorer nations. This rule, by virtue of which in times past those nearest us were to be helped in time of need, applies today to all the needy throughout the world. And the prospering peoples will be the first to benefit from this. Continuing avarice on their part will arouse the judgment of God and the wrath of the poor, with consequences no one can foresee (article 49).

With Psalm 146 we respond with praise of our God who is always faithful to the poor and is the source of our hope in situations of injustice when we are bowed down and helpless. What really makes for "beautiful people" in God's eyes is not material riches, but fidelity to the demands of our Christian life that we professed at baptism. At every baptism, but especially those celebrated at the Easter Vigil or the "weekly Easter" of the Sunday Eucharist, the people of God witness and support the ones being welcomed into the rich heritage of the church.

The reading from the First Letter to Timothy gives us a checklist against which the rich of the parable, or of Amos' Israel would be the lowest scorers. And how would we rate on the good confession of "righteousness, godliness, faith, love, endurance, gentleness" which Jesus Christ witnessed for us even in the pain and passion of his trial, and which will enable us to win the greatest and most enduring riches of eternal life?

Twenty-seventh Sunday in Ordinary Time

• Hab 1:2-3; 2:2-4 • Ps 95:1-2, 6-9 • 2 Tim 1:6-8, 13-14 • Luke 17:5-10

This Gospel comes immediately after some hard words of Jesus to his disciples: warnings about being a stumbling block for others on the journey of discipleship. What is needed is correction, repentance, and forgiveness that is generous and uncalculating, even in aggravating circumstances. It all seems a bit too much for the disciples, so, "Lord, increase our faith!" they cry. "Quality, not quantity," is a cliché that we often use, seriously or frivolously, with reference to many different situations. In this one, the apostles (not the larger group of disciples) are asking Jesus for "more" faith, but Jesus responds with a qualitative image of faith: faith that is like a tiny mustard seed which the Sower God plants in our hearts. Buried deep, it germinates in darkness, but if we fail to tend the seed it will never break through its protective membrane and push into our lives. When disciples do live by faith, even "mustard seed faith," they can continue to do extraordinary things like persisting in the forgiveness about which Jesus has just spoken in the verse preceding the Lectionary text.

To impress us with this truth, Jesus uses another image: an uprooted mulberry tree. These trees can grow up to seventy feet high, and their root system is extraordinarily invasive. Those of us who have coped with root damage to plumbing systems would appreciate the first-century Palestinian law that prohibited the planting of mulberry trees near cisterns. Using exaggeration to make his point, Jesus says that the word of a disciple empowered with mustard seed faith would be able to lift up a mulberry tree and transplant it into the sea! Such is the metaphorical strength that God bestows on the person of faith, even in impossible, ridiculous situations.

Our faith is to be the faith of "slaves," not in the punitive sense, but in the way that Paul refers to himself as "a slave of Jesus Christ, called to be an apostle, set apart for the gospel of God" (Rom 1:1). Since Jesus' audience comprises those who are to be the apostolic leaders of communities, the "parable of the slave on duty" is directed first to them and then, by further extension, to all Christians. The duties of the slave are described as shepherding, plowing, and serving his master at table. The ministry of Christian leaders is to care for their flocks, plow the field of their communities to make them ready for the sowing of God's Word, and feed their people at the Lord's table. There is to be no self-adulation or congratulations, no expectation of special rewards or entitlements, no elevation of themselves to domineer over "their flock," as this always belongs to the Master. Such slaves are to consider themselves unworthy of any special reward, because what they do is to be expected of them in response to the grace of God that has been so generously given to them. A significant title of the pope is "servant of the servants of God." A lack of humility can result in leaders becoming self-righteous and adopting an attitude of spiritual superiority that hinders their shepherding and serving of the Christian community, and makes it difficult for the "little ones," especially, to approach and trust them. No disciple is exempt from personal sinfulness and immersion in the sin of the world. To judge ourselves as more worthwhile, more deserving than others, puts us under the judgment of God. In the center of this parable is the master's table; at the center of our lives, at this Sunday Eucharist, is the table before which, priest and people together, we profess: "Lord, I am not worthy." For our integrity as disciples, our lives must witness what our lips proclaim.

On December 6, 1273, while Thomas Aquinas was at the eucharistic table celebrating Mass in the Chapel of St. Nicholas at Naples, he had an ecstatic experience that profoundly affected him. From then on Thomas, the great theologian, refused to write another word of his *Summa Theologica*. His secretary, Br Reginald, said to him, "Father, are you going to give up this great work undertaken for the glory of God and to enlighten the world?" But Thomas replied, "I can do no more. All that I have written seems to me like straw compared to what has been revealed to me." He left the third part of the *Summa* unfinished, his own profound expression of the truth that "We are unworthy slaves. . . ."[30]

In the seventh century B.C.E., the prophet Habakkuk was also concerned with faith: how could people maintain faith in a God of justice in the midst of the injustice that was rampant in Jerusalem and Judea at that time? This is a question that transcends any particular place or time, and can provoke anguish, doubt, passionate questions in our own day. The opening verses sound like a psalm of lamentation, crying out "How long?" and "Violence!" to a God that seems deaf. But lamentation and complaint are not indicators of the loss of faith; Habakkuk does not cry out to a God who is not there, but to a God in whom he hopes, a God whose ways he is trying to accept, a God with whom he even dares to argue on behalf of those who suffer from injustice. The prophet's agony is an acknowledgment of human powerlessness and desperate need of God. And so he waits on God who seems passive and indifferent. Habakkuk stands firm in his grief, watching and waiting—and God does answer with what is described as a "vision" that Habakkuk is to write down. What the vision is we are not told; sufficient that it is from the God of steadfast love and faithfulness, and that Habakkuk is commissioned to write it down. To have a record of the message enables it to be taken by a runner and announced speedily to those who are waiting in hope. Putting something "down in writing" is like an affidavit, a witness to the trustworthiness of the prophetic word, and an enduring point of reference as the vision of what is "not yet" evolves into the reality of "now." In the New Testament, the last verse of this text is quoted by Paul in his Letter to the Romans: "The one who is righteous will live by faith" (1:17). For Paul, this is faith in the vision of the Gospel of Jesus Christ, who is the power and salvation of God. The struggle of Habakkuk and the people of Judea, of the apostles, of Paul and his Roman church, of each Christian today, is to hold onto and nurture the mustard seed faith.

The Second Letter to Timothy was probably written soon after Paul's death as a last testament and farewell to him by a close friend and fellow worker who was familiar with the closing chapter of Paul's life. In the section read today, Timothy is challenged to rekindle, to "fan to a flame" the gift of God, the gift of faith that is in him through the laying on of Paul's hands—probably a rite of anointing to strengthen him for his ministry of witnessing to Christ and enduring everything for the sake of the Gospel. And so Timothy, too, joins the company of those engaged in the struggle of faith. The greatest support of faith comes from the example of other people's commitment, and this is what Paul has shown Timothy. Like Paul, Timothy should never be ashamed to witness to the Lord or suffer for him. Given the importance of the affirmation we receive from the faith and courage of others, it is again surprising that the compilers of the Lectionary did not begin one verse earlier, where Timothy's grandmother Lois and mother Eunice are named as those in whom the faith that Timothy inherited first lived. This is feminine faith that Paul applauds. To be women and men of faith in any age, we need to listen to God's voice today and harden not our hearts, as we are challenged by the response to Psalm 95.

Twenty-eighth Sunday in Ordinary Time

• 2 Kgs 5:14-17 • Ps 98:1-4 • 2 Tim 2:8-13 • Luke 17:11-19

With Jesus we are traveling along the border between Galilee and Samaria, still "on the way to Jerusalem." No one would really take such a devious route, but Luke is not interested in geography except as it serves his theology. He wishes to remind us that Jesus is at the territorial boundary of Samaria whose people were despised by the Jews for their "hybrid" faith. The Samaritans reciprocated with their own expressions of hostility to the Jews who considered them religious and social outcasts. In the miracle that follows, Jesus is a marginal person with the marginalized: with the ten men who must keep their distance because of an infectious skin disease, referred to in the Scriptures as "leprosy," but not to be equated with today's leprosy (Hansen's Disease). So abhorrent was this condition that description, taboos, and rituals connected with it were detailed in the Book of Leviticus (Lev 13–14). The Greek text and some contemporary translations describe them not just as "lepers," but also as *men*. It may seem a subtle point, but it is a humanizing note that respects personal dignity, just as today we preferably refer to "people with disabilities," and not to "the disabled." What is more significant is the personhood, not the disability.

Keeping their distance, the men do not shout the prescribed warning words, "Unclean! Unclean!" (Lev 13:45-46) or ask for alms, but as one they call out for Jesus' mercy. They name him as "Master," a title not found on the lips of anyone except the disciples in Luke's Gospel. Jesus offers no healing touch, no eyes raised to heaven, no prayer over them; there is no tugging at his robe with diseased fingers. All he offers is his word that crosses the gap between them. *Before* they are healed, Jesus challenges the ten lepers to the obedience of faith in his word. He tells them to go and observe the ritual that was observed *after* the healing of a leper when a clean bill of health that would enable a person to reenter society was obtained from a Jewish priest. They obey. "And as they went, they were made clean."

Shared misery enables people to cross boundaries. The misery of leprosy had resulted in a hated Samaritan being admitted into companionship with Jewish lepers, and it is this one who returns to give thanks to Jesus. He would not have been welcome in the Temple or by a Jewish priest so, we might ask, what did he have to lose? But he had been doubly outcast: his polluting disease had gone, but not what Jews considered his polluting ancestry. Stranger and religious half-breed in Jewish eyes, he alone comes back. He praises God, not in an intimate whisper, but loudly and publicly, just as the ten had called out for mercy at the beginning of the narrative. The healed one sees in Jesus the power and presence of God and so, with no need for physical distance between them, there is another healing: a Samaritan throws himself at the feet of a Jew and thanks him.

Over the man at his feet, Jesus asks questions that are almost like a soliloquy. Hadn't he seen ten lepers on whom he had mercy? What about the other nine? Were they so overcome by their healing that they could see only their own new skin and new future and failed to see the goodness of God at work in them? Was it only "this foreigner" who could see with the eyes of faith and return to praise God? His gratitude is an expression of faith, Jesus tells the Samaritan, and this is what saves him. The other nine would have heard the words of the priest confirming their bodily healing. Only one foreigner heard from Jesus the words of salvation.

The significance of "seeing" is repeated throughout this Gospel. Jesus sees those who need mercy; the lepers see that they are healed; and one of them sees the power and presence of God in his healing by Jesus. Disciples need to learn how to "see" and be moved with the compassion of Jesus and the gratitude of the Samaritan. In *The Sign of Jonas*, Thomas Merton describes being overwhelmed on a street corner in Louisville in one of his infrequent excursions outside the monastery of Gethsemane in 1948:

> I found that everything stirred me with a deep and mute sense of compassion. Perhaps some of the people we saw going about the streets were hard and tough—but I did not observe it because I seemed to have lost an eye for merely exterior detail and to have discovered, instead, a deep sense of respect and love.[31]

Do we see today's "lepers" in the isolated, the alienated, the "untouchables" in our society, and respond with compassion? And what of the "leper" in each one of us: that weakest, least acceptable, and most unattractive aspect of myself that seems to put me at a distance from God, from my sisters and brothers, and from my own self-acceptance? For all this we, too, need to cry out with faith, "Jesus, Master, have mercy on us!"

At the beginning of his public ministry in the Nazareth synagogue, Jesus had infuriated his hometown congregation with the mention of the foreigner, Naaman, an Aramean commander and leper, who was healed through the word of the prophet Elisha. It is this Old Testament miracle that is so appropriately twinned with today's Gospel. To appreciate the miracle we really need to read this delightful story from the beginning of 2 Kings 5 through to verse 19, rather than bouncing in and out at verses 14-17. Naaman is a leper but of course, as a non-Jew, he is not subject to the taboos and penalties of the Mosaic Law. He goes on military expeditions, associates freely with his men and his own household. In this household was a young Israelite girl who had been captured and given to Naaman's wife as a servant. She is treated with respect, and when she tells her mistress about the prophet Elisha whom she believes could cure her master, her words are listened to. Naaman, in his turn, tells his king about this possibility of a cure, and consequently is sent with a letter and many gifts to present to the king of Israel. But the king misreads the Aramean king's intentions as asking the Israelite king himself to cure Naaman. When he failed, as he certainly would, this would provoke a political crisis! But Elisha hears of his king's distress and sends for Naaman to come to his house. When he does so, Elisha remains at a distance, does not come out to greet him, nor does anything spectacular. He simply offers Naaman his words, telling him to go and take seven dips in the Jordan river, and he will be healed. Naaman is indignant! He expected some spectacular treatment befitting his status. There were Aramean rivers at home, better than the Jordan, in which he could wash! Both Naaman's ego and his national pride are wounded by the idea of such a silly ritual. But this war hero is also approachable. He has already listened to the unimportant servant girl and now he calms down and listens to his own servants who lovingly address him as "My father." They convince him that if Elisha had asked him to do something difficult, he would have done it readily, so why not do the simple thing that the prophet had told him?

Naaman listens, goes and bathes in the Jordan, and rises up from the waters with his flesh like that of a little child. Before Elisha he confesses his faith in the God of Israel, an inclusive God of all the nations. Naaman offers Elisha gifts that are refused, but then asks if he may take back with him to his own land some of the earth of Israel. Religiously unsophisticated, Naaman assumes that the God of Israel can be worshipped only in the land of Israel, so he plans to transport back to his own land his little bit of Israelite soil on which to worship. Elisha accepts the right intentions and simplistic ideas of the one whom he recognizes as a good man and sends him away—with the soil and with a blessing of peace.

How do we match up to the recognition of God as a God of all nations? Do we really sing the responsorial Psalm 98 with genuine joy because our God's faithful love is not limited to any one nation? If ours is a multicultural society, can we look around our eucharistic assembly and praise God for the kaleidoscope of peoples with whom we are in communion? Or if they are not there, do we wonder why? And are we as good as Naaman at listening—especially to the wisdom of those without much status, or those who are not afraid to offer advice that dints our self-image?

Paul, in chains, writes to Timothy from prison. He is no longer able to travel, but stresses passionately that the word of God that he preaches cannot be chained. Paul's suffering gives his good news an extra urgency, his faith in Christ Jesus a new credibility. Perhaps there comes to mind the image of John Paul II, the traveler, in the last weeks of his life: a prisoner of his sufferings, but a witness to the world by his silence which spoke so loudly of fidelity, dignity, and hope in his faithful God and the promise of eternal glory.

Twenty-ninth Sunday in Ordinary Time

• Ex 17:8-13 • Ps 121:1-8 • 2 Tim 3:14–4:2 • Luke 18:1-8

As Jesus travels with his disciples to Jerusalem, today's Gospel describes how he tells stories that smash some stereotypes. We meet an insistent widow and an unjust judge whom she gets the better of. The parable, variously called "The Unjust Judge" or "The Persistent Widow," is prefaced with Jesus' comment about the need to pray always and not lose heart, but it is not only a parable that illustrates the importance of persistent prayer; it is also about the persistent pursuit of justice. The world of the parable is a difficult world, especially for a woman who is widowed and apparently without any sons or male relatives, since she represents herself before the judge. It is a world of injustice, suspected bribery, contemptuous judiciary, struggling and marginalized women. Yet if we look beyond the cultural context, we can recognize similarities in the way human beings relate to one another today. Huge backlogs of court cases for the poor who cannot afford expert legal help; judges who jockey for positions behind the scenes while cultivating the government that appoints them; charges of bribery among keepers of law and order that are either upheld or dismissed: such are often the headlines in our own daily papers.

The judge of the parable is everything that he is *not* supposed to be according to Sirach (Ecclesiasticus) 35:14-19, which is a portrait of a just judge who is especially attentive to the supplications of widows and orphans. The widow of this parable, however, does not dissolve into tears at her unjust treatment. She is no silent figure hovering in the shadows of her disregarded gender and marital status. She comes in from the margins of society loudly demanding justice of the judge who fears neither God nor anyone else. He is apparently shameless in a culture where honor and shame largely defined one's social response and reputation. There is also a lurking suspicion that the widow's opponent may have bribed favor from the judge. In the end, the judge gives in to the woman, admitting that what she asks are her just rights and she is "worrying him to death." This is a phrase from prizefighting vocabulary, and a much more colorful (and valid) translation would be "lest she give me a black eye"! That would very obviously shame the judge in his public appearances, especially if it became known that a supposedly helpless widow had doggedly resisted injustice, and had faced, named, fought, and won the bout with him. The widow reveals the power of weakness, as Jesus himself will soon do in his passion, death, and resurrection, and has already done in his empowering encounters with the poor and marginalized throughout his public ministry. In his Gospel and in the Acts of the Apostles, Luke has more references to widows than any other evangelist, perhaps a reflection of the significance of widows' ministry and presence in the Lukan communities.

The judge is described as dishonest and contemptuous in order to put him in sharp contrast with God, and to establish the argumentative technique of "from the lesser to the greater." If even a judge like this one gave in to the widow because of self-interest and suspect motives, how much more, suggests Jesus, will our compassionate God do justice for those who persist in their prayer and their faith. The destitute and the despised, those with no voting power, those on the losing side, are offered in the person of Jesus the presence and grace of God. Jesus' disciples, therefore, are to persist in prayer and be accountable for justice, advocating for people on the margins and enabling the defenseless to find their own voices, because what is not just is not of God.

To prayer that is persistent and constant must also be added the qualities of trust and patience that support the belief that God answers persevering prayer when and how God wills. That the time line may be lengthy is suggested by the "sandwiching" of the parable between the preceding narrative about the "last days" (Luke 17:20-37) and the last verse of today's reading (Luke 18:8). Our faith should be "night and day" faith like Anna's, the first widow whom we meet in Luke's Gospel (Luke 2:37), faith that endures until the coming of the Son of Man at the end of both our own personal life and the Second Coming at the end of human history.

By putting the first reading from the Book of Exodus in tandem with the Gospel, the Lectionary suggests that we focus not on the God who seems to endorse and direct aggression, but rather on the ritual endurance and persistence of Moses as he stands on the mountain, staff in hand, arms raised in prayer and growing painfully heavy as the hours pass. Because the Hebrews were God's people, their enemies were considered to be God's enemies. This is not a justification of militancy, but an attempt to explain the Hebrew perspective on it. Commenting on this text, Walter Brueggemann writes that as well as what happens on the battlefield: "battles require passion, energy, and sheer adrenalin which are usually generated by public leaders who can mobilize imagination and play on the passions of the military community."[32]

Moses' passion is his prayer, and it is this, not the military power of Joshua and his army, that overcomes the Amalekites. God, in fact, is not mentioned in the portion that we read, although the mention of the staff suggests the memory of the God through whom Moses performed wonders before Pharaoh (Exod 4:2-5) or parted and gathered back the waters of the Sea of Reeds (Exod 14:16). In what is like a massive, enduring sculptural formation on top of the mountain overlooking the battle, Moses' arms are supported by his companions, Aaron and Hur, for when Moses lowered his arms the Amalekites advanced. This is an image of how difficult it is to persevere in prayer without the support of others—even though the widow managed to persevere in her cause.

Psalm 121, our response to the reading, raises our eyes to the mountains, symbols of closeness to the heavens and that larger, different perspective that leads us to reliance on God, our creator and ever-watchful guardian. For this reason, mountains were considered sacred sites in many religions, and the Temple was built by Solomon on the highest point in Jerusalem. And there was also that "garbage dump" mountain on which Jesus one day stretched out his arms, supported only by cruel nails, and became passionate for the victory over sin, which is our salvation.

Timothy is encouraged by Paul to be persistent and insistent in his proclamation of the Word of God. He has the example of those who have witnessed the faith to him from his childhood in his family and throughout his adult ministry. The other great source of wisdom and fidelity are the Scriptures that Timothy has studied since his childhood. By this, of course, Paul means the Old Testament—a reminder to us that these did not become obsolete when the New Testament was written, but they have "enduring value for guiding the lives of Christians."[33]

Like any good Christian teacher, then and now, Timothy studied these Scriptures not just for the sake of his own salvation, but also for the sake of others whom he will teach and guide, challenge and correct. This is a sacred trust and responsibility given to Timothy in the name of God and Christ Jesus, a preparation for the return and appearing of Christ and the ongoing establishment of the reign of God. Such a sacred trust continues to be held by all those who preach and teach the Word of God.

Thirtieth Sunday in Ordinary Time

• Sir 35:12-14, 16-19 • Ps 34:2-3, 17-19, 23 • 2 Tim 4:6-8, 16-18 • Luke 18:9-14

In the homily that he preached at the funeral Mass of Basil Hume, O.S.B., the Cardinal Archbishop of Westminster and former abbot of Ampleforth, his friend Bishop John Crowley described the cardinal's reaction when he had learned of his terminal cancer two months earlier. Hume told him that at first he was tempted to feel: "If only . . . If only I could start all over again I would be a much better monk, much better abbot, much better bishop. But then I thought, [these are Hume's own words] then I thought how much better if I can come before God when I die not to say thank you that I was such a good monk, a good abbot, a good bishop, but rather, 'God, be merciful to me a sinner.' For if I come empty-handed then I will be ready to receive God's gift. 'God, be merciful to me, a sinner.'"[34] For that reason, Basil Hume himself chose for his funeral Mass Gospel the parable of the Pharisee and toll collector that we hear this Sunday.

Last Sunday's Gospel spoke about persistent prayer; this week it is about both presumptuous prayer and humble prayer. The parable praises those who, like Basil Hume, realize the wisdom of coming before God not only with awareness of their sins, but also with abiding trust in God's mercy. Luke notes that Jesus told this parable to those who trusted in their own goodness and regarded others with contempt, but there is no indication in the text that Jesus' audience consisted only of Pharisees.

The setting for the parable is public Temple worship, not private devotions. From beginning to end, Jesus draws a sharp contrast between the two men who go there to pray. The Pharisee, a pious lay leader, stood and prayed "about himself." His prayer is a litany of self-congratulation, self-advertisement, and self-aggrandizement, a litany of "I . . . , I . . . , I . . . , I . . . , I . . . ." Exalted in his own eyes, the Pharisee looks down on others, adding the toll collector to his list of undesirable companions or worshipers. In the custom of the time, the Pharisee's prayer would be audible, a litany of moral virtue for which he himself, not God, is responsible. It is announced not only to God (in case God doesn't know) but also to the other worshipers around him. His tithing and fasting are beyond what was required, but his boasting gives the lie to his claim to virtue. If we are regular churchgoers, reasonably generous financial supporters of our parish, it might be rather shocking, but sobering, to stand with the Pharisee, rather than the toll collector, and look into our own hearts. How dependent on God do we acknowledge ourselves to be? How self-satisfied are we about our religious observance? Are we dismissive of or mean-spirited about those who are on the margins of church and society, or outside both? And how do such attitudes and judgments affect our relationship with God and our prayer life?

The first shock with regard to the toll collector is that he would even be going up to the Temple to pray! Toll collectors were much further down the social ladder than a chief tax collector like Zaccheus, whom we will meet next week. They were minor functionaries of the Roman bureaucracy, often driven to this job in desperation of finding any other employment, and practicing small extortions to keep themselves and their families from starvation. Toll collectors were despised and underpaid by their employers, although useful to them. Consequently regarded as collaborators and cheats, they also found no favor among their own people. Dislocated and distanced on all sides, it is no wonder that in this visit to the Temple the tax collector stands far off from the Pharisee and the other worshipers. But he does not despise other people; he despises himself. So he prays, "God, be merciful to me, a sinner!"

Like the Pharisee, the toll collector's physical stance expresses his inner attitude. Nothing about him is lifted up: his eyes are lowered in shame, he is bent over and beats his breast, a gesture more typical of women than of men in Middle Eastern culture. Only one other time in the Gospels is such a gesture described: when the crowd returns home after the crucifixion of Jesus (Luke 23:48). The toll collector's prayer, in contrast to the Pharisee's, is brief, simple, and truthful. He needs the righteousness of God because he has none of his own. And because he acknowledges this, he receives it as God's gift. Two men went up to the Temple to pray; only one really did, and so went home justified, "for all who exalt themselves will be humbled, but all who humble themselves will be exalted."

Again we have a parable of reversals. The love of God can so easily turn into idolatrous self-love. If we regard God's gift as our possession, the gift is canceled out. Prayer is distorted into boasting by comparisons with and judgment of our sisters and brothers. The Pharisee becomes another kind of "tax collector" of exorbitant self-adulation.

The first reading from the Book of Sirach (Ecclesiasticus) assures us that God hears the cries of those who wholeheartedly serve him, no matter what their social status. It is the prayer of the humble ones that pierces the heavens. Such humility is not a groveling attitude, but a realism about one's relationship with God. There can be good Pharisees and rogue toll collectors—to whom we can give contemporary names. In every age, God the reader of hearts, is concerned with justice, not favoritism. Sirach could be called a collection of wisdom for the "middle classes," and therefore there was need to remind such people that they have a responsibility for justice toward the poor and disadvantaged. When society fails in this, God intervenes as a faithful covenant partner, especially on behalf of the defenseless such as widows and orphans. Our response to Psalm 34 echoes this belief that God hears the cry of the poor who call out to him in faith and praise.

A much later rabbinic story reflects the wisdom of Sirach. A man was outraged by the treatment of some of the poor in his village. He took to the street, shouting to the heavens, "God, why haven't you done something about this?" And a voice replied, "I have. I made you."

In the poignant conclusion to the Second Letter to Timothy, Paul is simple and truthful before God about his achievements, but without boasting, because unlike the Pharisee he knows that God has been the source of any success he may have had. Paul wants to pour out his life as a holy sacrificial offering to God as he prepares to make his departure from this life. The Greek word used for this "departure" suggests a soldier breaking camp or a sailor weighing anchor after a tour of duty. Paul has fought hard for the victory of the Gospel, has run the race as an apostle as well as he could. Now, as death approaches, he waits for the laurel wreath of victory which he trusts God will give him—and not only to him, but to all faithful competitors in life's olympiad. Companions may have disappointed and deserted him but, like the toll collector, Paul has the trust of the humble in the merciful love of God who during his life has rescued him from so many a "lion's mouth." God will now rescue him from the jaws of death. All glory belongs to the Lord, not to himself, says Paul.

Thirty-first Sunday in Ordinary Time

• Wis 11:22–12:2 • Ps 145:1-2, 8-11, 13, 14 • 2 Thess 1:11–2:2 • Luke 19:1-10

We are introduced to Zacchaeus as a short man, disdainful on this occasion of whatever dignity he has as he perches in a sycamore tree, literally and figuratively "out on a limb" because he wants to see Jesus. His height and the crowd milling around him have blocked his view, and no one is going to make room for Zacchaeus. Unlike last Sunday's toll collector, he is a chief tax collector and a rich one, heading up those who worked in Jericho for the occupying Roman force and taking money from the people of the land. As such, Zacchaeus was despised, socially and religiously, by the Jewish population. But he was also a single-minded seeker, "and was trying to see who Jesus was." What is suggested here is the biblical concept of "seeing," of discerning to depths beyond one's physical sight. From the beginning of Luke's Gospel it is important: for the shepherds (Luke 2:10-11,15-17), for John the Baptist (Luke 7:18-23), not only to hear but also to "see."

Jesus passes through the city of Jericho and into Zacchaeus' life, plucking him from the tree like good fruit ripe for discipleship. He looks up and sees Zacchaeus, and the urgency of his call adds to the vitality of this encounter. Even with the crowd following him, Jesus stops for just one person, up a tree, and calls him by name. He tells Zacchaeus to hurry and come down, because Jesus *must* stay at his house, and do so *today*. This imperative is associated with the urgency of Jesus' mission: for example, with the prediction of his passion (Luke 22:7) and the preparation of the Passover lamb (Luke 22:7). "To seek out and save the lost" (Luke 19:10) is also the demanding and continuing mission of the Son of Man.

Zacchaeus responds to Jesus' call with eager joy and ready hospitality that shine out against the dark background of the crowd's judgmental murmuring. Throughout Luke's Gospel and down the ages, the prophecy of Simeon will be fulfilled: Jesus is destined for the falling and rising of many, and will be a sign to be opposed (Luke 2:34). The murmurers oppose both Jesus and Zacchaeus; they are not able to see either of them for what they really are. They stereotype Zacchaeus as a sinner and, by association with him, Jesus is also judged as contaminated. When Zacchaeus stops on the way home to make a public profession of his financial dealings in front of the crowd, he speaks in the present continuous tense which suggests that his determination to give to the poor and make restitution to anyone he has defrauded was not going to be a one-shot burst of enthusiasm, but an ongoing conversion and commitment over and above the demands of the Mosaic Law. The fault does not lie in being rich, but in how one had become that way and what is done with one's wealth, as Luke reminds us in the Acts of the Apostles where Barnabas, Lydia, and Dorcas are all acclaimed disciples and people of economic means who generously share their wealth.

Jesus does not respond to Zacchaeus with any probing questions about his dealings; he gives no lengthy sermon or moralizing instruction; he just accepts his seeking and his longing to see Jesus. Are there implications here for the way in which we ritualize and celebrate the sacrament of forgiveness in today's church?

The crowd's stereotyping and judging of others are sadly familiar and contemporary. Despite the pleas of just and discerning civil and religious leaders, too many "unseeing" people are ready to categorize and condemn others. We may, for example, melt down Muslims and terrorists, Islam and evil, asylum seekers and profiteers into one hated and homogeneous group, dismiss all the unemployed as welfare cheats, or decide that those in trouble were "just asking for it."

Jesus invites himself to Zacchaeus' house; he is host rather than guest, offering the tax collector the hospitality of salvation and, calling him "son of Abraham," worthy of the inheritance of the Abrahamic promises, such is the dignity of the forgiven Zacchaeus. Jesus longs to be welcomed into our homes, our parishes, our communities, and be received there with joy—the expansive Lukan response to the Good News. Then, to our surprise, we too will find ourselves hosted into new life and love.

The murmuring crowd is nameless, and we can ask ourselves if we are in its midst: rejecting others because of prejudice and cynical superiority that "knows" what certain people are like and that they cannot change. Yet Jesus keeps company with "the lost," and the vividness of the account gives Zacchaeus a very human face. Although a meal at Zacchaeus' house is not part of the narrative, it is only a threshold away. Because Jesus so often encounters despised people and offers them hospitality, questions are surely raised for the church: "Who should we welcome into the reign of God?" and "With whom should we eat?" The answer to the first is universal; the answer to the second is an ongoing quest that dares to question.

If the story of Zacchaeus is like a small cameo portrait, the reading from the Book of Wisdom is an immense cosmic canvas that depicts God's loving concern for both the vast and the most insignificant realities in creation. Our concept of the cosmos continues to expand so far beyond the limits of second century B.C.E. wisdom, and in a way that evokes such awe and wonder that it is not surprising that some physicists and scientists are regarded as among our modern mystics. The grain of sand, the drop of morning dew, or our planet Earth, which we have seen hanging like a peaceful opal against the blue velvet of space: all this is loved by God who is "the lover of life" in its myriad forms. Because God loves what he has created, he is also merciful to it, as God in Christ is merciful to Zacchaeus. There is no contradiction between divine power and mercy; both are unlimited. Into this web of life, in which even the tiniest thread is precious,

God has woven humanity. Everything in creation is mutually dependent; we should not fail each other. In any work of art, there is always something of the genius and imagination of the artist, but these are not contained in and exhausted by any one work. So it is with the Divine Artist. Because all comes from the hand of God and his creativity, his touch is on everything and his immortal spirit in everything—but it is also infinitely more and beyond.

Psalm 145 is one of the "acrostic" psalms, which means that in the Hebrew text each line begins consecutively with a letter of the twenty-two-letter Hebrew alphabet. It is like the saying, "Everything from A to Z," when we want to express the idea of completeness. To fashion this psalm "from *aleph* to *tav*," suggests the universality of the God who is praised for his kindness and compassion—a fitting response to the Wisdom reading. Perhaps we should hear Zacchaeus singing it down in Jericho?

In the first eleven verses (not read today) of the Second Letter to the Thessalonians, Paul has been praising this church for their endurance in the face of suffering and persecution. When Jesus comes again, they will inherit the reward promised to those who are faithful. At the beginning of the second reading, Paul prays for the ongoing fidelity of the Thessalonians so that they may be worthy of their call by God. Baptized into Christ, they already share *now* in the glory of his resurrection, and their lives must give witness to this truth. Therefore, the Thessalonians should not be looking for anything spectacular, or be worried about a sudden and extraordinary intervention of God. The Day of the Lord, the Second Coming of Christ, is *not yet.* Our surprising God may come to us in apparently ridiculous places, when we are up in our own "trees," in our family or workplace, in the relationships of respect and care that we have for one another. This is how we prepare for Jesus' return in glory and the final harvesting of the fruits of discipleship . . . all in God's own good time.

Thirty-second Sunday in Ordinary Time

• 2 Macc 7:1-2, 9-14 • Ps 17:5-6, 8, 15 • 2 Thess 2:16–3:5 • Luke 20:27-38

Not *Seven Brides for Seven Brothers* in the Hollywood musical style, but one bride for all of them, death after death, is the setting for this Sunday's Gospel. Jesus is confronted by the Sadducees, the members of the religious-political party that claimed descent from Zadok, the high priest during David's kingship. Probably by the first century C.E. they were not all priests, but they were articulate, conservative and aristocratic, successful cultivators of lucrative contracts with the Roman governors and others in positions of power. This earned them privileges and the consequent desire to keep things as they were. They could smell danger to their status in the air around Jesus and in the company he kept, and so the Sadducees were determined to show that he is either crazy, irrelevant, disobedient to the Mosaic teaching and traditions, or a threat to established authority, especially their own. To have the common people excited about possibilities of change and a new quality of life is the last thing the Sadducees want. To disturb the status quo would threaten their powerful influence in the comfortable world that they have created for themselves, and this world is all that matters to the Sadducees who, unlike the Pharisees, held that there could be nothing as radically new as resurrection from the dead. A concept of an afterlife had only been clearly articulated in Judaism about two centuries before Christ, in the Second Book of Maccabees (which is today's first reading) and in Daniel 12:2, but the Sadducees' rejection underlines their conservative stance.

In the midst of all the concerns with social oppression that were current in Palestine, it is surprising that the Sadducees should raise an issue based on reference to Deuteronomy 25:2-6. They use this text as the basis of either cynicism or absurd exaggeration with which to provoke Jesus. Deuteronomy taught that if brothers live together and one of them dies leaving no son to carry on his name into the next generation, his brother must marry the widow. The first son of this marriage will bear the name of the dead husband. This was known as the "Levirate law" (from Hebrew *levir*, meaning "a husband's brother"). Its original purpose, though seeming strange to us, was to strengthen family bonds and provide for the widow. The Sadducees push the brotherly mortality rate through the six other brothers! To ridicule the idea of resurrection from the dead, the Sadducees put the question: "Whose wife will this woman be at the resurrection?"—with the implication that this question could only be considered by those who are stupid enough to believe in a such a resurrection. Any answer that Jesus gives, therefore, will show up the absurdity of this belief. About this question Walter Brueggemann comments:

> They sense, as Jesus surely knows, that resurrection is a dangerous business. It is not just about the dead person being resuscitated. It is about God's power for life that moves into all our arrangements, shatters all our categories by which we manage, control and administer. It speaks about God's will for new life working where we thought our tired deathliness would prevail. And the Sadducees plead: Please tell us that such dangerous life will not come among us.[35]

Jesus refuses to play number games or indulge in trivial biblical pursuit. The power of resurrection is utterly new and overwhelmingly transforming. To be children of the resurrection is to be ready to commit ourselves into the hands of God, accepting that our relationship with God surpasses any other human relationship, no matter how intimate and loving. Jesus shows the Sadducees that they are playing with fire when they try to use the Word of God against him. He replies in a traditional Jewish method, answering their reference to one biblical text with another, and giving it a meaning that extends beyond that of the original author. Unlike the Sadducees' biblical reference, the text that Jesus quotes is radical and central to Jewish faith: the event of the burning bush (Exod 3). Here, says Jesus, God names himself as the "I AM," the God of Abraham, Isaac, and Jacob, a God in a continuing and personal relationship with the Hebrew ancestors which transcends death. This is "a God not of the dead but of the living; for to him all of them are alive" (v. 38). This is the fierce faith that is the central focus and challenge of the Gospel. To his face, the Sadducees admit that Jesus has spoken well, has gone to the heart of the matter—but not to their hearts. It is the fear of being outwitted by Jesus that in the following two verses (not in the Lectionary reading) holds them back from asking him any more questions.

The life that transcends death is also affirmed by another family of seven brothers, the Maccabeans, who with their mother were martyred for their fidelity to their Jewish identity as it was defined by dietary laws, circumcision, and Sabbath observance during the years of the Maccabean revolt against the Syrians (165–142 B.C.E.). The Syrians were determined to force the Jews to abandon these religious traditions, and the martyrdom of four of the brothers and the strong faith they professed are described in this reading. In the responses of these brothers, the beginning of faith in the Resurrection is proclaimed: faith in the King of the world who will bring life out of their obedience to the Mosaic teaching, faith in the resurrection of the body that is being mutilated, faith in the promises of God who is a God of the living. Although it is not in the Lectionary excerpt, it would be well to read to the end of the chapter and reflect on the description of the magnificent faith of the mother of the Maccabees who encourages her sons. The Creator who shaped them in her womb, giving them life and breath, will, she says, give them life and breath again after death. Psalm 17 is a cry of the innocent to their just God that they may be saved. In the Liturgy of the Word it is a psalm that is put on both the lips of the Maccabean martyrs and our own lips, so taking on a new significance beyond the original intent of the psalmist. The Maccabeans are confident in the midst of their sufferings that they will awake in the presence of God's glory. As once they were sheltered in their mother's womb so, in the psalm's imagery, the innocent are sheltered, like vulnerable little fledglings, under the protective wings of their Mother God.

Paul also prays for the comforting and strengthening of his Thessalonians and asks for their prayers, because it is the mutual support of prayer and solidarity in action for the Gospel that will enable the community of disciples to withstand the attacks of wicked and evil people. Externals are not important; it is the heart, our deep inner conviction, that must be continually turned to God. For most of the Thessalonians, like ourselves, suffering will not be as dramatic as that of the Maccabean martyrs, but unswerving fidelity to our faithful Lord will inevitably bring its own share and type of suffering.

Thirty-third Sunday in Ordinary Time

• Mal 3:19-20a • Ps 98:5-9 • 2 Thess 3:7-12 • Luke 21:5-19

Given our contemporary technology, we are almost instantly aware of global crises—social, ecological, political, and even in outer space, that would have been beyond the imagination of the Lukan communities. Related to this can be an awareness that nothing in this world lasts forever: not the Second Temple refurbished by Herod, not the twin towers of the World Trade Center, not the idyllic holiday resorts of southeast Asia, not human lives. On the other hand, our awareness and mindfulness can be anesthetized by the bombardment of technology and the mass media. At times we seem to be citizens of a rather random, chaotic, and disordered world, desperately in need of encouragement and hope. It is such a hope that is central to this Sunday's Gospel and the discussion that is precipitated by Jesus' words about the destruction of the Temple. It would appear that from the perspective of Luke's Gospel this event lies in the future, but when Luke actually wrote his Gospel this cataclysmic event had happened about fifteen years earlier in 70 C.E. It may have been witnessed by many of those to whom Luke is writing the good news, and so the purpose of this narrative becomes not prediction but hope—hope for those who profess the Gospel in the face of its opponents. But no matter what the disasters, Jesus promises that spiritual resources to remain faithful will always be available.

Jesus warns his followers of every age against opportunists who will claim leadership in his name but, in fact, are only concerned in exploiting people when they are most frightened and vulnerable. Jesus tells those around him to watch out for, but not to be deceived by or panicked because of prophets of doom. There will be persecutions and suffering, betrayals even by family and friends, but these are opportunities to bear witness to one's faith with the eloquent wisdom that is the gift of the Spirit of Jesus, and so there is no need to worry about what to say. The One who knows us so intimately that, as

Jesus has already told his disciples, "even the hairs of your head are counted" (Luke 12:7), will never allow his faithful witness to perish.

Jesus is not forecasting the end *of* the world, but is urging his followers to confidence in and obedience to God in the face of the tough demands of their present and future discipleship that is *for* the world. In the Acts of the Apostles, Luke describes how the early church suffered the various trials Jesus speaks about in this Gospel: imprisonment, persecution at the hands of Jews and Gentiles, hatred of those who held political power. But this was countered by the bold wisdom of Stephen, the empowerment of the apostles to work miracles on hearts and bodies, their steadfastness in prison or under flogging and, ultimately, martyrdom. This is what Jesus himself suffered, and with Jesus we can let go of our precious, protected selves, confident that, no matter what the disaster, if we die into his love we will also rise with him.

Often false prophets arise who claim that the end of the world is near and that Jesus is about to come again. The turn of the millennium saw such pseudoprophets announcing specific dates for disasters, for planes to fall out of the sky, or for everything to be taken up to the heavens. It did not happen, and these people and their sects were exposed as charlatans. Yet someone, somewhere, will persist in proclaiming such sensations in the media or write about them in popular novels. On the other hand, those who are concerned about a new heaven and new earth according to the hope and vision of Vatican II, are men and women who "nurture on earth the values of human dignity, community and freedom, and indeed all the good fruits of our nature and enterprise." Then at the Second Coming of Jesus, we will find these present realities again, "burnished and transfigured" in the kingdom that Jesus will hand over to his Father.[36] Paralyzing fascination with the end time at the expense of active involvement in the present is also condemned by Paul in the Second Letter to the Thessalonians. Even though the Second Coming of Jesus was expected in the Thessalonian community's lifetime, this was no excuse for present idleness. A way of life that does not contribute to the building up of the community, weakens the community. The favorite occupation of idle people, Paul believes, is to interfere with what everyone else is doing. Paul offers his own example, not arrogantly, but quietly reminding the Thessalonians that he did not impose any financial or personal burden on them when he stayed in their communities, but paid his way, even though he was working day and night on their behalf as the servant of the Gospel (Acts 18:3).

In Chaim Potok's novel, *The Chosen*, the gentle and progressive Orthodox scholar, David Malter, speaks to his son Reuven about the pain that is in human life and its short span when measured against eternity. It is, he says, like the blink of an eye. A blink of an eye is nothing but, he continues, the person who blinks, no matter if that person's life is long or short, is of infinite value. It is not the quantity but the quality of a person's life that is important.[37] And quality consists in filling the life we are given with meaning. This is always hard work—a continuous, active endeavor before and with God, not just passive expectation that meaning will be given automatically.

Both Jesus and Paul want their followers to fill their lives with the meaning that comes from enduring in the present time of the church, not escaping into pointless and idle fascination with the future. The future is God's secret already revealed in Christ but not yet revealed in the total cosmic transformation of all creation that will come at the end of the ages. This endurance is hard work, but the reward is eternally great. Psalm 98 is an orchestration of praise for this "not yet" universal kingship of God. All the musical instruments used in the Temple liturgy, all the seas and rivers, all land and mountains, are summoned to give their voice to acclaim the justice, not the domination of the King, the Lord.

In Judaism, the short, fifty-five-verse Book of Malachi is known as "the seal of the prophets" because it closes the books of biblical prophecy in the Old Testament. Central to Malachi is the question that verse seventeen of the second chapter asks, "Where is the God of justice?" All the images in the reading are of light of varying intensity. For those who were beguiled by sorcery or adulterers, who disregard the Mosaic teaching, who had no concern for justice or for the plight of the widow, the orphan, and the poor laborer (Mal 3:5), there will be the hard punishment imaged as purifying or destroying fire. For the just, the light is healing and joyful, imaged as a winged sun disk (familiar in ancient iconography) that will rise over and shine upon them. It is a pity that the reading does not continue into the next verse and the delightful imagery of the righteous leaping freely around like young calves released from their stalls. Joyful freedom on the Day of the Lord at the end of the ages is what will come for those who seek and do justice.

Thirty-fourth Sunday in Ordinary Time

The Solemnity of Our Lord Jesus Christ, Universal King

• 2 Sam 5:1-3 • Ps 122:1-5 • Col 1:12-20 • Luke 23:35-43

Stumbling along, sometimes backtracking, we have tried to follow Jesus through another year of grace. With the many people we have met along the Lukan way we have accepted or refused the hospitality of God that invites us each Sunday to be fed at the tables of both word and sacrament so that we might go out to nourish with compassion our sisters and brothers, especially the most hungry and thirsty whose lives are in ruins. And so we come to the Sunday that closes Year C and are confronted with the stark realism of the Gospel choice for this Solemnity of Our Lord Jesus Christ, Universal King.

The end of the Jerusalem journey is not Mount Zion, "the stronghold of David" (2 Sam 5:7) and the site of Solomon's Temple and the Second Temple. We finish outside the city walls, on an unremarkable outcrop shaped like a skull, a place of execution of criminals. There Jesus is brutally enthroned and reigns as king from the cross that can never be separated from his resurrection. As was customary with crucifixion, a notation of the crime for which the person was condemned is placed on the cross, so above Jesus could be read: "This is the King of the Jews." For some this will prompt abusive derision, for others it will be a proclamation of faith. And Simeon's prophecy of division, of people's falling or rising because of Jesus, will be played out around the temple of his body (Luke 2:34). We listen and watch, knowing where we should be as his disciples, but also knowing at times the temptation to join the jeering, the mocking, the raging, or to be among the absent ones.

To the end, Jesus endures the wilderness temptations, not on the pinnacle of the Temple but from the height of the cross: "Are you not the Messiah? Save yourself" (Luke 23:39). The leaders glory in their shabby triumphalism; the soldiers hang around Jesus in a kind of bored representation of officialdom and offer sour wine to this One who drinks our sinfulness to the dregs; one of the criminals who was crucified with Jesus derides him as no good to himself or anyone else.

Around Jesus, too, are the people who will rise because of him: those who stand by not just watching, but "contemplating" their crucified king, and the other criminal who recognizes in Jesus an authority so different from that which has condemned them both. Luke gives to this man the voice of a traditional Jewish hope for the end time that was envisaged as a return to the primeval innocence and peace of the garden (or "Paradise" in the Greek translation of the Hebrew Scriptures). Throughout his life, Jesus had associated with and befriended outcasts; again and again he sought out and forgave the lost and the sinners, and he will do this even as he is dying. One of the crucified criminals rebukes the other for his cynical messianic taunting of Jesus, and dares to ask Jesus for a late invitation into the kingdom. This criminal addresses him not with the title of the inscription, but simply and familiarly as "Jesus." And then a faint, future hope becomes a "today" event of salvation for the one whom we have come to call "the good thief," the man for whom the compassion of Jesus throws open the door of the kingdom and allows him to steal paradise.

Both the first reading and the Gospel are climactic moments of king-ship in the history of the people of God. On Golgotha, Jesus is the reconcil-ing King, anointed with his own blood; at Hebron, David is royally anointed with oil. David had already been anointed king over the southern tribes of Judah (2 Sam 2:1-11), and now the elders come to him, appeal to their kin-ship with him, their "own bone and flesh," and ask him to be a reconciling king over the northern tribes of Israel also. From being the shepherd of his father Jesse's flocks, David becomes the shepherd of a united kingdom, with the special biblical concern that was expected of a king: the tender shep-herding of the weak and poor. David's authority will come from the cove-nant God makes with him, not from political power. From his house and lineage will one day come an offspring, a son whose kingdom will be estab-lished forever (2 Sam 7:11-13). On this feast the church asks us to remem-ber that royal descendant, faithful to the end as the shepherd who leads a poor criminal into the green fields of paradise.

Jerusalem was the city of King David and also the city into which Jesus was welcomed as king a short time before his passion and death (Luke 19:35-38). But it will not have him, a crucified king, within its walls. In the verses of Psalm 122 that is our responsorial psalm, the psalmist expresses the joy of the pilgrims who come to the Jerusalem Temple. Significant as it was, the Temple will be destroyed and the golden years of David's kingship will pass away, but Jesus makes the royal promise that those who are faithful in following him will be built into the new and eternal temple of his body.

We are covenanted into a spiritual kinship that is deeper than that of "bone and flesh" when, by water and the Holy Spirit, we become members of the body of Christ. As such, we are called to reconciliation and to seek-ing out and shepherding and forgiving the lost. One of the most moving and contemporary examples of forgiveness was offered by Dom Christian de Chergé, a monk of the Trappist monastery of Our Lady of Atlas, Thi-birine, Algeria. With six other members of his community, he was mur-dered on May 21, 1996, by a radical faction of Islamic fundamentalists—to the horror of the other Muslims in Thibirine. Suspecting that such an at-tack might occur, two years earlier Christian had written his *Testament*, to be opened only after his death. Opened by his family and read on what happened to be Pentecost Sunday, the closing words were addressed to the one who might be his killer:

> And you, too, my last minute friend, who would not have known what you were doing, yes, for you too I say this "THANK YOU" and this "ADIEU"—to commend you to the God in whose face I see yours. And may we find each

other, happy "good thieves" in Paradise, if it please God, the Father of us both. AMEN. IN SH'ALLAH![38]

In the reading from the Letter to the Colossians we hear a magnificent hymn to Christ. It is introduced with three verses that are clearly baptismal in origin, and remind the Colossians that through the love of God the Father they now belong to the free and forgiven community of the saints in the kingdom of the Son who enlightens and separates believers from the powers of darkness. The huge and cosmic event of Christ's universal kingship is proclaimed in the titles given to or implied about Christ.

Most commentators believe that the hymn was a pre-existing hymn, already familiar to "the saints and faithful brothers and sisters in Christ at Colossae" (Col 1:2), a region that had been evangelized from Ephesus. Originally the hymn would have had a liturgical context, and it was later pieced into the Letter. Listening to this hymn, we can easily feel that we have been transported from our simple parish churches to worship under a glorious mosaic of Christ the Pantocrator (Creator of All) that adorns so many ceilings of ancient churches and basilicas. Poetic in form and profoundly theological in its height and depth, this hymn has been the subject of so much commentary that perhaps the best way to savor it is to reflect briefly on the titles with which it names Christ.

Like all poetry, the language of the Colossian hymn is both affective and educative, urging us as a liturgical assembly to move out of the mundane to an alternative world—not an "other world" with no relevance to this world, but a "Gospel world." On this last Sunday of the church year, therefore, we praise Christ as "the image of the invisible God" who, as our bone and flesh, makes God known to us. He is "the firstborn of all creation," preeminent in his loving authority and eager to shepherd all that exists into the new creation. Because Christ is "source of all created things," creation is to be cherished. "Head of the body, the church," he is intimate with all those who, like the Colossians, are baptized into him. "Firstborn of the dead," and affirmed in his resurrection as the Beloved Son, he is the pledge of eternal life for all the sons and daughters of every age who follow him through suffering and death into a share of his eternal life. As "reconciler and peacemaker," Christ stretched out his arms on the cross to embrace everything in heaven and on earth, but especially the abandoned ones who, like the "good thief," are saved by the last Spirit-Breath pumped from his pain. During the week we might use these titles of Christ as a personal and fitting "lectio litany" with which to bid farewell to this church year.

Notes

1. Vatican II, *Constitution on the Sacred Liturgy*, article 14.

2. Cf. Patrick Kavanagh, "The Great Hunger," in *Collected Poems*, The Norton Library (New York: W. W. Norton & Company, Inc., 1973) 38.

3. George Herbert, "Ungratefulness," in *The Complete English Works*, Everyman's Library (New York: Alfred A. Knopf, 1995) 79.

4. Normand Bonneau, *The Sunday Lectionary: Ritual Word, Paschal Shape* (Collegeville, MN: Liturgical Press, 1998) 161–162.

5. Photina Rech, O.S.B., *Wine and Bread*, trans. Heinz R. Kuehn (Chicago: Liturgy Training Publications, 1998) 50–51.

6. Anselm Grün, O.S.B., *Jesus: The Image of Humanity: Luke's Account*, trans. John Bowden (New York: Continuum, 2003) 136.

7. Oscar Romero, *The Violence of Love*, trans. John R. Brockman (Farmington, PA: Plough Publishing House, 1998) 181.

8. Dianne Bergant with Richard Fragomeni, *Preaching the New Lectionary. Year C* (Collegeville, MN: Liturgical Press, 2000) 237.

9. John Paul II, Apostolic Letter, *Novo Millennio Ineunte*, January 6, 2001, art. 1.

10. Gustavo Gutierrez, "Song and Deliverance," in R. S. Sugirtharajah, ed. *Voices from the Margin: Interpreting the Bible in the Third World* (Maryknoll, NY: Orbis, 1991) 131.

11. Viktor Frankl, *Man's Search for Meaning: An Introduction to Logotherapy* (New York: Washington Square Press, 1969) xiii.

12. Shabbat 31b, cited in Lewis Browne, ed., *The Wisdom of Israel* (London: Four Square Book, 1962) 129.

13. The original of this prayer is held in the Holy Innocents Chapel, Norwich Cathedral, UK. Used with permission of the Sacrist of Norwich Cathedral.

14. Julian Burnside, Uniya Lenten Lecture, Xavier College, Melbourne, February 23, 2005.

15. Timothy Radcliffe, O.P., "Preaching to the Perplexed," *Priests and People* (December 2002) 442.

16. John Paul II, *Universal Prayer, Confession of Sins and Asking for Forgiveness*.

17. Jonathan Swift, *Gulliver's Travels* (Harmondsworth, Middlesex: Penguin Classics, 1985) 55–56.

18. Gerard Manley Hopkins, "As kingfishers catch fire," *Poems of Gerard Manley Hopkins*, ed. W. H. Gardner and N. H. MacKenzie (Oxford: Oxford University Press, 1970). By permission of Oxford University Press on behalf of the British Province of The Society of Jesus.

19. Elizabeth Schüssler Fiorenza, *But She Said: Feminist Practices of Biblical Interpretation* (Boston: Beacon, 1992) 56.

20. Cited by Dorothee Sölle in *Great Women of the Bible in Art and Literature* (Grand Rapids, MI: William B. Eerdmans Publishing Company, 1994) 272.

21. André Schwartz-Bart, *The Last of the Just* (New York: Athenaeum Publishers, 1960) 421.

22. A story shared in a night of conversation between Jews and Christians. Source unknown.

23. Augustine, "Sermon sur la porte étroite," trans. in *Bible et vie chrétienne* 51 (May–June 1963) 16.

24. Flannery O'Connor, *The Complete Stories* (New York: The Noonday Press, Farrar, Strauss & Giroux, 1972) 507–509.

25. Vatican II, *Pastoral Constitution on the Church in the Modern World*, article 45.

26. Dietrich Bonhoeffer, *The Cost of Discipleship* (London: Macmillan, 1959) 66. Gender of the 1935 original respected.

27. R. S. Thomas, "Via Negativa," *Collected Poems 1945–1990*, 4ᵗʰ impression (London: The Orion Publishing Group, 2002) 220. Used with permission of The Orion Publishing Group.

28. Henri J. M. Nouwen, *The Return of the Prodigal Son* (New York: Doubleday, 1992).

29. Henri J. M. Nouwen, *The Road to Daybreak: A Spiritual Journey* (New York: Doubleday, 1988).

30. *New Catholic Encyclopedia*, vol. XIV (Washington, D.C.: The Catholic University of America, 1967) 108–109.

31. Thomas Merton, *The Sign of Jonas* (London: Hollis & Carter, 1953) 87–88.

32. Walter Brueggemann, "The Book of Exodus," in *The New Interpreter's Bible*, vol. I (Nashville: Abingdon Press, 1994) 820.

33. Pontifical Biblical Commission, *The Jewish People and Their Sacred Scriptures in the Christian Bible*, 2002, article 5.

34. Transcript of sermon given at Westminster Cathedral, London, June 25, 1999, by Rt. Rev. John Crowley, Bishop of Middleborough.

35. Walter Brueggemann, *The Threat of Life: Sermons on Pain, Power, and Weakness* (Minneapolis: Augsburg Fortress Press, 1996) 146–147.

36. Vatican II, *Pastoral Constitution on the Church in the Modern World*, article 39.

37. Cf. Chaim Potok, *The Chosen* (Harmondsworth, Middlesex: Penguin Books Ltd, 1970) 214–215.

38. "Spiritual Testament of Dom Christian de Chergé," in *Cistercian Studies Quarterly* 32.2 (1997) 188–189.

6

"With the Gospel as our guide"

Short conversations between the Sunday Lectionary and the Rule of Benedict

At the beginning of his Rule, St. Benedict encourages his followers to "set out on this way, with the Gospel as our guide" (RB Prol 21), and in the last chapter he expresses his conviction that ". . . what page or even word of the divinely inspired Old and New Testaments is not a completely reliable guidepost for human life?" (RB 73.3). The placement of these two significant references to the importance of Scripture, the Good News or gospel of both Testaments, makes it the "bookends" that hold the Rule in place as a particular interpretation of Christian discipleship. It is also a reminder of what Benedict knew well and demonstrated in his Rule: that all our words are under obedience to the Word of God.

The first Prologue reference is in the context of "faith and the performance of good works," the practical living out of the gospel which is applicable to all the people of God, not only those who follow the monastic way of life. In his last chapter, Benedict refers to Scripture as the guidepost for *human* life, and so again universalizes the relevance of his Rule.

The following reflections, therefore, are offered as a kind of liturgical and biblical "chat room" into which those who are interested in a conversation between the Lectionary readings and the Rule of Benedict may enter to deepen their practical and human responses to the Word of God, no matter what their life situations. Like our conversations, one may be very short, another may be longer. Inevitably, over the fifty-two weeks of the year there will be some repetitions, but these will be in different contexts and can serve to emphasize what Benedict considered important.

Benedict was convinced that the biblical word cannot be locked in the past. In his own sixth-century life, he hears it speaking to his concerns for a new vision of community at the heart of a decadent society and in the midst of great social change. In such times there can be a temptation to withdraw nostalgically behind the barricades of the past, or to storm ahead into the future. Benedict was seduced by neither option. He chose a middle way, a lifestyle in which he tried to hold in dynamic balance both individual differences and commitment to community, work and prayer, nature and grace.

Originally written for men and for monastic life in the Roman church, its wisdom has also been inclusive of women who for centuries have lived and adapted the Rule to the feminine. Beyond the monastery, the Rule has proved to have ecumenical appeal for those longing for an often undefined, but strongly felt "something more." It is hoped, therefore, that there will be no gender, lifestyle, or faith tradition barriers preventing anyone's entry into this liturgical, biblical, and Benedictine "chat room." Given its original genesis and out of respect for this, references to and direct quotations from the Rule are left in the masculine.

Quotations from the Rule of Benedict (RB) are from Terrence G. Kardong, O.S.B., *Benedict's Rule: A Translation and Commentary* (Collegeville: Liturgical Press, 1996); Timothy Fry, O.S.B., ed., *RB 1980: The Rule of St. Benedict in English* (Collegeville: Liturgical Press, 1982); George Holzherr, *The Rule of Benedict: A Guide to Christian Living* (Dublin: Four Courts Press Ltd., 1994).

First Sunday of Advent

At a most significant moment in the rite of profession as described by Benedict (RB 58.20-23), the newly professed faces the altar on which he/she has placed the promises, and sings or says the *"Suscipe,"* "Uphold me according to your promise, that I may live, and let me not be put to shame in my hope" (Ps 119:116). Then the newly professed prostrates at the feet of each member of the community, for this hope lies both in God and in the very human men or women with whom he or she will live the daily challenges of fidelity to the way of life just professed. As Paul writes so clearly to his Thessalonians, it is love for one another that binds a community together. But when this love fails, and we walk through the rubble of our relationships, it is hope that can reshape our lives. This hope is not false optimism or pseudo-cheerfulness. Hope is always humble and frequently disappointed, but it is also strong.

Halfway through his chapter on "What Are the Tools of Good Works?" Benedict encourages us "to look death daily in the eye" (RB 4.47), not to be obsessed with it, but with honest directness to regard it as an untiring partner as we run toward our greatest hope: eternal life in God's kingdom.

Second Sunday of Advent

For Benedict, what cleared the way for his followers to be always on the move, yet running toward the same goal of the kingdom (RB Prol 49–50), were the three Benedictine promises. Stability of place for some but, more importantly, stability of heart for all, committed one to a continuous seeking of God in a particular way of life and a readiness to sink one's personal roots into a community, standing firm with its members in the joys and tears that are harvested in daily life. Yet because the realities of life change, stability is also a promise to accept change. Conversion of life is the constant turning and being turned to God through the gift of divine grace. In words that echo today's responsorial psalm, the Desert Mother, Amma Syncletica said:

> In the beginning there are a great many battles and a good deal of suffering for those who are advancing towards God and afterwards, ineffable joy. It is like those who wish to light a fire; at first they are choked by the smoke and cry, and by this means obtain what they seek (as it is said: "our God is a consuming fire" [Heb 12:24]): so also we must kindle the divine fire in ourselves through tears and hard work.[1]

Benedict begins his Rule with the word, "listen," a listening that is not just auditory, but is done with the ear of the heart. To listen (*obaudire*) is to obey, to be tuned in to the Word of God in the Scriptures, in those in authority, in our companions, and above all in the Word made flesh in Jesus Christ. With the "powerful and shining weapons of obedience" (RB Prol 3), Benedict's followers are to fight for that which Advent keeps before us: the establishment of God's reign over the territory of the human heart (RB Prol 49–50).

Third Sunday of Advent

John the Baptist understood his place in the world. He is able to be honest and direct with the crowd about his own limitations—he is not the Messiah—and his own gifts as one called into and out of the wilderness to listen to and proclaim the Word of God to Israel. He is also realistic about the moral limitations of those who question him, but John does not humiliate the soldiers or tax collectors; he urges them to right relationships with their God and other people. Benedict, too, understood that humility is the foundation of human relationships because it is counter to the self-love and narcissism that are still contagious modern maladies. To read the long and difficult, although central, Chapter 7, "On Humility," from this angle is helpful.

Benedict believes that the whole of the monastic life should be permeated with joy. Obedience is to be a response of gladness, a positive attitude to life rather than that characterized by grudging negativity and grumbling, for "God loves a cheerful giver" (RB 5.16-17; 2 Cor 9:7). Basic to such joy is the awareness that God has bestowed on us such unsurpassed gifts. The cause of our joy is above all the paschal mystery of Christ's passion, death, and resurrection, and so Benedict refers to this twice, not in any Advent context, but in his chapter on "The Observance of Lent." Just as John the Baptist speaks of the Holy Spirit and purification from sin, so Benedict knows that the discipline of Lent will enable the "joy of the Holy Spirit" (RB 49.6; 1 Thess 1:6) to work in the hearts of those who yearn for God and "await Holy Easter with the joy of spiritual desire" (RB 49.7; 4.46). As RB 49 takes much of its inspiration from St. Leo the Great's Lenten sermons that, as Bishop of Rome, he addressed to the wider church, Benedict's words have relevance beyond the monastic community to every Christian.

Fourth Sunday of Advent

Care of those whom society considers of little importance is part of the Advent mystery; it is also significant for Benedict. For the sick (RB 36), the poor beyond the community (RB 31.9; 66.3), there is to be special care. For the aged and children, the Rule adds its own urgency, even though "human nature is indulgent toward these two groups" (RB 37.1-2).

In the meeting of Mary and Elizabeth there is reverent love and mutual support between youth and age. Although in the monastic world there is a certain hierarchy (RB 63.1-9), Benedict twice repeats the positive relationships that should exist between the generations. The seniors are to be respected by the young, and the seniors are to love the young (RB 4.70-71; 63.10).

Christmas Day

Nowhere in his Rule does Benedict mention Christmas as such, but central to his spirituality are humility and humanity, two words deriving from the Latin *humus*—earth, soil. In the Incarnation, the Word of God takes on our human clay, earths himself in our humanity with a humility that is so radical that it can only be grasped by faith. Christ's humanity is the new "Jacob's ladder" that is stretched between heaven and earth (John 1:51; RB 7.6). It is, therefore, out of deep and faithful love of Christ, says Benedict, that one can be truly humble and true to one's humanity which matures in relationships with others. What so often makes us miss a rung as we climb the ladder of humility are the difficulties that arise in our relationships with other people, especially those with whom we live closely.

This is a prism through which we may read Chapter 7, "On Humility" with contemporary significance that extends far beyond the monastic walls.

The Feast of the Holy Family

Benedict names the abbot as "father" (RB 2.24; 33.5), usage that may have grown out of Egyptian reflection on the biblical use of *abba*. Jesus uses this to express his intimate, loving relationship with his Father. We do this relationship a disservice when we translate *abba* as "daddy," for it was not childish terminology but an expression of adult endearment between son or daughter and father. Benedict does not want an infantile relationship between the one who is abbot and the members of his community. But parents, both *abba* and *amma*, can see reflected in RB 2, "The Qualifications of an Abbot," the personal relationships which are so important for today's "holy families": the need for wise teachers who educate more by their example than by their words (RB 2.11-13); love which accommodates to individual differences; the avoidance of favoritism; respect for different personalities. And above all is the call to give birth to each other, to beget each other by the good zeal of the Gospel.

The Epiphany of the Lord

Benedict must have been very fond of the Magi, or wise men, because he believes that one of the most important signs of the validity of a person's monastic vocation was that he/she "really seeks God" (RB 58.7). This seeking is, of course, a response to God's seeking, without which the search could not begin (RB Prol 14). It is a journey of a lifetime, a journey of love (RB Prol 49-50), which makes daily demands of fidelity (RB 7.27-29) until we come to that which we seek: a share in God's kingdom.

The Baptism of the Lord

John the Baptist's call to the crowds is for a change of lifestyle. Such a change is also at the heart of Benedict's Rule and clearly expressed in the Prologue with its baptismal overtones. The monk promises to do what every other Christian is called to do by baptism: renounce sin and commit oneself to Christ (RB Prol 3), but in a particular way of life, the monastic way.

Conversion of life means readiness for a God who is often as unpredictable as a consuming fire and, through the Holy Spirit, can blow through an individual or a community to change what was thought to be the right and safe direction; to surprise with revelations of strengths and weaknesses; and to reveal Christ, the Beloved Son. This Sunday, for the first time in Luke's Gospel, we see Jesus in prayer that splits open the heavens and reveals his true identity. Benedict's twelve chapters on the Liturgy of the Hours/the Work of God (RB 8–19), reverence in prayer (RB 20), the oratory (RB 52), and the importance of the prayerful reading of Scripture or *lectio divina* (RB 48), proclaim prayer as essential to the identity of the monastic way of life and those who follow it. Every good work is to begin with prayer (RB Prol 4), and psalmody and *lectio* are to become so engrained in the monk's heart that they pulse through the whole day.

First Sunday of Lent

For Benedict, the season of Lent was to be a model for the whole life of a monk (RB 49.1). As mentioned in the reflection for the Third Sunday of Advent, the chapter "On the Observance of Lent" is influenced by several fifth-century sermons of St Leo the Great that were addressed not to monks but to all Christ's faithful. Benedict shows a compassionate realism about the lifelong struggle to be faithful to Christ. He does not expect constant perfection, but sees the days of Lent as a time of extra effort with regard to prayer, sacred reading, and fasting. Lent is also a time when we should allow our hearts to be "punctured" by love and consequently pricked into that self-denial which recognizes our sinfulness and urges us to be possessed more and more by God. This is no dour duty which is forced on the monk, but a free response "in the joy of the Holy Spirit" (RB 49.6) which has nothing to do with superficial hilarity or forced cheerfulness.

Only twice in his Rule does Benedict use the word "joy"—and both are in this chapter (RB 49.6-7). In the following verse, Benedict makes a crucial statement about the season of Lent: it is the season of "the joy of spiritual desire" because it leads us to Holy Easter.

Tears and joy, passion and resurrection, are intimately related; so too is the individual and the communal Lenten effort. Benedict strikes a delicate balance between both; if he is not to falter, the individual monk's heart needs to beat in rhythm with others who are also purposeful about the Lenten discipline. Like long-distance runners, each one paces and supports the other along the way.

Second Sunday of Lent

As Benedict well knew, no one should be content with an initial perception of Jesus, no matter how sincere or persuasive. Before each one of us lies a lifetime of seeking the God who first seeks us (RB Prol 14-15). The basic question to be asked about the genuineness of a monastic vocation is whether the newcomer truly seeks God (RB 58.7). In our own situations, the same lifelong question can be asked of every baptized Christian.

To seek God requires that we listen. "Listen" is the first word of the Rule, and it is a listening with the ear of the heart by which we try to hear the truth, God's truth, of a situation and then respond to it "with the gospel as our guide." God's truth became flesh in his Beloved Son, and to listen to him was what God asked of the disciples on the mountain of the transfiguration. For Benedict, it is also and always "Jesus alone" (Luke 9:36). Love of him must be the center of the monk's life (RB 4.21); nothing is to be preferred to Christ (RB 5.2; 72.11).

Benedict says nothing of Moses and Elijah, but he says much about the need for taking counsel. In important matters, the abbot is to do nothing without seeking the counsel of the whole community, from the youngest to the oldest, and even in lesser concerns the counsel of the senior advisors is required (RB 3.12-13). No leader is exempt from listening, although the ultimate decision will be his or hers; no one can continue to seek God without the support of sisters and brothers in the Christian community.

Third Sunday of Lent

In both the first and second Lectionary readings today there are warnings about grumbling. Benedict knew well the negative effect of this on the solidarity of a community, whether in the exodus wilderness, the Corinthian church, or his own monasteries. It may well start in a person's heart, but soon finds expression in discontented words and behavior that not only weaken an individual's ready and cheerful obedience but also infect others who live in close communal relationships (RB 5.14-19). Benedict's comments are certainly relevant to other situations beyond the monastery walls. The biblical background to Benedict's attitude we hear on this Sunday reminds us that grumbling, complaining, murmuring (all synonyms that are used in the Rule) show a lack of gratitude for the liberating grace into which we have been baptized in Christ.

The avoidance of grumbling, and the criticism of others to which this vice can lead, is a tool of good works that Benedict hands to us early in the Rule (RB 4.39-40). He recommends practical and positive ways in which grumbling may be prevented in the community: make extra help available for those who are stressed by overwork, for example, in the guesthouse (RB 53.18); give some extra food and drink to the kitchen servers before they have to attend to their brothers' needs (RB 35.12-13); be flexible and respect the climate and the local conditions when determining the amount of drink that is served, or the best times for the community's meals (RB 1980 40; 41).

On the other hand, there is the individual's responsibility to avoid grumbling by accepting that needs differ, and that according to the biblical principle in the Acts of the Apostles, "It was distributed to all according to need" (Acts 4:35). Grumbling with regard to attention to individual differences was not acceptable in Benedict's community—just as it should be unacceptable in the family or other community contexts (RB 34.1, 6-7).

Like Paul, Benedict makes his own application of the symbolism of Christ as "rock." Just as Moses struck the desert rock, which Paul interprets as Christ, so the monk is to dash any temptation to turn from following Christ. And, adds Benedict, the spiritual counsel of a wise elder may also be a helpful "rock."

Fourth Sunday of Lent

Reconciliation and forgiveness, both between God and the monk and between members of the community, are essential aspects of the monastic life. Benedict is a realist about human failings that can tempt a monk to settle down passively into a lifestyle where he obeys his own willfulness, rather than the will of God. But although he understands this, Benedict does not accept such "inertia of disobedience," which distances one from God. To turn and return to God by the labor of obedience is part of the ongoing struggle to serve Christ that Benedict puts at the beginning of his Rule (RB Prol 2-3).

Because to some degree we are all prodigal sons and daughters, Benedict frames each day with the recitation of the Lord's Prayer at both morning and evening prayer, drawing special attention to the words: "Forgive . . . as we forgive. . . ." By this each one makes a pledge to the others that he will not allow the "thorns of quarreling" to spring up in himself, and too easily and quickly spread through the community, choking its growth in holiness (RB 13.12-13; 17.8). Of course there will be failures, but no one should go off into the "far country" of sleep at the end of the day without having made peace after a quarrel (RB 4.73). Because this may be very hard to do, inside or outside the monastery, Benedict immediately adds: "And never despair of God's mercy" (RB 4.74).

Fifth Sunday of Lent

Benedict wants his monks to be good runners. Three times in the Prologue, he uses the word "run" to express the eagerness to turn away from sin that he wants his community to have (RB Prol 13; 22; 44). If the monks run from the darkness of sin into the light, energized by their good deeds and unswerving in their commitment to God, they will reach the finish line and break through to receive the prize of the kingdom (RB Prol 49-50). Just as Paul described how he was willing to share in the sufferings of Christ so that he would also share in his resurrection, so Benedict assures his followers that although the race is tough and demanding, the prize is worth the struggle (RB Prol 50).

Again in the last chapter of his Rule, Benedict uses the language of hastening toward perfection—a perfection that will take a lifetime of eager effort (RB 73.2, 8). Just as the support teams for the marathon runner are always on hand with carefully chosen sustenance for the competitor, so Benedict tells his monks what is to be their special sustenance: the Old and New Testaments, the writings of the Fathers of the Church, and his "little rule" for beginners, through which Christ will be their nourishment and guide (RB 73.3, 8).

Palm Sunday of the Lord's Passion

In his chapter on humility, Benedict quotes from Paul's great hymn in the Letter to the Philippians that we hear today. Jesus "became obedient to the point of death" (RB 7.34). In the biblical tradition, Benedict always links obedience to love of God, even when it seems that what is asked of a monk by his superior is impossible. He illustrates the painful process of arriving at responsible obedience (RB 68), not as a robot or as someone spiritually blind and immature. Dialogue with the one in authority, discernment devoid of self-interest, obstinacy, or pride—all these are acceptable, but the final and radical response is that of Christ: trust in God's help and love. Even in the encounters between juniors and seniors, the former is to obey the latter with loving concern (RB 71.4), while Benedict assures us that such obedience is no encouragement of the tyranny of the old over the young (RB 70.6)!

Given the richness of the Lectionary during the Holy Week, to abide in this word will be obedience to Christ, the Suffering Servant, to whom absolutely nothing is to be preferred for he will lead us to the everlasting life that is the promised joy of Holy Easter (RB 72.11-12; 49.7).

Easter Sunday

In the *Dialogues* 2.1², Gregory recounts that as a young hermit distanced from other Christians, Benedict had lost track of the date of Easter. Our Lord appeared to a priest and told him that while he had his Easter dinner prepared, Benedict was hungry.

Hearing this, the priest immediately went to search for Benedict—not an easy task as Gregory describes it, "amongst the steep hills and the low valleys and hollow pits"!

Eventually finding him in his cave, the two of them prayed together and talked about spiritual things. After this, the priest said to Benedict: "Rise up, brother, and let us dine, because today is the feast of Easter." Then came Benedict's charming response: "I know that it is Easter with me and a great feast, having found so much favor at God's hands as this day to enjoy your company." How wonderful it would be if we could all recognize the Easter mystery in our sisters and brothers, in their companionship and their conversation, and they could have the same experience with us.

Second Sunday of Easter

When Benedict first speaks of faith in the Prologue (21), he uses a Jewish Passover image. On that exodus night the Hebrews were to eat their meal "your loins girded, your sandals on your feet, and your staff in your hand" (Exod 12:11), in urgent readiness to obey their God who was calling them forth from slavery into freedom. So Benedict tells his community: ". . . let us belt our waist with faith that leads to the performance of good works" (RB Prol 20), in readiness for their new exodus of obedience to the Gospel. It is a faith that makes Christ visible by loving service of one another, both within and beyond the monastery.

As the way of life is faithfully followed, the monk's heart will expand and he will come running toward the kingdom. It will not be without the pain of patient effort, but this will be overcome by an overflowing love, like that which Thomas experienced before his wounded and risen Lord. Esther de Waal writes at the conclusion of her chapter on the Prologue that what the Prologue teaches us is the Paschal Christ:

> . . . the Christ risen in fullness from the grave, the risen Christ who has come through death embracing love into his fullness which is our liberation from the dark powers within and without. In Benedict's school we shall learn Christ, not in any intellectual or cerebral way but in heart and mind and feeling.[3]

Third Sunday of Easter

Columba Stewart, O.S.B., remarks that it would be fair to say that the early readers of the Rule "had a livelier sense than we do that Christian life is preparation for heaven."[4] Consequently, they were more conscious that when they were engaged in the Work of God (the Liturgy of the Hours), their choir and the choir of heaven were most present to one another (RB 19.1-2).

When there is little sense of the presence of God and his angels, when psalmody becomes a mindless monotony, and "Glory be" and "Alleluia" a routine murmur, to raise one's eyes to the vision of the Seer and the heavenly liturgy helps hearts and voices to be in harmony to the praise of God (RB 19.6-7). Indeed, in describing the dawn liturgy of praise, Benedict recommends that there be a reading from the Apocalypse (Revelation) that was known by heart (RB 12.4).

Fourth Sunday of Easter

Benedict uses the image of the shepherd to describe the role of the abbot in the community and the relationship he is to have with this "flock." This relationship is loving and compassionate, but not sentimental. Benedict is a realist about the community flock. At times it can be restive and disobedient, and the abbot must take responsibility for doing what he can to restore order, but if his efforts fail because of the recalcitrance of the sheep, he is not to blame (RB 2.7-9). Like Christ the Shepherd, the abbot should know and respect the individual differences of those in his flock so that he can call them forward to the kingdom in the way best suited to each one: "some by encouragement, some by rebuke, some by convincing argument. Let him tailor his approach to meet each one's character and understanding" (RB 2.31-32). No wonder that Benedict requires that the one elected as abbot should himself "not be restless and troubled, not extreme and headstrong, not jealous and oversuspicious," because otherwise he will drive his flock too hard and destroy them (RB 64.16-20). There is also the unstated implication that constant interference by the shepherd is not good for the flock, and this will be avoided if the abbot knows his monks well.

One of the most moving aspects of Benedict's portrait of the abbot as shepherd comes in the middle of what is often called the "penal code" section of the Rule. Although the biblical reference is to the earlier "Good Shepherd" section of John and not today's later Lectionary portion of that chapter, so significant is this image of the abbot as shepherd that it repays repeated reflection. It is with the monk who is seriously failing in his commitment that the abbot is to show the greatest compassion. Confidentiality, the counsel of other wise and experienced members of the community, the prayers of the community, all these are significant for the restoration of their brother into the heart of the community. But it is in making sure that the one who has strayed feels the strong heartbeat of his shepherding abbot's love for him that Benedict places his greatest hope for the return of this erring sheep to the flock of the community (RB 27). That flock is always, the abbot must remember, the flock of Christ, and not an exclusive abbatial possession.

Benedict's wisdom with regard to the shepherd style of leadership has many implications for today's leaders in both the workplace and across the spectrum of ecclesial communities.

Fifth Sunday of Easter

It is often easier to love those we don't have to live with every day in the family, community, workplace, but it is exactly daily, patient, warm, and mutual love that Benedict stresses. The "good zeal" about which he writes is expressed in love among those who are committed to a stable life together and will lead them to the love of God and everlasting life (RB 72). This zeal is to be both "fervent" and "practiced" love. It does not take into consideration seniority or community roles (RB 63.16-17 or 71.3-4). All the brothers are to honor one another with the practical love that bears with the unattractive personality traits or physical and psychological weaknesses of the other members of the community. Preference is to be given to the good of the other rather than one's self. Citing Eugene Manning, O.C.S.O., Terrence Kardong comments that mutual respect, support, and obedience are the horizontal expression of love in the first half of Chapter 72 of the Rule. In the second half of the chapter (RB 72.9-11), Manning sees the love of God, of the abbot as the representative of Christ, and of Christ himself, to which nothing is to be preferred, as the vertical dimension. "Finally, v. 12 summarizes and amalgamates these two 'crossbars' into the synthetic image of Christ leading the community to eternal life."[5] This is the sign that all Christians must follow, together, on our way to the kingdom.

Sixth Sunday of Easter

For the creation of a loving community (see last Sunday), Benedict adds another essential ingredient as Jesus did at the Last Supper: the seeking and pursuing of peace (RB Prol 17; Ps 34:14). He has just urged his community to "avoid evil and do good," and immediately follows this with the double biblical imperative to underline what he knew so well, and what our own experience teaches us: that no individual or community ambles mindlessly into peace. It demands what is often painful perseverance, because it is the peace of Christ that is being sought and pursued, not just an escapist or superficial harmony.

Benedict's words about peace are in social contexts that are easily transplanted outside the monastery. He is aware of the importance of details of life together that can make or break peace: the insincere greeting which is at best thoughtlessness and at worst mockery (RB 4.25); the sharp words that can slice a relationship to pieces (RB Prol 17); the effort required to make peace before the end of the day lest the wounded relationship fester (RB 4.73); the need for people in leadership positions to be peacemakers, with themselves and others. Nonviolent daily living is especially important for Benedict's abbot because to maintain peace in himself and the community, he "should not be restless and troubled, not extreme and headstrong, not jealous and oversuspicious" (RB 64.16)—a valuable checklist for leaders in any situation. Nonviolent relationships are also important for the cellarer (RB 31.1, 17), for so often peace is broken over material things. Love is well companioned by peace in any community situation.

The description of what is often called the Jerusalem Council also reminds us of how seriously Benedict took the calling together of the brothers for counsel (RB 3). This was an expression of solidarity and co-responsibility, an occasion of respectful listening to all, young and old, for the Holy Spirit may surprise by the person through whom he speaks. The abbot has the responsibility for calling to counsel, setting the agenda, listening reflectively, and making the final decision after searching his own heart. Selfish contention and defiance of the abbot's decision destroy both the counsel and peace of the community.

The Ascension of the Lord

Seventh Sunday of Easter

Benedict ends his Prologue with encouragement to persevere energetically in the race to God's kingdom. To reach this goal will mean suffering, but also companionship with Christ (RB Prol 49-50). Benedict closes the last chapter with the mention of the homeland of heaven where the monk, and every disciple, long to be (RB 73.8). The desire to be at home with Christ is not just a hazy, undefined longing, but an incentive to dynamic progress that demands the continual conversion that Benedict has spoken about in "this modest Rule for beginners" (RB 73.8). Gazing into the heavens has no place in monastic life, or any other Christian way of life, except to whet our spiritual appetite for the perfection that, although unattainable in this life, is the promise to which Christ has ascended.

Pentecost Sunday

Early in the Rule, and quoting Revelation, Benedict reminds his followers that: "Whoever has ears for hearing should listen to what the Spirit is saying to the churches" (RB Prol 11; Rev 2:7). He saw his community as an ecclesial community that must be sensitively attuned to the words of Scripture, roused and energized for running out of the darkness of sin into the light of life.

Benedict ends his chapter "On Humility" with an acclamation of the Holy Spirit as the one who works within us, healing us and making us passionate lovers of God rather than fearful slave drivers of ourselves (RB 7.67-70). Life is to be seen in positive terms of the love of Christ and the everyday disposition to do what is good—and delight in it.

As Pentecost ends the Easter season, we might well reflect again on what Benedict says about the Holy Spirit (RB 49.6). Even though he is speaking about the observance of Lent, it is the joy of the Holy Spirit that urges the monk to be generous and self-disciplined in his preparation for Holy Easter, the central mystery of faith. If such a joy should permeate Lent, then there is never any time for sadness that cannot be healed by the memory of Christ's triumph over sin and death.

The Most Holy Trinity

When Benedict's monks prayed the Work of God (the Liturgy of the Hours), at the end of each psalm they were to bow their bodies when they added the "Glory be . . . ." This was to reverence the Trinity and to make some sign that we are humbled before the immense love of the Triune God (RB 9.7; 11.3). The body has always been considered important in liturgy, for we worship as whole persons, not just talking heads.

The other significant invocation of the Trinity that Benedict mentions is at the profession of a member of the community. After the newly professed has placed his promises upon the altar, he sings the *"Suscipe"* ("Receive me, Lord") three times. The whole community repeats this verse of Psalm 119:116, adding after the third repetition the "Glory be . . . ." With the praise of the Trinity, the icon of every Christian community, ringing in his ears and heart, the newly professed then prostrates at the feet of each member of the very human community in which he is committing himself to God. Symbolically, he throws himself on the merciful love of God—love that is present, he trusts, in this community (RB 58.20-23). In different circumstances, in different communal situations, we have the same responsibility to, and trust in, one another. It is tragic if it is disappointed.

The Body and Blood of Christ

In *RB 1980* the comment is made that: "To the modern reader the scarcity of references to the Eucharist in RB may seem scandalous."[6] The reference to approaching the altar "for the kiss of peace and for Holy Communion" (RB 63.4) and the discussion of rank in the community (a custom considered inappropriate after Vatican II) probably refers to a Communion service, possibly daily. The only other time that *communio* is mentioned, in the discussion of the weekly reader (RB 38.2, 10), Holy Communion is not the central issue.

Given Benedict's balance between adaptability, his sense of the importance of listening to what the Spirit is saying to the churches (RB Prol 11), and the significance of the liturgical life in his monasteries, he would surely approve of the adaptation of the liturgical tradition which gives it "new vigor to meet the circumstances and needs of modern times"[7] when the celebration of Eucharist may not always be available. But what is always available and necessary is that which makes for communion in the Body of Christ: our love for one another, which is taken to and flows from the liturgical action of Eucharist. Without this, no matter how often the Eucharist is celebrated, there is only an empty ritual and, as Paul says even more strongly, ". . . all who eat and drink without discerning the body, eat and drink judgment against themselves" (1 Cor 11:29).

Second Sunday in Ordinary Time

The mother of Jesus is not mentioned in Benedict's Rule, but today we have heard the last words that she speaks in John's Gospel: "Do whatever he tells you." For Benedict, such obedience to Christ is the hub of the monastic life, an obedience that "is characteristic of those who hold Christ more precious than all else" (RB 5.2). A few words, a lifetime of living them without any obviously spectacular achievement, an unflinching acceptance of her unique share in the suffering and glory of Christ: this was the calling of the mother of Jesus. In this she is a model and guide for all who follow the "unspectacular" monastic way of life.

In communities that follow the Rule of Benedict, therefore, the tradition has developed of always turning to an icon of Mary at the conclusion of Night Prayer (Compline) when the "Salve Regina" or another seasonal

Marian anthem is sung. Guests in the community often comment about how moved they are by this moment of communion with the Mother of the Church, with the community, and with one another.

Third Sunday in Ordinary Time

The poor, the "little ones," those considered not very important as members of the body politic or the Body of Christ, were a special concern for Benedict. As Jesus did for the synagogue assembly at Nazareth, he holds up a mirror to our social consciences. Early in his Rule, in the chapter which asks and answers "What Are the Tools of Good Works?" his communities are urged "to assist the poor" (RB 4.14), named in the next verses as the naked, the sick, those who have died. The latter part of the chapter is a summary statement of what we should work hard at: "Come to the aid of those in trouble. Console the sorrowful" (RB 4.15-19).

Paul would approve of Benedict's awareness of the Body of Christ and the communion of members in it, which he shows by his attitude to the sick and to guests. "The sick are to be cared for before and above all else, for it is really Christ who is served in them" (RB 36.1). All guests who arrive at the monastery are to be received "as Christ" (RB 53.1, 15). The cellarer, the "business manager" of the monastery is one who "should lavish great care on the sick, the children, guests and the poor" (RB 31.9). What Benedict says about "The Aged and Children" (RB 37) adds its own Christian urgency to human concern for the young and the old (RB 37.1-2). It is the poor who are to be greeted by the porter with "Thanks be to God!" or "Bless me," for they are truly a blessing for the community (RB 66.3-4).

Today there is need for us to listen to Jesus, Paul, and Benedict in the face of the tragedies of child abuse and slavery, the too common disregard for the frail aged and people with disabilities, the fear of strangers, the people who are "different" to us in culture, ethnicity, or religion. For those with any kind of authority, the abbot is a model of good news for the physically, spiritually, or socially weak. He is to love, heal, absorb the hurt, even to the extent of laying down his life, as did the Good Shepherd (RB 27.6).

Fourth Sunday in Ordinary Time

The importance of love permeates the Rule of Benedict. He puts love of God and neighbor at the head of the fourth chapter, "What Are the Tools of Good Work?" and, as so often in the Rule, the quotation of the biblical word guides and governs the whole chapter, as if to place under *the* Word all Benedict's other words about the way in which lives are to be shaped.

Love of one another is expressed in the everyday service of those in the kitchen (RB 35.6), the mutual respect between the young and the old (RB 63.10), and the love of the abbot for his brothers, despite their faults. In this love he is to be just and impartial (RB 2.22; 64.11), but for those who are struggling with their religious commitment, the abbot has the added responsibility of reaffirming his love and leading the community to prayer for them (RB 27.4). With a lovely turn of phrase, the porter is encouraged to greet all those who knock at the door, but especially the poor, "with the warmth of love" (RB 66.4).

It is in chapter 72, "The Good Zeal That Monks Ought To Have," that Benedict's concern with love becomes a hymn of praise, as it had for Paul. The brothers, the abbot, Christ, God—all are wrapped together in language that is warm and energizing but also makes tough demands. Like Paul, Benedict knows that he is addressing a community of saints and sinners, with a potential for love or evil, good zeal or bitterness. Beyond the monastery, in ourselves, we know the truth and challenge of that.

Fifth Sunday in Ordinary Time

In the Prologue to his Rule (RB Prol 14), Benedict describes the initiative that God takes with his workers. To seek God is the strong focus of the monastic and Christian life (RB 2.35; 58.7), but before we can begin this search, God comes seeking us, just as he sought Isaiah, Paul, and the first apostles. The Isaian phrase, "Here I am," is also quoted in the Prologue (RB Prol 18), but here the speakers are reversed, and it is God (as in Isa 58: 9) who assures the faithful disciple of his loving presence.

Terrence Kardong comments on this call:

> Since the worker is called "out of a multitude," this may seem like a symbol of a special vocation, but the content does not suggest that meaning. If it (the Prologue) is a baptismal catechesis, it is addressed to all Christians. And since it offers nothing less than life (v. 15), it is addressed to all persons without exception.[8]

Sixth Sunday in Ordinary Time

It is perhaps surprising, given Benedict's emphasis on *lectio divina*, that Benedict does not quote from Psalm 1 in his Rule, but the importance of being rooted in and at home with God that the psalm stresses is the first of the Benedictine vows (RB 58.17). Mobility rather than stability is a characteristic of much contemporary life. We move to second and third or more careers; we buy and sell houses more frequently; business may involve several international flights each week; the phones we carry are mobile. But what is also familiar for many of us is the restlessness of spirit that the monastic writers described as *acedia*.

For women and men that pronounce this vow, it does not necessarily mean lifelong physical stability in one monastery, although for some that will be their particular expression. Whatever the external expression, it is stability of the heart that is more important and deeper. Paul Wilkes, a husband and father of two sons, speaks of his discovery of monastic wisdom, especially through the Cistercian community of Mepkin Abbey, South Carolina, and its relevance for him in his own family life. Of stability he writes:

> Stability is woven of the ability to stay put and yet never lose the explorer's desire for new experiences. It is not merely a leaden weight meant to anchor us so securely that we might never go astray . . . Rather, stability's goal is that we might see the inner truth of who we are and what we are doing.[9]

Then, says Benedict, our hearts overflow with unspeakable, expansive love, urging and enabling us to continue running toward the kingdom of God.

That love is expressed in active concern for the poor, the "blessed" of the Beatitudes. Luke's "Sermon on the Plain" repeats the good news to the poor that he proclaimed in the Nazareth synagogue (Luke 4:18), and so we might return to the reflection for the Third Sunday in Ordinary Time to remember how important the presence and service of the poor are to a Benedictine community. We could meditate on this, rock and chew its sweetness, and allow ourselves to be permeated with the wisdom of the Word which will help us to accept the challenge that we become a stranger to the world's ways and "woes," and "prefer nothing to the love of Christ" (RB 4.20). So often he comes to us in the poor and pilgrims, those who have nothing but are seeking something or Someone, "for Christ is more especially received in them; for the very fear of the rich wins them respect" (RB 53.15).

Seventh Sunday in Ordinary Time

One effective but dangerous tool that Benedict hands his monks is to "Love your enemies" (RB 4.31), quoting directly from Luke and Matthew (Luke 6:27 and Matt 5:44). To ensure that this is not just a romantic idea, Benedict adds a series of maxims that make this love explicit and practical. They are easily recognizable as copied from the Sermons on the Plain and on the Mount: no repaying wrong with wrong, but suffering what is done to oneself with patience; not returning insult for insult, but rather offering a blessing. It is mindfulness of the love of Christ and his overwhelming mercy that enables us to pray for our enemies or pray to the Father for his forgiveness of them. "And finally, never lose hope in God's mercy" (RB 4.72-74)—for us, in difficult situations, as well as those who are difficult.

Living a nonviolent life makes daily demands in every lifestyle. Every morning and evening Benedict called for the Lord's Prayer to be recited in choir "on account of the thorny scandals that have a habit of springing up" (RB 13.12). The verse to which Benedict draws particular attention is "Forgive us as we forgive" (RB 13.13), for he saw this was to be a pledge the community made to each other, and a very necessary one in any situation of close living. Whether monastic, married, or single, this is the privileged prayer with which to frame our lives.

It is told of Abba Moses that he was invited one day to a council at Scetis which was called to pass judgment on an erring brother, but he refused to go. When they pleaded with him, he got up and took with him a leaking jug filled with water. When he arrived and the other brothers asked him, "What is this, Father?" Abba Moses replied: "My sins run out behind me and I do not see them, and today I am coming to judge the errors of another." When they heard this, they forgave the brother.[10]

Eighth Sunday in Ordinary Time

Already in his Prologue, Benedict is warning his followers that vicious, deceitful talk can damage the spiritual quest (RB Prol 17). By ending this verse with the encouragement to make peace one's quest and aim, he establishes a link between just and gentle speech and peace in the monastery and the desire for eternal life. For "monastery" we can easily substitute family, workplace, friendship—wherever our own experience teaches us the damage that can be done to our relationships by a vicious, uncontrolled tongue.

Benedict recognizes that both false and truthful speech are matters of the tongue and the heart (RB 4.27-28). Early in his Rule he devotes a whole, if short, chapter to "On Silence" or as *RB 1980* entitles the chapter, "Restraint of Speech" (RB 6). This chapter may not be very attractive to a noise-addicted society, nor is it particularly rich in its spirituality, but in its practicality it is significant. Garrulous speech must be discouraged, for this makes for an audience of one—the speaker. The mouths of those who tell crude jokes and psychically enervating banter are to be "clamped shut" with the gag of obedience. Benedict does not intend his monasteries to be dour, unhappy places, but laughter *at* and *about* others can be cruel (RB 7.59-60).

Speech is related to silence, and just and gentle speech rises from a quiet heart. It is the kind of speech that Benedict expects from the cellarer who, if he cannot supply what a monk asks for, should at least offer him a kind word (RB 31.13-14). The porter, the "first impression" person, is to greet all who come to the monastery with a blessing, with gentleness, and with the warmth of love (RB 66.1-4). We all know what a blessing it is when someone offers us the proper word for the proper time; on the other hand, we also know the pain inflicted by those who have an almost psychotic compulsion to respond with the negative, judgmental, or bitter word.

Ninth Week in Ordinary Time

Solomon, Paul, and, above all, Jesus, are hospitable to the stranger, ready to welcome the "outsider." For Benedict, too, hospitality was a significant aspect of his community's life, to be extended especially to the pilgrim and the poor; a Benedictine community without guests is an atypical community. Benedict places the whole of chapter 53, "The Reception of Guests," under the obedience of the Gospel precept: "All guests who arrive should be received as Christ, for he himself will say, 'I was a stranger and you took me in'" (RB 53.1). "To receive" here has the meaning of "to cherish," and is indicative of a hospitality that is not manipulative or controlling.

Kathleen Norris affirms this quality of hospitality when she writes of her own experience:

> For the guest the most refreshing thing about monastic hospitality is that it does not seek to turn you into a 'monklet', a celibate, or a Roman Catholic, but guides you into honoring your own vows, in my case as a married Presbyterian lay preacher and deacon.[11]

In a guest house we might well find a bag lady, a theologian, a backpacker, a contemporary pilgrim or two on a journey of self-discovery, a regular retreatant . . . all are treated with equal respect, all are equally welcome.

Tenth Sunday in Ordinary Time

In his Letter to the Galatians, Paul describes himself as being "zealous" (sometimes more weakly translated as "enthusiastic") for the traditions of his ancestors, a zeal that led him into violence against the followers of the Way (Phil 3:6). The seeds of intolerance, present in all religions, need to be plucked out by humility and mercy. Yet there is also another zeal to which

Paul was converted: the loving, forgiving zeal of his crucified and risen Lord. This is the subversive zeal that destroys violence, but not the violent, with the mystery of the cross, which is a mystery of love.

The mention of zeal prompts a memory of Benedict's wonderful chapter 72, "The Good Zeal that Monks Ought to Have," which begins with a contrast between good zeal and bitter zeal. Good zeal means that the members of a community have a sacrificial and selfless love for one another, just as Christ had for us. This will happen if Christ's way of acting is their absolute preference (RB 72.11). The opposite to this is the bitter, aggressive zeal that can lead to the "persecutions" in any human group—and especially in the family, religious community, or parish where the good zeal is to be expected. Many of the Fathers of the Church describe the "violence" of evil zeal as the bitter or hostile silence which puts someone "on ice," or the dismissive words or gestures which accompany an attitude of aloofness and pained patience. None of this is as dramatic as Paul's persecuting zeal but, as we probably know from experience, it is a violence that can be devastating and destructive of relationships.

Eleventh Sunday in Ordinary Time

In the house of Simon the Pharisee there was both hospitality from the uninvited guest and inhospitality from the one who was supposed to be the host. The hospitality that Benedict teaches is a holy event; Christ is to be welcomed with warm love rather than polite boredom (RB 66.1), with friendly words rather than officiousness (RB 31.13-14). Hospitality is costly, not in terms of money, but in the demands it makes on our hearts, our time, and our personal resources.

As Luke makes clear in the gospel of this Sunday, first-century Palestine had its socio-religious rituals of hospitality; so did fifth-century monasticism as a sign of "all courtesy of love" (RB 53.3). There was prayer, the bow, the prostration, the kiss of peace, and the abbot's washing of the guest's hands, and the most significant washing of feet by both the abbot and the whole community. Never must Christ, present in the guest, be ignored (RB 53.1, 7, 15), and especially in those who might be judged unfavorably by society: the poor and the strangers.

To respect and forgive one another is an act of hospitality, a response to the hospitality of God who welcomes the sinner into divine love. After Benedict's condemnation of hatred, jealousy, envy, quarreling, and arrogance, he encourages his community to handle the last tool of good works: "And never lose hope in God's mercy" (RB 4.65-74).

Joan Chittister comments that "Hospitality is the way we turn a prejudiced world around, one heart at a time,"[12] a way in which we may spread the peace with which Jesus sent out the woman of this Sunday's gospel.

Twelfth Sunday in Ordinary Time

"Deny yourself in order to follow Christ," is the gospel tool which Benedict hands us in his Rule (RB 4.10). But true Christian self-denial is never a matter of asceticism divorced from practical charity. Packed beside the tool just quoted are those instruments for shaping a better life for the poor, the naked, the sick, and to offer support and comfort at the times of death and other sorrows or troubles (RB 4.14-19).

Benedict encouragingly describes his Rule as "a modest Rule for beginners" (RB 73.8), and the way of life that he encourages is not one of dazzling spiritual experiences or dramatic suffering. These may come, but what is more important is the apparently "unexciting" reality of fidelity to the gospel, a willing commitment to the "daily-ness" of sharing in the sufferings of Christ. This will happen especially through patience: that vigilant, active endurance demanded of a follower of Benedict from the time of seeking entry into the community (RB 58.3), through perseverance when challenged by the hardships of injustice (RB 7.35), sickness (RB 36), honest but difficult dialogue with those in authority (RB 68.2), and in the bearing of weaknesses of body or behavior which are inevitable in close relational living (RB 72.5). When such vigorous effort fails, there sets in the insidious *ennui*, that unenergetic boredom, dreaded by spiritual guides, that slowly erodes commitment.

Thirteenth Sunday in Ordinary Time

Benedict quotes from Galatians in his chapter on "What Are the Tools of Good Works?", warning about the danger of carrying out "the urgings of the flesh" (RB 4.59; Gal 5:18). We are too readily inclined to put a sexual or hedonistic interpretation on this Pauline reference, but for Paul, "the flesh" referred to all that is opposed to God in the human person, especially that self-seeking desire that can destroy a community. Immediately after this, Benedict hands us the tool with which his monks are to work: "Hate your own will" (RB 4.60), a rather startling injunction, but one that highlights the common concern of both Paul and Benedict for the Other, the will of God, and for the community. This is obedience.

Just as Paul assures the Galatians that if they allow themselves to be led by the Spirit they will not be self-indulgent, so Benedict ends his chapter

"On Humility" with one of his few references to the Holy Spirit. As Esther de Waal comments on this verse: "It is through the cleansing and leading of the Spirit that I shall stay open to growth, growth into freedom, growth into love."[13]

Fourteenth Sunday in Ordinary Time

Benedict has some interesting comments that echo the missionary instructions in today's gospel, although he is thinking more of the ministry that his followers owed to one another in community. It also has implications for our relationships in the family, the community, and the workplace.

Early in his Rule he is critical of those monks whom he calls "gyrovagues" (RB 1.10-11). They are the ones who drift around aimlessly, never settling down. They have no desire to stay in the same house, no intention of stability of mind or heart, no commitment to people or place as Jesus requires of those sent on his mission. This is not to be confused with the genuine seeking of God, but with the temptation that, then and now, can make us contemporary gyrovagues, circling around in a dizzy attraction to the latest alternative spirituality, only to drop it and move on to another when the demand is too great or a more appealing option presents itself.

Benedict well knew the importance of our words, and would have nothing to do with time-consuming social dallying and gossip, what he describes as the habit of long-winded conversations, empty babbling, and the kind of joking that provokes raucous laughter (RB 4.51-54). This can become both psychically exhausting and destructive of a hospitable or contemplative atmosphere.

Fifteenth Sunday in Ordinary Time

Although Benedict only uses the word "compassionate" twice, when speaking of the care of the elderly and children (RB 37.1), and the attitude of the abbot to the brother who is failing seriously in commitment to the monastic way of life (translated as "sympathy" in RB 27.9), the attitude of compassion is woven into the whole fabric of Benedictine life. After references to the handling of specific tools: "Assist the poor. Clothe the naked. Visit the sick. Bury the dead" (RB 4.14-17), Benedict widens his vision to include those who need their lives to be handled gently when they are in any kind of trouble or sorrow (RB 4.18).

The sick, says Benedict, are to be the special care of the community, "before and above all else" (RB 36.1), because in them Christ is served with a personal as well as a functional relationship. The sick, however, are not excused from their own particular challenges of overcoming self-centeredness, petulance, and excessive demands (RB 36.4-5). The abbot is to be merciful and so exercise authority in a way that puts mercy before judgment (RB 64.9-10, 12). The cellarer, the manager of the material resources of the community, has to lavish great care on the sick, the children, the guests, and the poor, because he, like the innkeeper of the parable, will be asked by Christ for an account of his service to these vulnerable people when he returns (RB 31.9). One of the most beautiful expressions of love is the way in which Benedict wants the poor person to be greeted by the porter: "Filled with the gentleness of the fear of God, he must quickly respond in the warmth of charity" (RB 66.4) to those who, in their need, are a blessing to the monastery.

Benedict holds up a mirror to our social consciences in which we may see the need for compassion reflected in the tragedies of child abuse and slavery, in disregard of the frail aged and people with disabilities, and in the emphasis on productivity as an indicator of a person's worth. And in the exercise of the Church's authority, at all levels, mercy should surely be put before judgment.

Sixteenth Sunday in Ordinary Time

In his Prologue to the Rule, Benedict quotes from today's responsorial Psalm 15 four times (RB Prol 22–24, 39). He sees the "tent" to which we are running as the kingdom of God and, repeating the words of the psalmist, the right relationships with other people as the track on which we must run to reach this goal. We heard how Abraham was eager, quick in his response to the strangers; Benedict also uses the language of haste to impress on his followers the eagerness with which they should welcome the opportunity to return to God, running unswervingly and lovingly, until the end of the race in the kingdom (RB Prol 2, 13, 44, 49; 73.8).

Chapter 53, "The Reception of Guests," is modeled on the hospitality of Genesis 18. The superior or the brothers hurry out eagerly to meet the guests, and offer them a warm, courteous, and enthusiastic welcome, for in the guest, especially the poor and pilgrims, Christ is welcomed. Through rituals and personal contact, the members of the community extend to the stranger the merciful and reconciling hospitality that has been offered to them—and to all of us—as strangers and people without hope who have been brought near to God through the sacrifice of Christ (Eph 2:12-13). But the practicalities that will enable a community to integrate a ministry of hospitality with the other demands of their way of life are not forgotten.

Benedict's chapter on hospitality is one of the best loved and perhaps most relevant to society beyond the monastery, especially in our own time that knows so much loneliness and hostility. A listening ear, a quiet place for prayer, a healing space to balance the frenetic clutter of everyday pressures, an environment of simple beauty, are what many people are seeking today. Monasteries and religious communities are surely called to be open places of hospitality, oases in a world that knows so much alienation and hostility.

Seventeenth Sunday in Ordinary Time

Benedict says little about the nonliturgical prayer of his monks, but that does not mean he considered it unimportant. Rather, the Work of God (the Liturgy of the Hours), sacred reading (*lectio divina*), and personal prayer flow into and out of each other. Personal prayer and communal prayer were but the continuing ebb and flow of the sense of God's presence that was to seep through the whole monastic day.

The oratory of the monastery, although primarily the place of the Work of God, was also available for the monks' quiet private prayer (RB 52.4). When Benedict wrote about prayer, he often linked this to the experience of tears that were the result of compunction (RB 4.56-57; 20.3-4; 49.4). Taken literally, this meant a sharp jab that wakes up someone and "punctures" their laziness or drowsiness. Spiritually, our hearts need to be goaded, awakened, and purified, especially by the Word of God. Benedict is not advocating dramatic or flamboyant behavior. "Short and pure" prayer (RB 20.4), with a focused awareness of God's presence, is to be the norm. As Columba Stewart, O.S.B., writes: "Purity of heart, tears of compunction, intention of heart: these simple but deeply traditional synonyms for prayerful awareness of God shape Benedictine prayer."[14]

Benedict also encouraged his monks to "Pray for your enemies for the love of Christ" (RB 4.72), for those who are finding their commitment difficult (RB 27.4), those with demanding, if ordinary, community tasks such as kitchen service (RB 35.15) or the reader at meals (RB 38.2), and those who are sent on a journey (RB 67.1, 2, 4).

Eighteenth Sunday in Ordinary Time

Benedict was passionately committed to the community of goods, not self-sufficiency, as the ideal after which his monks were to strive. A monk was to receive everything that he needed from the abbot, the "father of the monastery" (RB 33.5). This lack of possessiveness flowed, therefore, from obedience. It can be seen as a reminder of the truth at the heart of the

Parable of the Rich Fool, namely, that God is the giver of all good gifts. Benedict recognized that material goods are required for work, study, personal needs of ministry and health, as is obvious from the positioning of chapter 33, "Whether the Monks Should Consider Anything Their Own," immediately after the chapter about the tools and goods of the monastery (RB 32) and before discussing respect for the individual needs of the members of community (RB 34). The cellarer's role in the community is founded on the way he treats and relates to those who ask him for material things (RB 31), making it obvious that relationships are at the heart of Benedict's concerns with material possessions: relationships which handle the goods of the monastery with the reverence due to the holy vessels of the altar, and handle people with humble service, offering a kind word as the best gift if, for example, the cellarer has to refuse material goods which are unavailable (RB 31.13-14). The cellarer is to handle himself without any greed, avarice, or extravagance. Benedict was very well aware that anyone who deals constantly with material goods can be tempted, like the rich fool, to avarice and greed, with disastrous results for family, community, and workplace relationships.

Nineteenth Sunday in Ordinary Time

Behind one of the qualifications of an abbot (RB 2.30) stands the last verse of this Sunday's gospel, for like the steward to whom much has been entrusted by God, much will be expected of him in return. The leader is to be *abba/amma*, a father/mother who loves and nurtures the community, and stands answerable to both God and the community for the exercise of his/her role. With them both, the abbot is still a servant. This reminder can be expanded to apply to any Christian in a leadership position: in parish, community, family, or business.

It is not easy to walk the tightrope between the stewardship of material goods that is as mundane, for example, as ensuring that the clothing and footwear distributed fit the monk (RB 55) or that the tools of the monastery are well cared for (RB 32.1-3), and also practice the delicate art of counseling those who are failing seriously in their commitment (RB 27; 64.10-15). If he is a good steward, the abbot neglects neither the practical nor the spiritual. He integrates both dimensions into his own spiritual life, or delegates aspects of his charge to other trustworthy members of the community such as the deans (RB 21.1-3) and, especially, the cellarer (RB 31).

When speaking of Benedictine stewardship, Norvene Vest uses a beautiful term. She names it a ministry of "tender competence."[15]

Twentieth Sunday in Ordinary Time

As we saw in the reflection for the Sixteenth Sunday, Benedict also speaks in the language of haste and running. Benedictine life is no lethargic stroll after Jesus. It is to be a zealous discipleship. In its derivation, "zeal" has the sense of a burning urgency, the spiritual energy about which Benedict spoke in the Prologue and which he links to the unswerving race toward the kingdom (RB Prol 44; 48-50). In her commentary on chapter 72, "The Good Zeal That Monks Ought To Have," Esther de Waal writes that Benedict:

> . . . does not want a collection of passive ciphers but a dynamic and alive people. This primary spiritual energy, which brings light and fire, passion and fervour, and which prevents what otherwise be simply plodding, he calls a very ardent love. The Latin *ferventissimo amore* suggests a burning, white-hot love.[16]

It is by love for other members of their community that the brothers cheer each other along in the race to the kingdom, despite their faults of character or weakness of body. Good zeal is also expressed in the love of God, of their abbot—and in Christ, to whom nothing whatever is to be preferred.

Self-love and bitterness are part of the "bad zeal" that will weigh down and hinder progress. It is an evil which all must guard against, even the abbot, lest "the flames of envy and jealousy" sear his soul (RB 65.22).

Twenty-first Sunday in Ordinary Time

The hospitality of Benedictines to the nations is witnessed by the inscription in the grotto of the *Sacro Specco* (Holy Cave) in the Monastery of St. Benedict at Subiaco. On the wall beside the steps that lead to and from the grotto, at this foundational place, there is a plaque which reads:

> Know that from this grotto in which St Benedict, anticipating the apostolic work of his disciples, used to teach the shepherds words of eternal life, came forth many monks who, imitating their master, either converted most of the western nations to Christ or, already converted, made them grow in their faith.

> St Augustine preached the gospel to the Angels
> St Boniface to the Germans
> Ss Ansgar & Rembert to the Danes and Swedes
> St Leander to the West Goths in Spain
> St Suitbert to the Frisians & Westphalians

Ss Ludger & Sturmius to the Saxons
St Adalbert to the Bohemians & Poles
St Willibrod to the Bataves
St Amandus & Livinius to the people of Flanders
St Otho to the Pomeraniums
St Gerard to the Hungarians
St Bruno to the Prussians
Ss Kilian & Rupert to the Franks
St Wolfgang to the Austrians & people of Noricum
St Boniface, surnamed Fiery, to the Russians
St Corbinium to many peoples of France & Germany

Later on, when America and Australia were recently discovered, the disciples of Benedict also went there to preach the faith.

In remembrance of the beginning of the Benedictine apostolate this monument is here consecrated A.D. 1854.

Since then of, course, the missionary spirit of Benedict's disciples has taken the gospel to many more places, especially in Asia, Oceania, and Africa.

Twenty-second Sunday in Ordinary Time

Benedict begins "On Humility" (RB 7.1), with the words that we hear in today's gospel: "All who exalt themselves will be humbled, and those who humble themselves will be exalted" (Luke 14:11). When Benedict begins in this way, it is as though he intends to put all his own words under obedience to the Word of God, and in fact his frequent references to Scripture in nearly every verse of that chapter underline the fact that Benedict gives priority to the Word of God for the understanding of and progress in humility.

Humility is an expression of hospitality that makes room for others and, like "humanity," is derived from the Latin *humus* (earth, soil). Humility is acceptance of being grounded in our own imperfect humanity, to accept that we are not gods, and to accept the imperfect humanity of others.

In *Truthful Living: Saint Benedict's Teaching on Humility*, Michael Casey, O.C.S.O., writes insightfully:

A first approach to understanding humility is to see it as that total self-acceptance typical of untarnished humanity. Those who are humble experience no shame. They do not need lies and evasions to inflate their importance in the eyes of their associates, or to buttress their self-esteem. They have overcome the tendency to regard others as competitors or rivals, and so they work with whatever they have, and waste no time envying those who possess different qualities. The humble are equally content with both the gifts and the limitations that come from their nature or their personal history. Humility brings with it a fundamental happiness that is able to cope with external difficulties and sorrows.[17]

Chapter 7 is, therefore, basically a chapter about right relationships with God and with one another. In this brief reflection it would be a disservice to this long and important chapter to do other than to encourage the prayerful reading of the "twelve-step" climb up to "that perfect love of God which drives out fear" (RB 7.57), reflecting on the biblical texts, the gospel reversals, and the wise human experience on which the ladder of humility is raised to help us in our climb to heaven.

Twenty-third Sunday in Ordinary Time

Just as Jesus wanted us to have no illusions about the demands of the gospel, so Benedict was also clear about perseverance if this commitment to Jesus was to be expressed in the monastic way of life. Wild enthusiasm was not what Benedict required. Newcomers to the monastery were not received as though they were God's gift fallen from heaven onto the monastic doorstep. Rather, they were kept on the threshold, knocking at the door for several days, until persevering patience was rewarded. Today's threshold experience may be expressed more in the way of spiritual direction and psychological testing, but there is still no bounding-over-the-entrance experience! When admitted to the novitiate, the candidate was to be left in no doubt about the hardships and difficulties that will lead to God—but realistic discussion of these is a kinder way of formation than dishonest fostering of immature fervor. Neither is the emphasis on perseverance only gloomy and negative. The goal of this commitment was described as the culmination of the Prologue: the race along the way of God's commandments, with hearts filled with the "unspeakable sweetness of love" until, through death, "we will participate in the passion of Christ through patience so as to deserve to be companions in his kingdom" (RB Prol 49-50).

For Benedict, perseverance is another expression of stability, the first of the Benedictine promises. It is that ability to keep on going through the desert stretches of our lives, first by our abiding in the God of steadfast love who is committed to the world in Christ; and second, through the encouraging companionship of those who also take up their cross daily, following Jesus and walking not so much side by side but heart-to-heart with one another. This is a reality not confined to the monastery, as a layman and father writes:

Which of us hasn't been tempted to give up emotionally when presented by an unpleasant, irrational child, parent, relative, friend, or an impossible situation? How often as a father have I silently vowed to do the minimum required of me? I would no longer invest myself; it was more than I can take! I would await the return of reason or changed circumstances.[18]

Stability calls us to do the best we can in the place where we are.

Twenty-fourth Sunday in Ordinary Time

In his remarkable Chapter 27, "The Abbot's Preoccupation With the Excommunicated," Benedict refers to the parable of the shepherd who left the ninety-nine sheep to go after the one that was lost (RB 27.8-9). To show special concern and love for those who were straying from the monastic way of life was to be the abbot's great and most heartfelt responsibility. Benedict is realistic about human failings and inadequacies, and what is born from this realization is a wonderful model of pastoral care for those in leadership roles, a model applicable both within and beyond the monastery. No Christian community—small or large, parochial or universal—is perfect; none should consider themselves an elite. If it is our weakness that calls forth for us the compassion of Jesus, the physician and shepherd, so this is what should call forth compassion for one another in those who follow Jesus' way.

The abbot's pastoral care is illustrated in a story told about Abbot Lupicinus (died c. 480). As he was praying one night in the oratory:

> Two brothers enter the oratory, having agreed to meet there in order to discuss how they can run away from the monastery under cover of darkness. They do not notice the abbot, who suddenly speaks loudly out of the darkness: 'At least give me the parting kiss!' They start up in fright. The holy man, however, addresses each by name, stretches out his hand, takes them affectionately by the chin, and kisses them. Then he says no more, but kneels down and, in his fatherly love, reaches for the weapon of prayer.[19]

Both monks call on Christ for forgiveness and go back to bed, their humiliation because of the abbot's love being considered sufficient penance!

Twenty-fifth Sunday in Ordinary Time

Benedict's "household manager" is the monastic cellarer, and the description of his personal qualities and his role in Chapter 31 is one of the most charming in the Rule. The abbot delegates to him not only the care of the material goods of the monastery, especially such essential items as the community's food and clothing, but also the care of those who must daily

approach him for material necessities. In Benedict's vision there is no dual-
ism between the material and the spiritual, things and people. Not only
should he "lavish" great and generous care on the sick, children, guests, and
the poor, but all the goods and utensils of the monastery are also to be
treated as "sacred vessels of the altar" (RB 31.10) in a holy house of God.
Benedict is making a fifth-century comment significant for our twenty-first
century environment, for the way we treat people is a good indicator of
how we will probably treat the precious world in which we live.

Whereas the manager of Luke's parable was a self-centered schemer who
had to extricate himself from the problems caused by his squandering his
master's property, the cellarer is one of the most attractive characters in the
Rule, similar in many respects to the abbot to whom, of course, he owes
his obedience. Among other qualities, the cellarer is to be wise, mature, God-
fearing, disciplined, not greedy or extravagant, not a "turbulent" person who
can so easily disturb his own and others' peace. If he cannot supply someone's
needs, he can at least offer them a humble and kind word.

But the cellarer must also handle himself well, being ready to accept
help when needed so that he also is at peace. The members of the community have a responsibility toward the cellarer, too, with a sense of suitable
timing for making requests. As a model for middle management, the cellarer has much to teach us today.

Twenty-sixth Sunday in Ordinary Time

Benedict's passionate denunciation of greed or avarice, seeing this as
the root of the vice of private ownership (RB 33), reflects the concern of the
gospel. Physical possession of material things is not Benedict's target, but
the way in which they are used. It is a shame that the Lectionary for this
Sunday did not begin the First Letter to Timothy one verse earlier so that
we would hear: "For the love of money is a root of all kinds of evil, and in
their eagerness to be rich some have wandered away from the faith and
pierced themselves with many pains" (1 Tim 6:10). Benedict wanted to dig
out the smallest weed of such destructive love from his community.

That every Benedictine community was to be, literally, very mindful of
the poor at their gates is highlighted by the beautiful chapter on "The Por-
ters of the Monastery" (RB 66). Here is a loving, warm description of the
sensible old man who can stay put at the entrance to the monastery, take
and deliver messages responsibly and sensitively, and greet those who come
to the monastery in a way that makes a very positive and genuine first impression. He is to be a person of easy approachability, and Benedict makes

a special point about the welcome that a poor person is to receive. The porter greets all, including the poor, with "Thanks be to God," and then asks him or her for a blessing, not vice versa, for the pilgrims and the poor at the gate *are* a blessing to the community. The porter is also described as gentle—one of the same and, perhaps more unusual qualities that the Letter to Timothy required of "a man of God."

The poor and pilgrims are to receive hospitality as guests, for "Christ is more especially received in them" (RB 53.15). The rich, on the other hand, have their own powerful ways of earning respect that has nothing to do with the example of the hospitality that the powerless and poor Christ offered to those for whom he lived, died, and rose again so that all might be welcomed into his Father's house.

Twenty-seventh Sunday in Ordinary Time

The biblical authors, the great religious founders like Benedict, the theologians past and present—all wrote their vision so that it might be heralded and announced to the people as a challenge to greater fidelity and a reference point for individual and communal reflection. Nowadays, most communal endeavors, from giant multinationals to the local parish school, have a "vision statement."

In his Prologue, Benedict declares that he is setting down his vision for "a school for the Lord's service" (Prol 45) so that those who enter it may begin to learn how to be strong-hearted and faithful runners on the way of God's commandments until the race ends in the kingdom (Prol 49-50). In his last chapter, Benedict returns to the theme of running to our heavenly homeland, energized by the Scriptures and the teaching of the holy Fathers of the Church, and helped by Christ to keep "this modest Rule for beginners" (RB 73.8). In this description, Benedict's own humility is evident. He is not a leader with a pompous, inflated opinion of himself, but one who is obedient to the parable demand to consider himself "unworthy," expecting no credit because anything he achieves flows from the gift of God in Christ. It is this conviction that is also behind the sixth step of humility where, although it is not directly quoted, the "parable of the slave on duty" seems to be in Benedict's gospel memory. It may seem a harsh rung on which to stand, but pretentiousness, power games, and the temptation to be judged by what we do rather than what we are, are not absent from monasteries or any other communal living and working situation, as Jesus warned his apostles in this Sunday's gospel.

To keep his runners in training and his workers content in the Lord's service, Benedict reminded his monks that his vision, his modest Rule, should be read often in community. No one could then offer the excuse of ignorance of its demands (RB 66.8).

Twenty-eighth Sunday in Ordinary Time

There are no mentions of miracles or dramatic healings in Benedict's Rule; these are recounted by Gregory the Great in his *Dialogues*. On the record of these miracles, Adalbert de Vogüé reminds us ". . . the right question is not 'Is it true?' but 'What is it trying to say?'"[20] But there are healings—healings of relationships—and in this the abbot is to be like a wise physician whose primary care is to those members of the community who are weak in their commitment to the monastic way of life (RB 28). Benedict suggests pastoral prescriptions for the abbot's use, prescriptions that are available to any Christian: "poultices" of words that draw out bitterness, the "ointment" of encouragement, the healing "medicine" of Holy Scripture—and only then the more drastic remedies of "surgery" which remove the offending member (RB 28.3-6). We would all admit the positive effect of the soothing and gentle remedy or "word therapy" of words that are offered with compassion. Above all, the abbot and the whole community are to offer prayer to the Lord, who can do all things, for the one who is failing.

We all have our infirmities of character or personality, as well as of body, and the way in which we deal with these makes a loud comment on the quality of our life together in any community of close living (RB 72.5), from monastery to family.

Benedict would certainly approve of the emphasis on "listening" in the Lectionary reading for this Sunday: Naaman and his wife listen to the words of an unimportant slave girl; the commander listens to his servants; Paul tells Timothy to listen to the good news of Jesus Christ and the witness of Paul's own sufferings; with faith the ten lepers listen to Jesus' words of healing for their bodies, and only one hears the words of salvation spoken over his grateful, healthy body. In contemporary life we may seem to spend much of our time listening, but often this may only take us across the threshold of "auditory overload" into a kind of mindless noise. The listening Benedict wants is listening "with the ear of your heart" (RB Prol 1) to God, to the Spirit moving in the churches (RB Prol 11), to the counsel of our brothers and sisters, and often to the youngest or least important among us (RB 3).

Twenty-ninth Sunday in Ordinary Time

Just as Paul impressed on Timothy the importance of reading the sacred Scriptures, so from the very beginning of his Rule, Benedict impressed upon his monks that Scripture is the energizing word that rouses us from sleep and makes us ready to respond to God (RB Prol 8-16). It is a personal word that "calls" (RB 7.1), and urges to conversion of life (RB 7.19, 41, 45)—to the teaching, reproof, correction and "training in righteousness" of which Paul speaks to Timothy (2 Tim 3:16). This is especially true with regard to significant members of the community such as the abbot, who is to use scripture as a healing "medicine" (RB 28.3), and to the cellarer—business manager—in the exercise of his practical love and wisdom (RB 31.8, 14, 18).

In chapter 16, "How the Divine Office Should Be Performed During the Day," Benedict sums up the prayer that is offered seven times a day as "praise to our Creator for the judgment of his justice" (RB 16.5), justice which is the covenant relationship between God and his people. The widow of the parable does not fit Benedict's reverent and humble person described in chapter 20, but she does fit the abrasive, rude, honest prayer of so many of the psalms that are the main component of the Liturgy of the Hours, or the Work of God, as Benedict names this prayer. The widow's voice dares to bring to consciousness her anger, grief, desolation, and disappointment over injustice. It is a wonderful voice that we can echo in our praying of the psalms and our working for justice.

Thirtieth Sunday in Ordinary Time

Benedict encloses the climb up the ladder of humility with two references to the gospel of this Sunday. In the very first verse, he places chapter 7, "On Humility," under obedience to the Word of God in what some have called the "free-floating" wisdom saying about the humble that Luke adds to the parable, and which occurs also in the discussion of Christian table etiquette (see 22nd Sunday) as well as in Matthew 23:12. Near the end of the chapter (RB 7.65), by a mixed reference to Luke 18:13 and Matthew 8:8, the toll collector stands on the last rung of the ladder of humility as an example to the monk of the right place in which he should be before God. Again there is the paradox and reversal of the gospel. Up to the last and twelfth rung is really down: down into the depths of wisdom where, because of his honesty about his sinfulness, the monk bows trustingly before the love and mercy of God.

When Benedict writes of "Reverence in Prayer" (RB 20), we could well suspect that the Pharisee and toll collector are again in the background.

Benedict applauds compunction (RB 20.3; 49.4), that short, sharp jab that pierces both our hearts and the heavens with few but intense words, and criticizes the excessive talking of the Pharisee that distracts from the praise of the "Lord God of the universe" in favor of one's own limited self.

Thirty-first Sunday in Ordinary Time

Benedict often indicates his awareness of the dangers of murmuring or grumbling. About the tool of good works in chapter 4, "Do not be a loafer, nor a grumbler, nor one who runs down the reputation of others" (RB 4.38-40), George Holzherr comments that Benedict sees grumbling as "a fault-finding peevishness . . . which feels obliged to run everything down."[21] Such an attitude indicates a disturbed relationship to one's environment. It was a serious fault for the Hebrews in their wilderness years when they murmured against God's plan for their salvation; it is the attitude which Luke attributes to the Pharisees and scribes (Luke 15:2) at the beginning of the chapter of parables about seeking and finding the lost sheep, coin, son; it is the reaction of the crowds to Jesus finding Zacchaeus.

To be a murmurer can be the beginning of the monk's disturbed relationship with the community that, in its extreme development, may end in excommunication from the table and choir, two privileged places of community gathering and relating.

Beyond the monastery, grumbling can lead to the same erosion of relationships, especially in situations of close living.

Thirty-second Sunday in Ordinary Time

The Resurrection was central to Benedict's way of life. Easter is the hub around which work and the prayerful reading of Sacred Scripture (*lectio divina*) revolved in the daily timetable (RB 48.3); it is the starting point for the arrangement of the psalms in the various season (RB 8.1, 4; 10.1), and Benedict even adds a special chapter on the use of the Easter song, "Alleluia" (RB 15), extending its use beyond what was customary for the Western Church at that time. In his chapter on "The Observance of Lent" (RB 49), Benedict does say that "At all times the lifestyle of a monk ought to have a Lenten quality" (RB 49.1), but this is only to heighten the awareness of Holy Easter, to which the whole community was to look forward "with the joy of spiritual desire" (RB 49.7). The Resurrection is, therefore, the center of Christian life and the goal of our search.

The suffering that Benedict envisages as inevitable in our seeking the risen Christ is not the dramatic suffering of the Maccabean brothers and their mother, but is it often the hard, more everyday way of patience. Derived from the Latin *pati*, "to suffer," Benedict links this virtue with the sufferings of Christ, which the monk shares as he tries to live faithfully in the monastic way of life until death and so enter the joys of the kingdom. Patience in and with community life may sometimes be encountered in the hard and even unjust demands that are made on a monk. Dialogue may sometimes resolve the issue (RB 68.2) but, if not, the suffering is to be embraced, and in that embrace the suffering Christ is held close to the monk's heart (RB 7.35, 38, 42). More often, the challenge to be patient comes in the daily rub of community life: patience with the sick (RB 36.5), with personality defects and conflicts, or physical distaste about aspects of those with whom we live (RB 72.5), and such challenges have a broader relevance than just to the monastery. Yet from the beginning of the monastic acceptance (RB 58.3) to the end (RB Prol 50), patience needs to be discerned.

Thirty-third Sunday in Ordinary Time

Like Jesus and Paul, Benedict expected energetic action of his followers. His Prologue calls for fighters, workers, and runners for the sake of the reign of God (RB Prol 3; 14; 49). He detested idleness, naming it as "the soul's enemy" (RB 48.1). This is to be understood in the context of that chapter on "The Daily Manual Labor," and the balance that is to be achieved between work and prayerful reading or *lectio*, the latter being mentioned eleven times. Understandably then, a well-known Benedictine motto descriptive of the life is, "Pray and work." Our human nature is very similar, whether we are in Thessalonica or our own present time and place, and both Benedict and Paul find that the idle person can be busy about distracting others, especially with "frivolity or gossip" (RB 48.18) that result in a kind of psychic exhaustion and hinder our focus on the seeking of God. This is not to be mistaken for a compulsion to fill in every minute of the day with the workaholic's fear of or inability to cope with leisure; it is, rather, a question of a balanced lifestyle.

Realizing that all his gifts came from God, Paul did not hesitate to offer himself as an example to his communities. Benedict wants his abbot to be the same for his community. The abbot is to teach in a twofold way: firstly by his deeds, and then by his words, but it is the deeds which are the more effective way of teaching, especially for the "recalcitrant or naive" (RB 2.11-12). There is contemporary wisdom here for leadership and middle management over a broad social spectrum.

Thirty-fourth Sunday in Ordinary Time

Solemnity of Our Lord Jesus Christ, the Universal King

Kingship is not held in high esteem in many places today, but it is on behalf of the very different King whom we celebrate on today's feast that the monk is urged to take up "the powerful and shining weapons of obedience" (RB Prol 3). Christ is to rule gently and justly over a monk's life, and be recognized as present to him in the other members of the community, in his abbot, in those who need special care: the guests, pilgrims, the sick, the poor, the frail aged, and the vulnerable young. Christ died the way he lived—forgiving a sinner. Likewise, forgiveness is to be characteristic of Benedict's followers, from the abbot in his dealings with the monk who is failing seriously in his commitment (RB 27), to the daily and petty nastiness that needs to be forgiven before the setting of the sun (RB 4.73). As the community's pledge to give and receive such forgiveness, the Lord's Prayer is recited every morning and evening (RB 13.13-14; 17.8).

"Seven times a day have I praised you," says Benedict, quoting Psalm 119 (RB 16.1, 3; Ps 119:164), when he speaks of the celebration of the Divine Office, or what today we more often call the Liturgy of the Hours. This prayer was to overflow into the whole of life like hidden leaven, enabling a monk to pray always and praise God, mindful of the divine presence even in the midst of daily work and demanding relationships (RB 19.1-5). The day begins at Vigils with the verse of praise from the Psalm: "Lord, open my lips, and my mouth will proclaim your praise" (RB 9.1; Ps 51:17), words that can be repeated as a mantra in the heart throughout the day by anyone.

It is appropriate that as we come to the end of the church year, our reflections on the meeting of Rule of Benedict and the gospel of "the Lord Christ, the true king" (RB Prol 3) should end on the note of praise.

Notes

1. *The Sayings of the Desert Fathers: The Alphabetical Collection*, trans. Benedicta Ward, S.L.G. Cistercian Studies Series No. 59 (Kalamazoo: Cistercian Publications Inc., rev. edition 1984) 230–231.

2. Gregory the Great, *The Life of Saint Benedict*, trans. Hilary Costello and Eoin de Bhaldraithe. Commentary by Adalbert de Vogüé (Petersham, MA: St. Bede's Publications, 1993) 10–11.

3. Esther de Waal, *A Life-Giving Way: A Commentary on the Rule of St. Benedict* (London: Geoffrey Chapman, 1995) 13.

4. Columba Stewart, O.S.B., *Prayer and Community: The Benedictine Tradition* (London: Darton, Longman and Todd Ltd., 1998) 33.

5. Terrence G. Kardong, O.S.B., *Benedict's Rule: A Translation and Commentary* (Collegeville, MN: Liturgical Press, 1996) 599.

6. Timothy Fry, O.S.B., ed., Appendix 3, "The Liturgical Code in the Rule of St. Benedict," *RB 1980: The Rule of St. Benedict* (Collegeville, MN: Liturgical Press, 1981) 410.

7. Vatican II, *Constitution on the Sacred Liturgy*, art. 4.

8. Kardong, *Benedict's Rule*, 13.

9. Paul Wilkes, *Beyond the Walls: Monastic Wisdom for Everyday Life* (New York: Doubleday, An Image Book, 1999) 69.

10. *The Sayings of the Desert Fathers*, 138–139.

11. Kathleen Norris, *The Benedictine Handbook* (Norwich: Canterbury Press, 2003) 126.

12. Joan Chittister, *Wisdom Distilled from the Daily: Living the Rule of Benedict Today* (San Francisco: Harper & Row Publishers, 1990) 131.

13. de Waal, *A Life-Giving Way*, 61.

14. Stewart, *Prayer and Community*, 50.

15. Norvene Vest, *Friend of the Soul: A Benedictine Spirituality of Work* (Boston: Cowley Publications, 1997) 71.

16. de Waal, *A Life-Giving Way*, 211.

17. Michael Casey, O.C.S.O., *Truthful Living: St. Benedict's Teaching on Humility* (Petersham, MA: St. Bede's Publications, 1999) 9.

18. Wilkes, *Beyond the Walls*, 80–81.

19. George Holzherr, *The Rule of Benedict: A Guide to Christian Living* (Dublin: Four Courts Press Ltd., 1994) 166–167.

20. de Vogüé, in Gregory the Great, *The Life of Saint Benedict*, viii.

21. Holzherr, *The Rule of Benedict*, 68.

"Verna Holyhead's *With Burning Hearts* is an elegant complement to the liturgical readings of Year C. It provides us with a frame which brings out the deeper artistry of the biblical selections used at the Sunday Eucharist. The author draws on liturgical and scriptural knowledge, poetry, common experience, and personal reflection to offer a counterpoint to the familiar texts and to start us off on fresh avenues of meditation. This wise and mellow book will become a valued companion as we journey through the Church's year, opening up the riches of the liturgy, and calling us to a more fruitful listening and a fuller practice."

Fr. Michael Casey, O.C.S.O.
Tarrawarra Abbey, Australia

"If it is especially in the sacred liturgy where the Church 'offers to the faithful the bread of life' found in the Scriptures, as Vatican Council II taught us, we need help in breaking the life-giving bread. The thoughtful worshiper at each Sunday's Mass depends on a well-prepared lector and a gifted homilist. These are precisely the readers who will benefit from Verna Holyhead's reclaiming of the Liturgy of the Word, together with parish groups in Lent and Advent that traditionally ponder and pray over the Sunday texts. Here every reading in the Sundays of the year of Luke comes alive with her impeccable grasp of the biblical author's intention coupled with a sense of readers' life situation. Her sureness of touch arises from long experience in mediating the inspired Word to people hungry for that bread of life."

Robert C. Hill
Australian Catholic University